The Craft of Professional Writing

The Craft of Professional Writing

A Guide for Amateur and Professional Writers

Michael S. Malone

ANTHEM PRESS

Anthem Press
An imprint of Wimbledon Publishing Company
www.anthempress.com

This edition first published in UK and USA 2018
by ANTHEM PRESS
75–76 Blackfriars Road, London SE1 8HA, UK
or PO Box 9779, London SW19 7ZG, UK
and
244 Madison Ave #116, New York, NY 10016, USA

British Library Cataloguing-in-Publication Data
A catalogue record for this book is available from the British Library.

ISBN-13: 978-1-78308-829-4 (Pbk)
ISBN-10: 1-78308-829-X (Pbk)

This title is also available as an e-book.

To every person who ever wrote a sentence and wondered if they could make a living from it.

CONTENTS

Introduction   1

Part One: Basics   5

1. Gathering Information   7
2. Words, Sentences and Paragraphs   13
3. Narrative and Composition   23

Part Two: Corporate Careers and Disciplines   27

4. Publicist   29
5. Advertising Copywriter   43
6. Speechwriter   67
7. Technical Writer   95

Part Three: Writing Careers in Media   109

8. Blogger   111
9. News Reporter   121
10. Critic   141
11. Essayist   161
12. Book Author   173
13. Television and Radio News Reporter   195
14. Screenwriter and Playwright   209
15. Fiction Writer and Novelist   221
16. Academic Track   255
17. Miscellaneous Writing   267

Part Four: The Work of Professional Writing   275

18. Pitching   277
19. Editing   283
20. Rejection   293
21. A Writer's Life   297

Further Reading   307
Suggested Assignments   309
Index   315

Introduction

This book is about the work—the craft—of professional writing. It is written for those who make writing their career and those who hope to do so.

There's an endless number of books about finding your inner writer, about how to write elegant sentences and how to call down the Muse to help you pen your novel. This book is about none of those things. It takes as a given that you know how to write, that you care passionately about writing, and that you make—or want to make—writing the centerpiece of your career.

It is that commitment to being part of the unofficial guild of professional writers that informs this book. It is not your typical textbook. For one thing, while it has an explicit structure, it is written in a more literary style than you may be used to. It also contains stories and anecdotes, both good and bad, from my own checkered career. Why? Because when veteran writers of every stripe get together, they swap stories. For the apprentice sitting in on one of those conversations the acquired wisdom conveyed in these stories is far more important than, say, the rules of grammar. They teach how to *live* as a writer: how to start your career, how to manage it and how to end it.

Central to this book is the belief that writing really is a craft. As such, all writing you do as a professional is the same, whether it is a press release or an experimental novel. Up close—which is where every writer finds himself or herself when writing—all writing is words and sentences. How much art you imbue those words with depends upon your talent and your ambitions. But first comes the work of writing: If you don't complete the task before you, you will fail. And you won't get paid. And you will have to find another career.

The craft of writing is about not letting that happen. It is about having the right tools and techniques to carry you to success and having the insider knowledge to guarantee that success over and over through the course of your career.

I am a college professor, but I am neither an academic nor a textbook writer. Rather, I have been a professional writer for forty years, much of it as a freelancer. During those years when I had a real job, I was, at various times, a corporate public relations professional, a newspaperman and the editor of the world's largest-circulation technology business magazine. But it is as a freelancer, like many of my peers, that I have had the most eclectic writing experiences. Over the years I have been a blogger, columnist, speechwriter, television host, producer and writer, music critic, movie reviewer, book reviewer, screenwriter, author, playwright, novelist and now, a textbook writer. It was, in fact, the remarkable range of my writing experiences (which, believe me, was never planned) that led me to write this textbook. Most of these experiences weren't driven by any particular creative desire, but more often by just the need to pay the bills and feed my family—motivations, I suspect, that I share with most of my fellow professional writers. Some of the work I created in these different disciplines was quite good, some of the rest was mediocre, but I can say that I always put the writing first, and gave it everything I had.

I used to fantasize about becoming a novelist, of writing what I wanted without the pressures of bosses, deadlines and the marketplace. Then I became one—and I still faced all of those pressures, and I still needed to make money. The Muse still shows up to whisper sweet sentences in my ear, but she is a very unpredictable goddess; she doesn't have a schedule and she never leaves her phone number. And so, while you wait for her to reappear, all you can do is keep writing in the most professional way. You will also probably win some of those awards you dream of, but probably too late to matter and not for your best work. That's how real-life, professional, writing works.

The second tenet of this book is that not only is all writing essentially the same, but that all writing careers are valid. Each discipline has its own rules, its own standards, its own professional tricks, and its own examples of exemplary work. As such, each of these disciplines calls upon its writers to be professional by following those rules, to take the work seriously, and to write to the best of their ability every day. If the corporate speechwriter doesn't enjoy the public renown of the famous playwright or the income of the blockbuster screenwriter, that doesn't make the speechwriter's career as a writer any less valid, or the work any less important. Indeed, more than almost any other form of writing, great speeches have changed the world.

That said, professional writing careers do often have different trajectories based upon the nature of the work and the client or employer. Some jobs, such as news reporting, start out strong and often slowly fade; while others, such as criticism, start slowly but grow stronger toward the end. Because of that, each professional writing career typically has different strengths and weaknesses and, just as important, each has different turning points, where the writer must make some crucial decisions about what to do next.

This book is divided into three parts. The first looks at writing careers in the business world, which is where most jobs for writers are found. The second, and largest, section looks at the wide array of writing work—full-time and freelance—that is found within the media, from blogging to reporting, columnist to book author. And the third offers advice on the day-to-day business of professional writing, including pitching, rejection, billing and editing. The final chapter offers advice on how to conduct your life as a writer.

The chapters are divided into an overview of each particular career, occasionally a brief history of the profession, a collection of tips and advice and then a list of the good and bad traits of the job and its turning points. I've also included examples of some of the best work in each field and templates for some of the tools of the trade (such as a standard-form invoice) that you may want reference in the years ahead. In some chapters—notably news reporting and novel-writing—I've added special sections in order to either look at a related specialty career (such as investigative reporting) or to provide more detail on the actual work (such as novel writing).

Finally, as already noted, throughout the text I've salted in stories from my own career that relate to the topic at hand. A few are stories of triumph or failure, but most exhibit the messiness of real life as a professional writer and, with luck, will spare you some of the same mistakes.

My hope is that, for the professional writer, this text will serve as a reference, not for your current career necessarily, but for when you are asked to step outside your usual writing work to take on a different writing task. With luck, the chapter on that type of writing will get you quickly up to speed. It is also for those times in your career—and every writer has them—when you want to stretch your talents and try something new, either as a hobby or as a brand-new career trajectory. The appropriate chapter should give you a good idea of how different that new direction is from your current path.

For students who dream of writing careers this book is designed to be a survey course—with a twist: It doesn't look at just the forms of professional writing, or even its standard tools. It also wanders off into the woods to talk about what it means to *be* a professional writer; to get up every day at 25 or 40 or 60 years old and stare once again at that blank sheet or at that empty, glowing display and face the challenge of once again writing words that matter. As such, it is as much a trade manual as it is a college textbook. And that is exactly what I set out for it to be.

This book is based on notes compiled over years of teaching juniors and seniors at California's Santa Clara University. That my students, sitting in the heart of hard-charging, empirical and expensive Silicon Valley, had chosen to consider a writing career was a testament to the power of language—and of determination. It was the sight of that determination in the first year I taught this course—Writing for Professionals—that made me quickly abandon theory and dive right into real-life application. I realized that traditional college education, at best, only teaches students *how* to write, not how to *be* a writer.

One course isn't much time to prepare students for the real world, but I did the best I could, stuffing as much real-life experience, tricks of the trade, object lessons and practical skills as possible into a score of career descriptions in a single academic quarter. This text reflects that same hodgepodge of content because, frankly, I don't know of any other way to do it. I don't know if my students thought I was a good teacher, but I think most will agree that it was an intense ten weeks—and that they never had a class like it. That many have gone on to successful writing careers suggests they did, at least, listen, which is more than I think I would have done at their age.

I was lucky to have my own practical teachers and mentors when I began my writing career. Christian Leviestro looked at my awful early fiction, pretended it was good, and goaded me on. Most important was James Degnan, whose class I inherited after a twenty-year gap. Degnan, a legend to those students lucky enough take him, was disorganized, opinionated and terrifying, but he was the real deal, a professional writer, and he demanded the same professionalism from his students. We didn't learn from Degnan how to be writers, but from trying to be him. Forty years later, his former students still tell "Degnan stories." I don't deserve to stand in his shoes.

If this book strongly stresses the guild-like nature of the writing craft, it is because at every step of the way in my career I was taught by men and women more experienced, and usually better, than I was. From the men at Hewlett-Packard corporate PR, my first real writing job, to Brenna Bolger at PRx Inc. decades later, I learned what it means to be a publicist. At the *San Jose Mercury-News*, my editors Jim Mitchell and Jack Sirard, and my investigative reporting partners Pete Carey and Susan Yoachum, demanded that my journalism be of the highest quality and integrity, and in the process transformed me from a clever dilettante into a serious professional. At Forbes, where I ran *Forbes ASAP* magazine, publisher Rich Karlgaard and co-owner Tim Forbes gave me absolute freedom to create one of the greatest magazines of the era—and then demanded I do just that. Working with the finest writers on Earth, including several Nobel laureates, was the ultimate writer's education.

I was middle-aged when I was offered the opportunity to teach at the university level by Dick Osberg. Then, after a few years hiatus to work on various books, I was asked to return to teaching by Simone Billings. Both took a huge risk on an untrained neophyte.

To all of them, and to all the others who, with one assignment or a score of them, made me a better writer, I give my eternal thanks.

Now, pull up your chairs, pour yourselves a drink, and let's talk about writing for a living.

Part One

Basics

Before we can even talk about writing careers, we need to do two things. First, look at how to gather the raw material for writing—that is, information in its many forms. Then second, look at the nature of writing itself and approach that subject not simply as communicators of our native tongues, but as people who use writing as their professional livelihood.

The reason we do this instead of just leaping into the much more exciting topic of making money from writing is that to do the latter you must be adept at the former. And that is a problem, because few of us are taught anything (other than "go to the library") for the former.

As for the latter—that is, our K–12 English education—most of what we are taught is misdirected, mis-oriented, wrongly prioritized, and just plain dreary. The truth is that most of the best writers we know were terrible English and grammar students, still can't parse a sentence, and could start a chain reaction with all the infinitives they split. So, in the course of a few pages, we are going to revisit and relearn your first 12 years of writing education.

Don't worry. It won't take long, and we'll try to make it fun.

Gathering Information

You can't write anything if you don't have anything to write about.

That observation may sound stupid and obvious, but you'd be amazed how many poets, columnists, feature writers and novelists try to force words onto the page without any real knowledge of what they are writing about. Some are even reduced to making up "facts" and sources that aren't real. Such are the demands of money, deadline and ambition. Sometimes they pull it off; but not for long.

Real, honest writing—even if it is fiction—requires real, honest *information* on what you are writing about. And the only way to get that information is to go out looking for it. That means interviewing sources or eyewitnesses, or visiting the sites of key events, or digging deep into official records, or searching far out into the hinterlands of the Internet. The closer you can get to actual participants or witnesses to the event you wish to describe, including the documents they leave behind—the more legally certified the documents you find, and the more verified and cross-referenced the file you find—the better off you are going to be.

Why do this? Because you owe it to yourself as a professional to get things right. And because you owe it to your readers, your client or your employer not to mislead them or place them in legal or financial jeopardy. Sound overdramatic? Wait until you get a story wrong.

We once worked for an editor who was the very model of a conscientious reporter—including checking and double-checking every factual claim made by his staff of young reporters. At first we thought he was overly careful, at the expense of stripping some of the power out of our stories. Then he told us of an experience from his own days as a young reporter.

It seems that, while still little more than a rookie, he wrote a profile of a fast-growing new company that had a hot new product, skyrocketing sales and the prospect of even better days ahead. The young reporter got this insider news from the CEO of the company itself and was flattered that this business superstar even took the time to talk with him. He went back to the newsroom and pounded out a breathless feature on the Next Big Company. He barely even took the time to gather a few guarded comments from competitors, industry analysts and trade-magazine reporters.

Roll forward a year, and our now not-so-young reporter found himself in the local courthouse covering another story. His editor had expressly assigned it to him as punishment. It was the trial of the CEO of that Next Big Company which, it turned out, was nothing more than a Ponzi scheme, with no real technology or products to show for the millions of dollars of investor money it had burned up—or had used to line the founder's pockets. Our future editor might have foreseen this had he dug a little deeper into the scam company's patent filings, the founder's (criminal) background or just asked around the industry.

Now, as the reporter walked toward the courtroom, he found himself passing through a gauntlet of furious investors who blamed him for their losses. Some even waved copies of his original article. But the encounter that shook him most, and that still haunted him a decade later as he spoke to us, was with the elderly couple who quietly walked up and told him, more crushed than angry, that they had invested their life savings in the company based on our editor's glowing article. Did he have any advice on what they should do now?

We reporters were never burned as badly by a story—perhaps because we were nearly as haunted by our editor's cautionary tale as he was. But on many, many occasions each of us had subjects not give the true story. Some subjects were just zealous employees who saw their employers through rose-colored glasses. Others were egomaniac executives who wanted to inflate their reputations. A few had something they wanted to hide—dwindling shipments, a late new product, an impending lawsuit. And a very few were simply lying sociopaths. A few got through our filters but, thankfully none did much damage. And, if caught, they got no pity from us.

Over time, like most reporters, we learned to grow a thick hide. A number of companies even complained that we were too cynical, too skeptical of the great story they had to tell. But, remember, this was Silicon Valley. At least 90 percent of those so-called great companies, with even greater stories to tell, died a quick death. We may have started out in journalism as romantics, but we soon learned to trust only the facts.

Facts are your friends. If you want to be a successful professional writer, learn how to find them.

So, where do you find these facts? Where do you go to get accurate information to underpin your writing?

There are a number of places—indeed, more than you probably know from watching television shows and movies about journalists and other writers. Here's a quick overview:

Source documents—In terms of accuracy, there are few information sources more trustworthy than those that derive from actual witnesses to (or participants in) an event or from official records about the event created by trained investigators. In fact, the latter may prove to be a more reliable source because, as any criminal investigator will tell you, eyewitnesses may have a distorted view through the lens of their own limited viewpoints, excitement and bias.

- *News coverage*—Newspaper stories, wire service stories, and local television coverage can often be good sources when working on a story, especially one being written well after the subject event occurred. But beware: you are essentially trying to overcome potential weaknesses in your own writing, but adopting the possible failures of others. Moreover, news reporters often get facts wrong because they are under a tight deadline, have little time to interview eyewitnesses, and even the officials they speak to may have an incomplete understanding of what just happened.
- *Official reports*—Official reports tend to get around the "Rashoman effect" of conflicting and confused eyewitnesses by using time, the luxury of conducting many interviews, and professional information gatherers to come up with the best description of the event, its causes and its aftermath. That's not to say that some reports are eventually proven wrong as additional evidence appears but, in all, they remain the most reliable of sources (especially if you follow up with some of the eyewitnesses). The downside of reports, especially those created by for-profit research companies, industry analysts and so forth, is that they can be hugely expensive—sometimes running into thousands of dollars. If that's the case, you may be able to get your employer (especially if it's a corporation) to pay for it. Short of that (if you are a journalist) you may be able to request a free copy. And if all else fails, look for the executive summary of the report, or a summary of it, on the Web.
- *Legal documents*—Because they are created as part of an adversary process, legal documents usually conceal as much as they disclose. But what they do offer is information that has been made under oath or the threat of legal penalties for misrepresentation. In the real world, it's hard to get more reliable information than that. That's why the libel lawyers publications and news stations keep on retainer, when they sit down with you to go over an investigative story, will ask you about every statement in your story: "Do you have paper to back that up?" If you do

not, and it is a high-risk story, you will have the unpleasant experience of having half of your work chopped out and thrown away.

The downside of legal documents is that they are a pain to get—and even more of a pain to decipher. Though some of these documents are now posted on the Web, most (notably court filings) remain in print form, which means you have to drive down to the courthouse or county records department, deal with the bureaucracy there, and then spend hours trying to find that one document that will support your argument.

And even then, you've only begun, because you have to read through the legalese (remember: these documents aren't written for you, but for members of specialized professions) to find the key statements you need. This can take days, even weeks, in a stuffy room searching through page after page until your vision blurs.

But it can be worth it. A former reporting partner of ours spent days going through real-estate documents and deeds in an obscure courthouse on Long Island (he worked for a California paper) until he found the handful of documents he was looking for. They helped pull down the Marcos regime in the Philippines, and earned the reporter a Pulitzer Prize. Not bad for a bunch of boring legal documents.

- *Oral histories*—For source information at least, one of the most positive developments of recent years has been the rise of oral histories.
  One obvious reason for this movement has been the technological revolution. Instead of taping an interview with a subject then spending laborious hours transcribing it, or taking notes by hand and then trying to decipher and flesh them out afterwards, these days it is possible to digitally record a subject, convert the interview into a file that even can be automatically transcribed via software. Combine that with the advent of permanent mass storage, either on personal media or in the Internet Cloud, and is possible for the first time to capture the life stories of millions of people—not least old folks being interviewed by their grandchildren as a family record.

  Needless to say, the key to doing oral histories right is to have the proper equipment—including a good microphone, digital tape recorder (or smart phone or personal computer), good translation software and permanent digital storage ready.

There are several tricks to capturing a good oral history:

a. Let the subject know in advance. With enough forewarning the human brain will dig up an amazing number of forgotten memories.
b. Make the subject comfortable. You don't want the subject worried about the setting or the equipment or fearful of the next question. You are not there to judge, but to coax out stories.

c. If possible, do multiple sessions. In our experience, once you've interviewed a subject more and more memories will surface for days and weeks afterwards. Some of them may prove very important. So, go back and follow-up, if you have time.

d. Index the interview. Once you are done, transcribe or software translate the audio track into narrative form. Go through and mark out key statements and divide the text up into chapters and subchapters while it is still fresh. That'll help with navigation later on—especially if the interviews are hours long.

Words, Sentences and Paragraphs

For the next two chapters we will look at the practical craft of constructing compelling phrases, sentences and narratives. Think of it as everything you were supposed to learn in language and grammar classes in primary and secondary school—but in only a few thousand words. This time around, we're going to teach you the actual stuff you need to be a professional writer, and make a living doing so.

For that reason, we aren't going to spend time on grammar: in the real world, the only rule of grammar is that it works in getting the message through to the reader. Nor are we going to discuss rhetoric, other than, once again, what works. Nor vocabulary: experience has shown that working every day as a writer will force you to expand your vocabulary if you are going to be able to effectively explain yourself. Nor punctuation: not least because that field has become increasingly fluid in recent years.

Rather, we are going to use these two chapters to look at how you use language in the most powerful way to capture and hold readers, enhance their emotional response to what you've written, and keep them reading through to the end. Compared to that, whether you've written a sentence fragment or split an infinitive is inconsequential. Indeed, in professional practice, there are good arguments to be made for both. So, let's begin our short course in Real-Life Writing—or, as the author prefers, *Writing for Money*.

The parts of language and their roles

Sounds are senses

Once, during a safari in Namibia, the author met a man, a tracker and guide, who was one of the most linguistically accomplished individuals on Earth. His father was a member of the Ovambo tribe, the dominant African people in that part of sub-Saharan Africa; his mother was Bushman, a member of the San people. Meanwhile, by the nature of his work, and his own native language skills, this man dealt regularly with people from around the world and had to learn to speak with them in their own languages.

One day, in idle curiosity, the author asked this man how many different languages he spoke. He paused for a moment, and then began listing on his fingers: German, Swahili, Dutch, French, Polish, Spanish, Italian, Russian, Japanese. He listed several more, then finally said, "English, but not very well." This last despite the fact that we had just been conversing in English for the previous hour—in his mind, his command of English was still incomplete. What about his mother's tongue, I asked. Ah, he reminded himself, of course, I speak three San dialects.

Linguists have found that human beings communicate, via language, with less than twenty distinct sounds. Most of us are lucky to regularly use a dozen of those sounds. Thus, for example, as a middle-aged American, the author will never be able to capture the 'lion' growl in Gaelic Irish (though I'm of Irish extraction), nor the trilled "r" of the Latin languages. By comparison, my Japanese friends will forever struggle with the hard "r" and "l" that are almost my Yankee birthright.

What made my African friend so remarkable—and something he didn't know about himself until it was explained to him—was that he had learned to use not only all of the important vocal sounds of the world's major cultures, but even the rarest ones. In particular, in his mother's arms he had first learned the precisely modulated clicking sounds that made Bushman dialects among the most unusual in human history.

Only a handful of people on the planet regularly use, like my guide friend, all the available human language sounds. For the rest of us, we must make do with a dozen or less. That may seem constraining, but the analogy is to music, where a comparably limited number of notes have been used to create an incredible range of music over the centuries. A professional writer is thus, like a composer or improvisational musician: to make your writing "sing," to tap into the deepest emotions of your readers, you need to be so competent with the use of these sounds that you do not just write with them, but perform with them.

You may be asking: Why are so few sounds used by humans in their languages? The answer is not entirely clear. One answer is that we don't really need any more sounds than that. Other animals typically use far less. And, because of our intelligence, we can use our tools—from musical instruments to digital technology—to create a nearly infinite range of additional sounds. The creation of language—and thus of writing, which is symbolic language—appears to have begun a couple of hundred thousand years ago with a remarkable pair of events: a thickening of the cerebral cortex in the brain of early man—and with it a greater aptitude for higher, logical thinking—and the evolution of the hyoid bone in the throat, which enabled hominids to generate more complex vocalizations.

Still, language didn't come quickly: Neanderthal man, for all his intelligence, probably was unable to make more than a few basic sounds. And writing (as opposed to pictography, such as Egyptian hieroglyphics), which evolved at the intersection of these sounds with artistic representations of nature, didn't really emerge in a recognizable form until just 6,000 years ago in Sumer. It was there that mankind's oldest surviving story, the *Epic of Gilgamesh*, appeared.

As we write today, the limited number of sounds that compose our words carry with them those millennia-old coefficients of emotion. There are a lot of technical terms for these different sounds—*obstruents, sonorants, stops and fricatives, approximants, liquids, trills*—but unless you are a linguist you do not really need to know them. What you do need to know as a professional writer is how these different sounds *feel*. That is, what emotional responses are elicited by each of these sounds, and how can you employ them to maximize the impact of your writing on the reader. Let's take a look at the most important ones:

1. *The sibilants*—These are the sounds of *s*, soft *c* and *z*. In many ways, these are the most powerful of language sounds, as they produce the effect of menace, danger and intensity. Sibilants enhance the drama of prose.

2. *M* and *N*—The closed-lips hum of these two letters give the impression of softness, calm, satisfaction, sleep. Think of the classic children's bedtime book, *Goodnight Moon*.

3. *Wh*—The classic start for a question—*who, what, when, where, why*. In English, because we don't have an inverted question mark to start a question, as exists in Spanish, we typically use a *wh* to warn the reader (or listener) of the query to come.

4. *P*—*P* is the sound of exasperation and dismissal ("Put that down! P– off!") as if the statement is being spit out. When spoken with a softer *p* it can signal a more positive judgment. Perhaps the most famous example of the hard *p* comes from *Macbeth:* "Tomorrow and tomorrow and tomorrow creeps in this *petty pace* from day to day."

5. *F, V, W*—The hissing exhale of the letter *f* (and to a lesser degree *v* and the hard *w*) usually signals aggression or intensity. Thus, you *fight* your *foe, flinging* your angry *words* into his *face*, then *vying with* your *weapons* until one of you is *vanquished*.

6. *De, dis*—These prefixes produce a kind of an aggressive reversal of an original thought or opinion, or of the status quo: She *denied* my claim that she *destroyed* everything she touched, *dismissing* me as a fool.

7. *R*—Because it resembles an animal's growl the *r* sound, wherever it appears in a word, tends to produce a sense of strength, toughness or dominance—as it just has in this sentence.

8. *Y*—At the beginning of a word, the letter *y* can (with some exceptions, such as *yesterday* or *young*) induce a sense of goofiness or casualness: *yep, yuck-yuck, yahoo!, yeah, yo-you.*

9. *L*—At the beginning of a word, the *l* sound is typically upbeat, melodic and/or emotional: *lark, laugh, lachrymose, la-la-la, lovely, lighthearted.*

10. *G*—With its Teutonic roots, expresses from deep in the throat; a hard *g* anywhere in a word produces an earthy, physical effect: *ground, guts, guttural, good, grand, God*. Put an *l* after that *g* and *gl-* is the sound of heightened activity or effect, or extravagance: *glee, glowing, glittering, glide, glassy, glop, gulp.*

11. *-rk, -sk, -sh*—These three letter pairs represent different ways to end words—from *-rk* for an abrupt ending; *-sk* for a regular ending; and *-sh* for a soft, extended ending.

Words are emotions

If individual letters and combinations of letters represent our senses, then words—multiple combinations of letter clusters, and thus strings of senses—represent the entire range of human emotions.

This isn't what you are normally taught. Rather, words are supposed to be the signs and signifiers for emotions, ideas or phenomena of the natural world. True enough, but for our purposes—as writers, that of producing narrative in all its forms that has the maximum impact on readers—words are also the emotions they produce in those readers.

Those emotions are achieved through a combination of *definition* (or denotation), *connotation*, *sound*, and *context*. One of the best things about the world's great languages—and English in particular, as it is the world's lingua franca—is that they have words that emphasize every combination of those factors. Put another way: whatever emotion you want to induce in the reader for a particular idea, experience or thing, there is a best word, *le mot juste.*

Ultimately, that's the reason why, as a professional, you need to develop as extensive a vocabulary as you can in order to precisely pinpoint the effect you want to create in the reader.

What makes English interesting is that, for many words, the synonyms for one idea or thing reflect the history of the language—from its Celtic and Anglo-Saxon roots, to the arrival of the Vikings, to the Norman invasion to the vast British Empire with its contributions from India, Africa and the Caribbean, to American English as the global language to influences from science, technology and pop culture. Thus, it is not unusual to find for one concept a half-dozen words, each identical in definition, but slightly different in nuance and connotation. The goal is to be able to use them all with facility—but short of that, to at least appreciate that we have all the words we need, and that there is the perfect word for every occasion. We'll never find ourselves with William Shakespeare's predicament of working with a much leaner English and having to invent hundreds of words to match our ambitions.

Here are some "Basic Rules" for choosing the right words to match your ambitions:

1. The simpler, Anglo-Saxon terms are usually best—that is, *use* vs. *utilize*—because they are earthier and stronger, and typically a lot less pretentious. Use those simpler them as your base, then add more complicated and sophisticated words where they best work, if at all. You can lose by keeping it simple.

2. The ratio of short words to long words should match your purpose: one-syllable words for punchiness, multisyllabic words when you want to slow the reading rate and produce more reflection.

3. Mix and match short and long words to change the velocity and the "music" of what you write.

4. When faced with using the same word over and over, occasionally substitute one of the available synonyms. But beware of overdoing it. Thus, there is nothing wrong with using "said" over and over, or even of occasionally substituting a more precise or descriptive word such as "announced" or "exclaimed." But too many substitutions begin to look obvious, forced and, worse, silly.

5. Always listen to the *sound* of words, even written ones. Go for the music. Read aloud what you've written—ignore the meaning and listen to the music of the words: does your prose sing?

6. Unless you are a poet, stay away from dictionaries and thesauruses. Use them only to check spellings or to find the right word that is already on the tip of your tongue. Never use words you aren't comfortable with— you'll inevitably get it wrong and look like an idiot.

7. Expand your vocabulary every chance you get. It is the one proven way to actually become smarter. It will also make your thinking richer. And it will make your words more precise.

8. If you want to be a professional writer, you must learn to *love* words.

Sentences are thoughts: A phrase is a fragment of a thought

Sentences are strings of words, and thus are strings of emotions. As such, they give logic and coherence to those emotions. A properly constructed sentence then completes this collection of emotions, capturing a complete human thought. Sentences achieve, in the most basic way, conclusions. Phrases, including prepositional phrases, are fragments—of varying completeness—of those complete thoughts.

Note that these complete thoughts do not have to be explicit in the word composition of those sentences. They can also be implicit, evoking the complete thought only in the reader's mind. That is why, while a sentence fragment may be bad grammar (because the required pieces are not all there), it can be perfectly acceptable for the writer or reader if both parties understand what is *not* being said.

Also note that a true sentence contains only one complete thought—a subject and an action—around which you can add as many modifiers as you need to round out that thought.

Experience has shown that sentences under ten words are usually better than sentences longer than ten words. That said, there are great sentences that run up to 500 words or more (see the works of William Faulkner, Marcel Proust or Victor Hugo). But you need to be a very good, and confident, writer to pull them off. And, if you use them too often in a text you will exhaust—and eventually lose—the reader, no matter how great your facility.

How long should a sentence be? As long as it needs to be.

That's not meant to be a facile statement (well, not entirely). The fact is that a 'sentence' is not yet a real sentence until the sum of its explicit and implicit emotions constitute a complete thought. That's why a phrase can't be a sentence, but a fragment can.

How short should a sentence be? As short as you can make it. If a complete sentence needs to include all the components required to make it a complete thought—whether it be two or two hundred words—your goal should also be economy of language while not compromising the message. That may mean cutting just three words out of that two-hundred word sentence or cutting seven words out of a ten-word sentence. If both are as short as those sentences can be without losing their intrinsic value, then you have done your job as a writer.

Keep in mind that you can still break apart sentences by splitting out ancillary phrases and adding subjects and (more likely) verbs. You can also expand sentences by removing a subject and/or verb and bolting two or more adjacent sentences together. Why would you do that? *Rhythm* and *pacing*. Reading that maintains a constant, unwavering beat is boring. It's like a song in which every line rhymes with every other line. Instead, you want enough variation to keep readers slightly stumbling so that they stay awake and maintain attention. One simple way to accomplish that is to regularly, and randomly, change sentence length.

Some tips:

1. If you write short and choppy, take a breather occasionally with a long sentence—otherwise the reader feels pummeled.
2. If you write long and languid, let the reader catch a breath with a short, crisp sentence: remember, reading is a physical activity.
3. *Sentence fragments*—As already noted, don't worry about them (unless you are writing an academic paper, where a priggish editor may punish you for it). If you've written a sentence where you've screwed up and forgotten the verb or object, that's one thing. But if your fragment implies a longer sentence—for example: "Nope." for "No, that is incorrect."—then use of the fragment is just fine. Indeed, depending upon the context, it may even be advisable.
4. *Run-on sentences*—These are only bad if you lose control of them—that is, if they contain more than one thought, they don't let the reader "breathe" and, worst of all, if they are boring and monotonous. If in doubt, break them up.
5. *Metaphor*—Metaphor is a complex concept and an even more complex mode of thought. But, in writing, a metaphor is the connection between two seemingly diverse ideas, concepts or things that somehow seem to work and, in the process, expand our understanding of the natural world. Metaphor is uniquely human—indeed, it has been suggested that, more than anything else, it is what makes us human. And it is what brings art to writing.

   But metaphors are also dangerous. Use them sparingly or they quickly become distracting. Use them carefully or they look labored or wrong. And if you can't be original, don't use them at all—otherwise you risk using clichés and becoming tiresome to the reader.

   Most metaphors are in the form of *similes*. Real genius comes from bolting two utterly different things together with a simple "like" and in the process expanding our understanding of the world and adding to the combined knowledge of mankind. Great similes are as close as writers come to immortality.

   Here are some examples of great metaphors:

   His bony hand drug its way like a squirrel into his overall pocket, and brought out a black, bitten plug of tobacco. (Steinbeck, *East of Eden*)

   A damp streak of hair lay like a dash of blue paint across her cheek and her hand was wet with glistening drops as I took it to help her from the car. (Fitzgerald, *The Great Gatsby*)

   Raw cold daylight fell through the roof. Gray as his heart. (Cormac McCarthy, *The Road*)

6. Tight construction, lively and active verbs, and mind-expanding metaphors—that's the key to great sentences [...] and great thoughts.

Paragraphs are ideas

By definition, a paragraph is a collection of sentences—that is, it is a construction of distinct thoughts that combine to create a complete notion, an *idea*.

A classic paragraph is constructed like a sentence. That is:

1. The subject/predicate of the sentence = the lede sentence in a paragraph.
2. Supporting phrases in a sentence = Supporting sentences in a paragraph.
3. Prepositional phrase at the end of a sentence = the closing sentence that summarizes the paragraph.

The author is not a fan of closing sentences in paragraphs. They usually are too neat and often stop the narrative. You are better off to keep up the momentum, saving your summary to the big closer at the end of the chapter, article or other narrative.

How long should a paragraph be? As long as it takes to get the idea across in a convincing way.

How short should a paragraph be? Short enough not to lose the reader.

By now, even this early in the book, it should be obvious to the reader that this textbook—and professional writing—is all about keeping the reader interested and engaged. Amateurs think the first goal of writing should be to present the best possible content. Pros know that if you haven't captured the reader with good, smart, and disciplined prose the quality of your content doesn't matter because *no one* will ever read it. And since paragraphs, even more than sentences, are the building blocks of good prose, you need to construct the most compelling paragraphs possible.

The fact is, there is no tried-and-true model for writing paragraphs. And that's a good thing, because it gives you the freedom to be creative and experiment. That said, if in composing a paragraph you get beyond four or five sentences—especially if they are long sentences—you should revisit that paragraph to see if you aren't trying to convey more than one idea. If so, you should break the graph into two or three smaller paragraphs.

Here are two basic rules for writing paragraphs:

1. We break up words into *heartbeats* (we naturally write in iambic— duh dum, duh dum); we normally break up sentences into *breaths*

(try writing for radio), and we naturally break up paragraphs into *conversations*. Imagine that you are talking with someone else: we tend to give each other a few seconds to make our point, then the other person gets to talk. Talk too long, and you begin to monopolize the conversation—you become a bore. The same is true with paragraphs.

2. We will revisit this, but reading isn't just a visual experience, but an esthetic one as well. When writing—and particularly when editing—pull back and look at your copy on the page. Do you see large, daunting blocks of paragraphs? So will your readers, and they will hesitate to take on the task of reading your work. Paragraphs, like sentences, should vary in size in order to create tension—let readers catch their breath—and to keep their attention. The great thing about paragraphs, as opposed to sentences, is that you can just look at the shape of the text on the page to see if you have accomplished this. And don't be afraid of one sentence or even one *word* paragraphs. Because there are no real rules for paragraphs, even the grammar police won't complain.

Here are some sample paragraphs, from fiction and nonfiction:

The Maltese Falcon by Dashiell Hammett—"Sam Spade's jaw was long and bony, his chin a jutting v under the more flexible v of his mouth. His nostrils curved back to make another, smaller v. His yellow-grey eyes were horizontal. The v motif was picked up again by thickish brows rising outward from twin creases above a hooked nose, and his pale brown hair grew down—from high flat temples—in a point on his forehead. He looked rather pleasantly like a blond satan."

Lives of a Cell by Lewis Thomas—"I have been trying to think of the earth as a kind of organism, but it is a no go. I cannot think of it this way. It is too big, too complex, with too many working parts lacking visible connections. The other night, driving through a hilly, wooded part of southern New England, I wondered about this. If not like an organism, what is it like? Then, satisfactorily for that moment, it came to me: it is most like a single cell."

The Night Country by Loren Eiseley—"Man, who bumps his head and fumbles in the dark because of his small day-born eyes, fears the ghosts of the dark above all things. Maybe that is the reason why men string lamps far out into the country lanes and try to run down everything with red eyes that happens to waddle across the road in front of their headlights. It is cruel but revelatory: we are insecure, and this is our warfare with the dark. It began when man first lit a fire at a cave mouth and the eyes he feared—very big eyes they were then—began to blink and draw back.

So he lights and lights in a passion for illumination that is insatiable—a poor day-born thing contending against one of the greatest powers in the universe."

In the next chapter we'll string together these sounds, words, sentences and paragraphs into actual narrative in its multiplicity of forms.

Narrative and Composition

Sounds are senses.
Words are emotions.
Sentences are thoughts.
Paragraphs are ideas.

Narratives are conclusions

A narrative is a collection of words, sentences and paragraphs that have a structure, a direction, and a start and a finish. It also has a point—a lesson or a piece of enlightenment or an increase in knowledge, or it advances a conversation or offers an explanation of an event. If your writing doesn't have that point; if it doesn't make some well-thought-out statement, then you are doing something wrong.

A question commonly asked by amateur writers is: *Do you have to know what the conclusion will be before you get there?* No, you do not. And even if you do have such a conclusion in mind, you may find that in the course of developing your narrative its logic will take you somewhere else. But what you do need to know is that you *will* reach a conclusion. That you will know that conclusion when you get there. And that the narrative won't be finished until you have arrived there.

Types of narrative—Narrative, being the basic form of creative writing, comes in a multiplicity of forms, fiction and nonfiction, and is as diverse as human culture. Here's a short list:

1. Essays
2. Letters and diary entries
3. News articles
4. Blogs
5. Columns and editorials
6. Nonfiction books
7. Memoirs

8. Biographies and autobiographies
9. Anecdotes and miscellanea
10. Songs
11. Poems
12. Short stories
13. Novels and novellas
15. Screenplays
16. Dramatic plays
17. Books for musicals
18. Marketing communications, which includes:
    a. Press releases
    b. Advertising
    c. Reports
    d. Annual reports
    e. Speeches
19. Research and academic papers

Note the sheer range of narrative forms. Yet all share the characteristics of narrative, not least that they have a direction and a conclusion. Most people who are not professional writers impute more diversity to these forms than they really have and are often astonished that professionals can write well in multiple narrative forms. Professionals know that all real writing springs from the same source and requires the same skills and are only differentiated by the rules by which they operate.

Moreover, each of these writing types exhibits a range of values according to how well they achieve their conclusions, how much they accomplish within the rules of their form, and the quality of their prose. There are great press releases and terrible ones, just as there are great and terrible poems and screenplays. And a true professional writer will treat all narrative forms with the same engagement and focus upon producing the highest-quality result.

But before you can be a professional writer you must first survive an educational system that emphasizes the distinctions, rather than the commonalities, between all narrative forms.

Ironically, the two types of narrative that, for all but the most talented young people, are the most difficult to do: poetry and essays. These forms, because of their demanding rules, take not only talent and a lot of training and practice, but typically also require the kind of experience and wisdom not reached by most people until middle age. Yet, essays and poems are typically what our educational system demands of students. The result is that most students do not write poems, but songs; and do not write essays, but reports.

Songs, by way of example, are almost always in iambic, which naturally lends itself to sing-songy rhymes and easy memorization. Lyrics are almost always designed to be understood. For example, take the lyrics from the musical "Oklahoma" by Oscar Hammerstein:

> *Chicks and ducks and geese better scurry*
> *When I take you out in the surrey*
> *When I take you out in the surrey*
> *With the fringe on top*

Poetry, by comparison, gets away from the melody. It typically exhibits complex rhythms and carefully chosen imagery. It is often non-rhyming (or uses very sophisticated rhymes) and makes use of complex structural elements such as enjambment and caesura. You may not always understand the meaning of the words (thanks to everything from the use of the poet's personal information, obscure references and play with the sounds of words) but you can still be carried along by the sounds and the meter. Here for example, is an excerpt from "Little Gidding," by T. S. Eliot:

> Midwinter spring is its own season
> Sempiternal though sodden towards sundown,
> Suspended in time, between pole and tropic.
> When the short day is brightest, with frost and fire,
> The brief sun flames the ice, on pond and ditches,
> In windless cold that is the heart's heat,
> Reflecting in a watery mirror
> A glare that is blindness in the early afternoon.

This is not to render a judgment on the relative value of the two narrative forms. On the contrary, each represents a high point in their respective twentieth-century forms. Yet they are not the same thing. But chances are this is what you have been taught.

A second example:

A *report* is a form of nonfiction writing characterized by: start at the beginning and keep writing until you've covered the topic. Your task is to show how much you know. And there can be penalties for being entertaining.

Essay—Theme statement at the beginning, supported by as many paragraphs as needed to support that statement, ending with a conclusion that brings it all together.

1. How to write narrative.
   a. Just start writing: Don't wait around for the perfect sentence or for inspiration. Writer's block is just ego, thinking you can write better than you are at that moment. Get rid of your ego and get started.

b. Focus on that first paragraph: The tendency is to inhale, to ramp up to what you want to say, and not to get the point until you're a quater way into the piece. Go ahead and do that, then erase it.

c. Once you get your opening down, just plow your way through. If you have an outline, learn it, then ignore it while you write.

d. Try to do blocks of writing—chapter, section, and so forth—in one sitting. But always start the next section, even one sentence before you stop a writing session.

e. Edit, edit, edit. Be ruthless. Cut out everything that isn't important or that hurts the flow of your writing.

How long should an essay be?

a. As long as the editor will let you.

b. Until you prove your conclusion to the reader

2. Fiction

a. Don't worry about the opening. Just get started.

b. Write down your characters' names and all proper names.

c. Don't stop. Write all the way through.

d. Put it aside for a few days, if you can, then go back and edit ruthlessly.

e. Show it to someone you respect, but more important, trust.

How long should a story be?

a. As long as you need to convince the reader to believe in the reality of the world you've created and follow the protagonist through a defining experience.

3. Poetry

a. Listen to your words, enjoy the sound of language.

b. Don't force rhymes or rhythms, ever.

c. Stay away from rhyming dictionaries and thesauruses unless you are utterly desperate.

d. Edit. Be willing to throw out everything, including the entire poem.

How long should a poem be?

a. As long as it brings pleasure or insight to the reader.

b. As long as you need to implant the right emotion.

Part Two

Corporate Careers and Disciplines

That completes a quick tutorial on language and basic writing. The next part looks at different forms of professional writing, and at careers that make use of those forms.

Each of the following chapters will address one of those careers. We'll look, in turn, at a definition of the profession, give a brief history of the field, provide a taxonomy of the different writing forms used by the profession, provide some standard forms that you can use in years to come, and tips for producing professional quality work. Finally, we'll also address the advantages and disadvantages of the profession, as well as common career turning points.

We will end many chapters with real-life examples (mostly from the author's career) to show the rules in practice.

The next three chapters will look at careers typically related to corporate life—all of which fall under the title of corporate communications. Public relations, advertising and speechwriting are often found as departments in large corporations, and as stand-alone jobs in smaller ones.

That said, this work is also found in independent agencies that serve the corporate world, as well as government, academia, and nonprofit institutions. A number of freelancers work in these professions, especially speechwriters. The result is very synergistic universe in which freelancers are contracted by agencies, which in turn provide corporate departments with content materials (press releases, speeches, ad copy) for which they are kept on retainers. In this world, corporate communications professionals may produce their own written materials or act as managers/editors for the contracted agencies or freelancers.

Also, note that there are other writing careers within corporate life that are not directly discussed in this book. In some careers, such as marketing, writing may play a sizable role but yet remain sublimated to the larger work of the profession. In others, such as editing and writing in-house newsletters and magazines, the work is so similar to their counterparts in the media that we discuss them in the chapters dedicated to those professions.

As you read these chapters please keep in mind one underlying theme of this book: all forms of professional writing are valid career choices. And all deserve the highest levels of ethics and professionalism.

Publicist

What is public relations?

Public relations is the art of influencing the media to carry stories under their own banners, thus conferring the highest possible level of legitimacy with the target audience. This distinguishes PR from advertising or sponsorship, which are forms of purchased promotion. The official definition of public relations is: *the practice of managing communication between an organization and its publics.*

How PR works

Public relations targets the editorial side of media, and is willing to sacrifice control over the end product for this degree of legitimacy. This makes PR the cheapest form of promotion. But the lack of control over the end content carries with it a certain amount of risk: you never know what's going to finally appear in print or on the air. Journalists guard their independence and rightly resist any overt attempts to influence them. What that means is that there is always a risk—and it will happen several times in your PR career—that the reporter or editor will publish exactly the *opposite* story you've pitched to them.

Public relations typically targets legislators, key decision makers, customers, employees, current and potential customers and the general public.

Why do we need PR?

Journalists don't like to admit it, but 60 to 80 percent of all the content you see in traditional media, and probably 90 percent of all "reported" news on the Web, is ultimately the product of public relations, from personal contact to prepared media materials. The media, especially today, simply don't have the resources to cover all the stories they need to meet the demands of their audiences. Meanwhile, companies, nonprofits, schools and social groups all need public attention to stay successful, and they can't wait until the media finds them or recognizes the value of their story. They have to be proactive, and the most cost-effective way to do that is through public relations.

History of public relations

Public relations, though the term is less than a century old, is old as printing. Read Balzac's novel *Lost Illusions* to appreciate how ambitious individuals have always tried to influence the content of books, magazines and newspapers. Public relations as a profession, with its own rules and standards, really begins in the 1920s, with the rise of mass media, Hollywood and consumer products. From the beginning, PR's impact has been controversial: educating the general public about pollution, hygiene, vaccinations and other good works but, also (among other things) convincing women to smoke cigarettes and producing many of the excesses of consumer culture.

The biggest transformation in the history of PR took place in just the last few years, as the traditional media began to fade and were replaced by the Web and social networks. This has led to a profound shift in the nature of public relations from essentially a printed press release/cover letter/ mail process to one of Internet memes, social network management and blogger relations.

Despite all these changes, the essence of public relations remains the same: influencing the intermediaries who influence public opinion. And if the modes of conveying this influence have changed, great PR still requires very good writing. A cogent, powerful message is just as important now as it has ever been—indeed, it is even more necessary today given the added noise that must be cut through to reach the target audience.

Unfortunately, that fact is increasingly lost on much of the public relations profession. This need for good writing began even before the rise of the Web with the first public relations majors and degrees offered at universities, first in the United States, then throughout the world. While, historically, most PR professionals used to come from the world of journalism—typically veteran newspaper reporters and trade press editors—the graduates of these programs rarely had any experience other than PR. In this new reality, the role of account executives was emphasized, and the job of writer was discounted. The result has been a degradation in the overall quality of PR writing, which is ironic, given that the need for quality messaging may be greater than ever before.

Types of public relations

People new to public relations—and even some veterans—are often surprised at the many types of PR being practiced. Even in a small company, or agency, where a PR professional is expected to wear many hats, the different types of publicity should still be in one's quiver. Here is a quick description of the most common PR forms.

- *Analyst relations*—Conveying and managing financial and product information to industry analysts who in turn influence company stock prices.
- *Media relations*—What most people think of when they hear the phrase "public relations." This work involves influencing reporters at newspapers, magazines, wire services, broadcast news and on the Web.
- *Investor relations*—Similar to analyst relations but reaches out directly to shareholders. Can include authoring a company's annual report.
- *Internal communications*—Reporting, writing, and editing in-house organs, including company magazines and newsletters.
- *Labor relations*—Acting as the public spokesperson for the company regarding layoffs, hirings and union contract negotiations.
- *Financial public relations*—Management of all communications related to the legally required publication of quarterly and annual revenue and profit results. As you might imagine, this is a job of great responsibility— as even a minor error in figures can have devastating impact on stock price.
- *Celebrity/VIP public relations*—When you hear the term "publicist," what may spring to mind is one form of this type of PR: getting the name of important figures (such as movie stars) into print—or out of it. This work, which has something of a sordid reputation, is extremely stressful, and thus is typically high-paying.
- *Consumer public relations*—This is educational/public service PR, typically undertaken by consumer-oriented nonprofits and government agencies to educate the general public on matters of policy and consumer interest.
- *Crisis public relations*—High-pressure specialty work that focuses on managing media coverage during everything from natural disasters to corporate layoffs. Few corporations, even the biggest ones (excepting airlines and oil companies) have in-house crisis PR experts, as the occasions for such skills are few and far between. Rather, most companies contract, for the short term, agencies and experts adept at this work. Needless to say, it pays very well.

- *Industry relations*—A relatively rare practice. Some industry associations either take "loan" PR executives from their member companies or hire a full-time specialist, with the duty of promoting, not a single company, but the entire industry. This duty is usually reserved only for the most veteran corporate PR professionals.
- *Government relations*—Most large corporations have an in-house specialist, often holding the title of vice president, who takes on the combined role of lobbyist (or managing lobbyists) and promoting the company among legislators at the state and (more often) national levels.

The press release

The primary instrument of public relations—then, now and into the indefinite future—is the *press release.* Traditionally, it is the key document sent out to the media, though it may be supported by other documents, including sidebars, photos and a cover letter.

These days, the press release serves more as a source document from which to create other, targeted-content materials. That doesn't minimize its importance; it remains the narrative that defines and organizes the overall message, and from which the spectrum of subsequent publicity efforts need to derive to maintain consistency.

The role of a good press release is to capture the key points in the publicity "pitch." The headline and lede should cover everything important the target reader needs to know. It also should include usable quotes (and the name and title of the speaker), product specifications and capabilities, basic background information, benefits to users or participants and a boilerplate final paragraph that acts as a quick reference for journalists reporting on the business of the sender.

Types of press releases

Just as there are multiple professions inside the world of public relations so, too, are there numerous forms of press release. Sadly, few modern PR professionals know this; instead they typically only work with a few of the most common types. That's a shame, because the goal of public relations is to maximize good media attention, and the only way to accomplish that is to:

1. Expand the publicity effort beyond the related trade press and local media to other trade publications and the national media; and
2. Reach other editorial sections, beyond "News" or "New Products," such as features, news photos and career news.

Here is a partial list of press release (and subsidiary) forms. Get in the habit of using them all:

- *News release*—See above. This is the core written instrument of public relations. Note that a good news release does not try to be inclusive, and comprise every little nuance of a story. Rather, it should be kept short and tightly written, and include punchy quotes. All other content can be distributed through supporting documents, from the cover letter to sidebar releases. Typically, news releases are first sent to the media—and then after a proper period of time (a day or up to a few weeks, depending upon the roll-out schedule to international markets) are placed on the company website, social media and, if a video news release (see below) on YouTube or similar site.

- *New-product release*—The second most important form of press release. The new product-release is designed to be the most cogent way to notify the media of the introduction of a new product, product upgrade or service. The new-product release is similar to a news release but focuses on a single product or service at the time of its public introduction. As such, the release contains sections on product specifications, performance data and likely markets and applications. Every new-product release must contain price and delivery information—any "clever" attempt to escape including this information will damage trust with the media and should never occur, even if your CEO or marketing VP demands it.

- *Feature/application story*—The most difficult, but also the most powerful form of press release. A feature story typically describes the application of the company's products in services in real life. As such, it needs to be more about the user than the product, and more about the use than the company. Feature stories require top-notch writing, equal or greater in quality than a newspaper feature story, which it is trying to convince a reporter to write based on its contents. Feature releases, which can sometimes run several thousand words and be accompanied by evocative photos, are so valuable because they can reach the parts of publications and e-zines that other forms of publicity can never touch: the hugely valuable feature sections and cover stories. They can also extend publicity efforts to other vertical markets and the mainstream press that are otherwise almost never reached by traditional PR efforts. For professional writers, feature releases are the most satisfying, and creatively demanding, form of PR work.

- *Financial release*—Financial releases are very formalized documents, in most cases required by law, by which corporations and other for-profit institutions announce quarterly and annual revenues, profits and earnings-per-share (or, conversely, losses in those categories). Because the government requires very precise data presented in a very specific way—and because any mistakes in this reporting can not only crash company stock but bring down the wrath of the government agencies—this work is only for the most responsible and precise public-relations professionals. It is also advisable to establish a review process, by which both PR and corporate finance offices work together to double- and triple-check the numbers before they are released to the public. The government also requires that these releases be delivered to an acceptable number of media recipients—so it is important to carefully develop the routing list for these stories, including the use of wire services, and even hard copies by mail.

- *Press kit*—For the most important announcements, especially for the biggest new product roll-outs, a simple news or new-product release is just not enough.
  - o *Cover letter*—Given the importance of the announcement, and the request that the reporter or editor plow through a number of different documents, it is always best to accompany a press kit with a personal cover letter. This is to underscore that your company or organization considers this announcement sufficiently important to create a custom publicity document for the recipient. It is also an opportunity to reinforce the message and its significance. Remember, be professional; even if the journalist is a friend, don't be too chummy or it will seem as if you are exerting too much influence. Also, keep it relatively short: leave the real message for the contents of the press kit: that's what it is for.
  - o *Folder*—There are basically three ways to deliver a press kit to a journalist: print, email or PR wire service (via the Web). The first of these is increasingly obsolete—however, many companies will still deliver a hard-copy to key publications in order to reinforce the importance of the announcement and, frankly, to make sure the journalist actually sees it (rather than hitting 'delete' on an email). If you do choose to create a hard-copy version of the press kit, you'll want to put the contents into a folder—not a cheap, store-bought report folder, but a glossy and heavy stock folder, preferably white, with your company's logo printed and/or embossed on the front.
  - o *Photographs*—It is almost always valuable to include imagery with a press release, especially a new-product release. If you choose to create a print version, you should include 3–6 photographs, preferably color in 8 x 10 inch and transparency (large) versions. If you are using a virtual press kit, include links to the imagery or attach files. Virtual press kits also have the advantage of allowing you to add videos. This

can be done either with embedded videos with the press release or as links to videos on YouTube or the company's web site.

In developing imagery try to create a mix of stand-alone shots of the product and its use in real-life applications. Hire a professional photographer and models to do the work—anything you attempt yourself will inevitably look amateurish. As for videos, use a professional videographer and a scriptwriter. Keep in mind that this will not be inexpensive—but the good news is that you can also use this production for a video news release (see below).

○ *Sidebars*—Sidebars in publicity are comparable to sidebars in journalism; that is, they are stand-alone documents designed to amplify and support the main story. Thus, if you are introducing a new smartphone, you might want to create a sidebar on the innovative technology in its new display, or on its library of applications, or how it achieves extended battery life or the company's long history in cellular telephony. Sidebars are not supposed to be long: they are rarely more than 500–1,000 words—mainly because anything longer will distract from focus on the main story.

○ *Backgrounder*—Corporate backgrounders might be considered a form of sidebar, but they are so much longer and distinct in their targeting that they are considered a different genre. The backgrounder in a press kit is designed with one specific goal: to brief the targeted journalist with whatever he or she needs to understand the company's sending out of the press kit. For that reason, backgrounders can number several thousand words in length and include separate sections on company history, physical locations, products, senior management and customers. In the best-case scenario, a well-written and complete backgrounder will not only be used by a reporter in preparing the back paragraphs of a news story, but also will be kept on file indefinitely by that reporter as a reference document for future stories about the company.

○ *Q&A*—The Question and Answer is another distinct form of sidebar. In this case, the goal is to anticipate the most likely questions to be asked by the media, and then answer them in advance. The goal, as with many of these instruments, is to minimize the amount of friction facing a journalist writing a story and, in the process, increasing the odds of obtaining coverage. A typical Q&A is no more than a couple of pages and less than a dozen questions.

• *Personnel release*—One of the most prosaic forms of press release, the personnel release, sees the greatest use. Most local newspapers, as well as trade magazines/e-zines, have sections (often called "transitions" or a similar title) that document, typically in a sentence or short paragraph, job promotions or transfers by prominent figures in the community or industry. These items typically take the form of "Mary Smith has been named vice president of marketing for XYZ corporation," and includes added information on who that person is replacing, the subject's prior positions at the company (or elsewhere), duties in the new job, education, family, and so forth and often includes a headshot photo. A personnel release should contain the same information and in the same format (these columns are usually written by rookie reporters or bored veterans, so the less work required adapting the release the better). Also, include a photo. These are the easiest releases from which to obtain media coverage, so generating them should be a regular task of every corporate PR department.

- *Milestone release*—Popular a half-century ago (not least because it lent itself to the world of mass-production factories), the milestone release today is all but forgotten. That's a pity, because the milestone release has a remarkable ability not only to reach audiences otherwise untouchable but also to produce some of the best prose in the PR profession. Milestone releases celebrate key events in the story of a company or its products: the one millionth device shipped, the retirement of an important (to the company or the market) product, the company's 50th or 100th anniversary, and so forth. Because they are celebratory, and not specifically trying to sell anything, milestone releases are an opportunity to indulge in nostalgia, to trumpet success and to pen some really evocative prose. Given the opportunity to create memorable and evocative prose, it's a wonder that more writing-oriented publicists don't fight for the opportunity to write this kind of release.

- *Photo release*—In the Internet Age, one forgotten form of press release awaits its revival. The photo release used to be a standard vehicle for organizations (as well as for government—think of all of the military photographs handed to the press during World War II). Essentially, photographers would be employed by institutions to go around and capture interesting imagery inside the enterprise: rows of new cars coming off the production lines, vast factory floors, huge machinery, intent assembly workers and so forth). These photos would then be given a clever caption (snappy first, informative second) and sent out, typically in hope of being picked up by a wire service, such as Reuters, UPI and AP. A number of distinguished photographers (notably Margaret Bourke-White) got their start, and trained their eye, this way. Today, with the Web exhibiting an unquenchable desire for novel images, and every company employee armed with a smartphone camera, there is no reason why companies and other institutions shouldn't be continuously generating interesting images and regularly capturing millions of views. And to this can now be added video, with its own set of outlets and platforms.

- *Event announcement*—This is the most elementary press release type. Basically, it is an invitation disguised as a news release. The difference is that this type of invitation is directed toward the media, and the format allows for a more detailed description of the event itself. On the other hand, while a typical invitation presents the opportunity for the recipients to attend an event for their enjoyment, an event release is offering the journalist the chance to cover an interesting story. An event release should be short compared to other releases, but still long enough to persuade attendance. It should also have precise details on location (include a GPS link), date and time, and a means to give an RSVP (though don't depend upon journalists to reply: their calendars are too unpredictable given the possibility of breaking stories, and they don't like to be beholden to publicists). And don't just describe the event; make the case for why it will be a good story for the reporters' readers.

- *Video news release*—This type of press release takes the form a video, and it may be the most influential—at least in terms of reach—of any of the publicity instruments on this list. When you see a medical story on your local evening news, chances are it was the product of a video news release, edited (sometimes) with some local inserts and a new voice-over by a local reporter. Video news releases are a rare PR tool, which is a bit surprising given their impact, probably because they are much more difficult (and expensive) to create compared to print releases. You need to prepare a good script, hire a camera crew, set up field shoots and a firm to create graphics and special effects, and contract an editor. That's a sizable sum—equal to a dozen written releases—and that doesn't include paying for satellite distribution. But a good VNR, beamed up to a satellite and then transmitted to interested media can reach an audience of hundreds of millions around the world, far greater than any other publicity campaign. Moreover, you can take the same video—and in a longer version if you choose—and use it on your corporate Web page, in marketing and sales, and on sites like YouTube. Altogether, that's a very good return on your investment. Try it; you'll get better, and more cost efficient, with experience. Your success rate will improve as you better understand the needs of local TV stations.

In-person events—Public relations isn't just about managing clients and writing and sending-out press releases; it is also about meeting face-to-face with members of the media. Though, strictly speaking, these are not occasions for writing, they are often occasions for the *distribution* of your writing. Thus, at a press conference, you will almost always hand out press kits along with all the various presentations.

As these activities may also include other types of writing—such as the event announcement described above, as well as invitation letters, speeches prepared for the event, scripts, and so forth—we include a brief description of each:

- *Briefings*—These are casual gatherings, often regularly scheduled, by which a spokesperson presents news and updates as well as answers questions from the media. Corporations use irregular briefings to bring the trade press up-to-date on product developments and new technologies as well to manage information during company emergencies (layoffs, disasters, stock crashes) or major business deals (mergers, major contracts). For the former you may be asked to provide a presentation on the fly; for the latter you will have time for preparation, but the responsibility will be as great as for a financial release. Either way, it will be a high-pressure assignment.
- *Media events*—Think of these as briefing events—press conferences, major product announcements, annual shareholder meetings, public user group conferences—only more formal, a lot more expensive, and with a lot more time for preparation.
  - *Press conference*—These are the most casual type of media event, and typically more news-oriented than the others. Unlike a briefing, which is designed to update reporters, press conferences are normally reserved for new announcements. The format is well-known: a podium or table in the front of the room facing the media, and a series of presentations. The media in attendance will typically receive their press materials (prepared by you) at the start of the gathering. Simultaneously (timing is important) the same press materials will be sent out to reporters not in attendance. You may also be asked to prepare the presentations of the speakers.
  - *Major product announcement*—These are often truly elaborate events, held in a conference center or a hotel's grand ballroom, and featuring videos, live music, food, celebrities and VIPs and multi-media presentations. Your duties will be the same as with a press conference, but typically with a lot more material.
  - *User group meeting*—Given the precedent set by Steve Jobs and Apple, user group meetings—long a sleepy gathering filled with speeches and break-out sessions—have now become as elaborate as major-product announcements.
  - *Annual meeting*—By their very nature—convincing shareholders of the continuing value of the company—annual shareholder meetings are

carefully orchestrated events for which you may be asked to prepare one or more of the speeches.

- *Press tour*—Despite their effectiveness, press tours have always been rare events. One reason is cost, another is availability. Even if a company is willing to pay the expense of flying you and a top executive around the country (or world) and putting you up in expensive hotels, there is still the matter of taking a valuable employee away from the front lines of the company for a week or two. Still, if you can pull it off, nothing beats going directly to reporters and editors in their offices, capturing their complete attention for an hour or two, and giving them direct and exclusive access to someone who can speak for your company. That said, the world has changed: reporters today are more likely to work out of their homes than in newsrooms and to be scattered all over the landscape. That's the bad news; the good news is that the need for physical travel has been largely replaced by Skype and teleconferencing. But there's bad news in the good: once you had an executive in person, you had his or her full attention; by comparison, the exec who commits to a "satellite" press tour is very easily called away to other corporate duties. Make sure you get their commitment ahead of time.

PR jobs

Careers in public relations take two paths—corporate and agency (or freelance), though those paths may intertwine over the years. By the same token, PR careers typically start from two distinct beginnings: from journalism or, more frequently these days, from a degree in public relations.

Corporate jobs

Media relations—You interact regularly with reporters and editors at publications or stations.

Writer—You compose and edit press releases and pitch letters.

Corporate level—You prepare the annual report, the company magazine, quarterly financial releases.

Divisional level—You write or edit the division newsletter, introduce new products, write news releases.

Speechwriter—A full-time position at the corporate level, part-time at divisional level.

Agency

Account executive—You manage some of the agency's clients.

Writer—You author press releases, pitch letters and publications for clients.

Pitcher—You regularly contact the media to offer them your clients' latest announcements and news.

Web

Pitcher—You offer story ideas to bloggers and news editors.

Blogger—You write a blog that supports the image and the strategies of your employer.

Commenter/astroturfer—A controversial, and often unethical, job in which you pretend to be an independent observer when, in fact, you are secretly making a case for your employer.

Career: The good

Corporate

Company benefits

Longevity—Corporate PR is one of most secure jobs in many companies.

Job security

Part of a team

Access to the top—You will regularly deal with the top executives in your company.

Travel

Staff—At the corporate level, you will likely have an assistant and/or secretary.

Nice work environment

Agency

Good money

Excitement/lifestyle

Access to the famous and powerful

Wide-ranging interests—You will get the chance to deal with clients from every walk of life.

Career: The bad

You will sometimes be treated like a flack, a servant.

You may be asked to compromise your integrity if you work at a bad company.

There is no real job security at an agency.

Depending upon your perspective, it is not real writing compared with media or literary careers.

It can be hard to cross over to journalism, if you want that career direction.

Turning points

You get tired of telling one side of the story.
You grow frustrated at being a second-class journalist.
You are expected to lie. (If this happens, *quit*.)

EXAMPLE: A typical press release for a high technology company. This is the standard format, notably the heading. Note the use and location of quotes, bullet points to telegraph attributes and section heads.

For Immediate Release

May 9, 2018

LifeSignals Launches Life Signal™ Processor Product Family, Developed with Support of 3M and STMicroelectronics

- ■ *A new class of wireless biosensor platform purpose-built for OEMs to create wearables for life-critical medical and healthcare monitoring applications.*

- ■ *LifeSignals worked with 3M and STMicroelectronics to develop and industrialize the LSP product family, targeting high-volume markets.*

Fremont (California), and Geneva (Switzerland) – May 9, 2018 – The Life Signal Product platform, the world's first family of semiconductor chips optimized for mobile and wearable applications in medical and health monitoring for life-critical applications, was introduced today by LifeSignals Inc. here. The product family was developed and industrialized in conjunction with STMicroelectronics (NYSE: STM) and 3M (NYSE: MMM) to meet the stringent needs of the medical market.

"The medical world is in desperate need of clinical-grade disposable and reusable wearables for a variety of markets ranging from human monitoring applications such as in-hospital patient monitoring, remote health monitoring, wellness, fitness, worker safety, and senior care, to veterinary healthcare such as pet, equine and livestock monitoring," said Surendar Magar, LifeSignals CEO and Founder. *"We are answering that need. We believe the Life Signal Processor Product family will become a cornerstone of an emerging 'Internet of Lives' – serving billions and billions of bodies generating billions and billions of bits of life-changing valuable information every second of every day."*

The LSP family currently consists of two silicon devices and developer support items:

- ■ **LC1100 Life Signal™ Processor, a single-chip solution for disposable clinical-grade biosensor patches** – The core chip of the product family, the LC1100 enables the creation of low-cost, low-power wireless biosensor patches, smart clothing and other wearable devices that can continuously capture multi-parameter life signals with clinical accuracy. The LC1100 can communicate that resulting data to monitoring devices, smartphones, tablets and the cloud, continuously operating for days with only coin cell batteries.

- ■ **LC5500 UWB, a companion receiver chip** – A receiver chip that is optionally used in mobile and certain fixed receiver devices. The LSP chipset's hybrid radio (featuring Wi-Fi, Ultra-Wideband and Medical-Band standards) was invented to deliver wire-grade connectivity across multiple parallel wireless channels when multiple subjects are being monitored wearing LSP-based biosensors.

- ■ **Developer Support Items for OEMs** – The LSP family is supported by a full suite of hardware and software development tools, including a development board and a software development kit (SDK) for customers to design desired customized devices based on LSP. In addition, production-ready reference designs are available for multiple product types – including patches, smart clothing-based designs, receiver devices, etc. Various apps are available for iOS and Android devices.

The LSP product family was developed in collaboration with two major strategic partners. Innovation giant 3M provided key inputs and vital resources to verify the applicability of LSP technology. Semiconductor leader STMicroelectronics provided resources for silicon development, manufacturing and quality assurance for high volume production of LSP devices.

"We are excited to further apply 3M science to advance connectivity while improving patient outcomes,"

said Cindy Kent, President and General Manager of 3M Infection Prevention Division.

"We have been working with LifeSignals to industrialize their innovative multi-radio architecture and bring it to market in high volumes while meeting clinical-grade requirements. The LSP is the perfect example of the benefits delivered by the complex combination of ultra-low-power wireless connectivity, highly accurate sensor interfaces, advanced analog features, and an ultra-efficient processing platform," said Benedetto Vigna, President of Analog, MEMS and Sensors Group, STMicroelectronics

Background for editors

The healthcare and technology industries have worked for decades to create monitoring equipment and analytical innovations that can manage the immense volume of data streaming off the last generations of medical devices – and make it useful for healthcare, wellness, and personal safety applications.

However, deployment of such technologies remains limited since bodies still must remain tethered by wires to the sensors still used by the healthcare industry. Meanwhile, customized monitoring equipment remains bulky and expensive. Ultimately, this digital/medical revolution will never fully succeed until wearable sensors become wireless and comfortable to wear, in a small, low-cost form factor, capable of matching the clinical accuracy of current wired sensors and providing wire-grade connectivity to various receiving devices.

Ultimately, a single wearable device must be able to capture several key vital signals from the body, such as multiple profiles of heart rhythms, blood oxygen levels, respiration signals, heart sounds, temperature, motion, and others. Until now, traditional wireless and sensor technologies have been too expensive in both cost and power consumption, or not reliable enough for their mission-critical applications to realize this vision. The LSP product family changes all that.

Suggested Interviews:

Surendar Magar, President and CEO, LifeSignals

Benedetto Vigna, President of Analog, MEMS and Sensors Group, STMicroelectronics

About LifeSignals, Inc.

LifeSignals (formerly HMicro Inc.) is the Silicon Valley based creator and producer of the patented Life Signal™ Processor, a semiconductor platform designed to faithfully capture and communicate vital life signals from humans and animals to the cloud. LifeSignals is a venture capital backed, fabless semiconductor company, enabled by equity investments from Flex, Uniquest, Dreamtech, Renew Group, Seraph Capital, Xseed Capital, and Reddy Capital. Further information can be found at www.lifesignals.com.

About STMicroelectronics

STMicroelectronics is a global semiconductor leader delivering intelligent and energy-efficient products and solutions that power the electronics at the heart of everyday life. STMicroelectronics' products are found everywhere today, and together with our customers, we are enabling smarter driving and smarter factories, cities and homes, along with the next generation of mobile and Internet of Things devices.

By getting more from technology to get more from life, STMicroelectronics stands for life augmented.

In 2017, the Company's net revenues were $8.35 billion, serving more than 100,000 customers worldwide. Further information can be found at www.st.com.

Media Contacts for LifeSignals
PRxDigital
Jennifer Spoerri
Brenna Bolger

STMicroelectronics
Alexis Breton – Director, PR & Media Operations

Advertising Copywriter

What is advertising?

Advertising is the profession of developing, and buying placement in the media, controlled messages designed to influence the behavior—typically the purchasing habits—of current and potential customers or users. Advertising, in various forms, is as old as civilization and as new as the latest technology.

Advertising is distinct from public relations in that the message is purchased by the advertiser as opposed to being "pitched" for free coverage; and can choose its location and form of presentation. Advertising is distinct from "direct marketing" because it is non-personal—that is, it is not directed at specific individuals, only at types of potential customers with shared characteristics.

Advertising is currently a $600 billion industry worldwide, making it the single largest venue for professional writing in the global economy.

Why advertising?

Advertising enables the advertiser to fully control the content, the experience and the venue of the message. Once an advertisement is accepted by the delivery platform, its content will not be changed before it reaches its audience. This means that, unlike public relations and most other forms of corporate communications, the advertiser has complete control of its messaging, removing the risk of an intermediary (reporter, editor, blogger, broadcaster) intercepting the message and changing, or even reversing, it. Advertising also takes advantage of the ability of the media to take a single message and scale it to millions of people simultaneously.

History of advertising

Advertising is as old as writing—indeed it might even be older: we can probably assume that Paleolithic man carved or painted a message in a high-traffic area to promote a service. We do know for certain that painted advertising began in India in about 4000 BCE, and in books in China about 1000 BCE.

As signage from Pompeii shows, the ancients made heavy use of signs, posters and various forms of early billboards to promote their businesses and manufactured wares. The rise of printing was almost instantly followed by printed advertising—handbills, posters, pages in books, then newspapers and magazines. In medieval villages, the largely illiterate populace was guided to vendors via signage that resembled the service being offered (such as a boot from a shoemaker). The explosion of newspapers in the eighteenth century, particularly in Great Britain and the United States; and of books, especially in France and Germany, was underwritten as much by advertising revenues as sales.

The transformative figure in the creation of the advertising profession was Londoner Thomas J. Barratt, who developed a hugely influential advertising campaign for Pears Soap. His philosophy found a home in the first advertising "agencies" developed by Volney B. Palmer in 1840 in Philadelphia. Palmer bought space in newspapers at a discount, then resold the space to advertisers at a tidy profit. Barratt, and those who followed, learned to also offer the service of creating content (at a fee) for those advertisers.

What we think of as "modern" Madison Avenue–type advertising began in the 1920s. Advertising agencies adopted the theories of Edward Bernays—not coincidentally the father of public relations—in which subtle messaging could be used to tap into the hidden desires and subconscious beliefs of consumers and instill in them a desire for the goods and services being offered. Not surprisingly, this technique proved extraordinarily powerful over the next few decades, both in government propaganda and in creating the vast consumer culture we know today.

By the end of the twentieth century, advertising was ubiquitous in the developed world, finding venues in every corner of daily life, from radio to television to the Web to billboards to print, even to logos on clothing and every other form of consumer good. And whereas advertising in the 1950s and 1960s was primarily an art form, the intuitive creations of account executives and art departments, by the twenty first century it was mostly shaped by empirical research, including surveys and focus groups.

Types of advertising

Not surprisingly, for such a venerable and creative professional the range of advertising forms is nearly endless. Here is just a partial list:

- *Fliers, postcards and handbills*—One of the oldest types of advertising, these advertising instruments regularly undergo revivals. Fliers and handbills are cheap to make and usually distributed by hand by volunteers or true believers. Needless to say, that limits the geographic range of their distribution. On the other hand, where they are distributed—on street corners (usually illegally), stuck to light poles, pinned on kiosks—they can have a powerful impact. This kind of writing is almost always contract work, often done through printers.

- *Point of sale*—This form is a kind of hybrid between advertising and marketing. Point of Sale tools include brochures, discount cards, fliers and other promotional items found, as the name suggests, and checkout counters and similar locations where products are purchased. Most of these items can also be used in *Direct Mail* advertising, which is sent directly to a pre-qualified mailing list of current and likely customers. For writers, this is typically agency or freelance contract work.

- *Billboards*—Increasingly considered a visual blight, billboards endure in controlled locations in cities and along major highways simply because they work. The idea is to present a simple, strong visual (and to a lesser degree, verbal) message to commuters trapped in their cars. Thus, the size of billboards: they are designed to be big enough to provide the commuter with enough time to assimilate the entire message being presented.

- *Radio*—The dominant advertising platform of the first half of the twentieth century, radio remains a major medium, with audiences for news, talk shows and certain syndicated productions exceeding even the audiences for their television counterparts. Radio advertising's greatest challenge is the human voice, which must convey information at a much slower rate than printed words. Cross this with the constraints on time, and radio advertising is, by necessity, limited in the content it can convey. Radio advertising is usually contract work done for clients by the radio station, the writer contracted for the job.

- *Print*—Newspapers, magazines and specialty publications (including catalogs, fliers, and brochures) enjoy a number of advantages, including portability, quality image reproduction, high information capacity and a comparatively low price of reproduction. That's why printed materials were the dominant format for advertising for centuries, from Gutenberg to the rise of the Internet. Unfortunately for professional writers, print advertisement copywriting, a major source of employment, has rapidly lost ground in the twenty-first century.

- *Television commercials*—With its ability to project not just words (print) and sound (radio) but also full-motion imagery, television became the dominant form of advertising within decades of its creation. Even today, television remains the locus of the most creative advertising, and though its platform may evolve away from the television itself to laptops, phones and embedded displays, television commercials will likely remain the dominant form of advertising for at least a generation to come. For all of its power, experience has now shown that television does have several major limitations when it comes to advertising. Two of these, image quality and portability, have been largely overcome: we've come a long way from grainy black-and-white broadcasts on fragile, vacuum tube console TVs to high-definition (and even 3D) broadcasts on sturdy flat-screen displays. But others, most notably production and placement costs, along with high viewer expectations, have only grown more pronounced with the years. TV commercials are *expensive*, with placement costs alone rising into the millions of dollars per minute during large-audience programming, such as the Super Bowl. Moreover, a jaded viewing audience demands ever more-elaborate productions and clever messaging—the modern Super Bowl commercial costs more per minute to produce than a Hollywood blockbuster film—which largely limits broadcast television commercials to only the biggest and most prosperous corporate clients. The proliferation of cable channels has somewhat counterbalanced this trend: late night, second- and third-tier cable network advertising space can be purchased very cheaply, hence the proliferation of traditional, low-budget/low-quality advertising to be found there. But the audiences also are usually very small, with limited disposable income and very specialized interests. National-level television commercials are almost always written by full-time professionals at major advertising agencies.

- *Television infomercials*—Infomercials, pioneered in the mid-1950s by the likes of Ron Popeil (the "Vegematic," "Pocket Fisherman" and so forth), were the result of a recognition by a few brilliant entrepreneurs that the following ad space costs of off-hour local television might be combined with a county fair type of hucksterism for advertising mass-market products directly to consumers without the need for costly distribution and retail channels. The real breakthrough by these pioneers was the realization that it was possible to go beyond the 30–60 second straightjacket of established television advertising and instead buy up the 30-minute blocks usually reserved for programming. The result was the Infomercial (though it wouldn't get that name until the 1990s) which, though often the butt of jokes, has proven to be a highly lucrative and (despite early attempts to ban them) enduring advertising institution. Infomercials, like televangelists, derive their effectiveness from a combination of intensity (Popeil's famous "Wait, there's more!") that makes them hard to turn off, their contrived amateurishness (the everyday-looking demonstrator who operates the product with carefully choreographed expertise), a cheering audience and repetition (unlike traditional commercials, infomercials can repeat their message a dozen times in a half-hour to drive the message home). In the age of digital cable, the opportunity for infomercials continues to grow as fast as the creation of new channels. Infomercials typically require very simple repetitive scripts, often written by the promoter to control costs. Contract work is limited.

- *Web banners*—The Internet, in part because it began as a free (or at most a subscription) experience, struggled for decades to overcome cultural resistance to any attempt to monetize the medium. Thus, advertisers had to all but sneak their products onto the Web. Thus, the "banner" ad, a baby step into Web advertising consisting of small, narrow ads designed to haunt the edges of on-screen content. Typically, they consisted of an ad headline and a simple image. In traditional media, this would have been a disadvantage, but the Web brought with it some distinct technical advantages—not least that the readers merely needed to click on the ad and be "hotlinked" to much more robust and content-filled web sites where the real pitch (and ordering) could be made. Web banner ads still exist but have mostly evolved into other forms (see below). There is little writing work available on the ads themselves (in fact, most just port over copy from other media), but there can be considerable writing work—captions, descriptions, and so forth—at the linked-to web site.

  A more modern variant of the banner is what is known by the pejorative term *clickbait*. Clickbait takes two forms. The dominant version takes advantage of the revenues that can be obtained by advertisers per page view by convincing readers (usually through an interesting image on a mainstream web site) to visit the clickbait site and page ("click") through scores of images on separate pages. There is little opportunity for writers in this work, as most is done in poorer economies (as the literate reader quickly discovers). The second form looks exactly like the first but is, in fact an actual sponsored advertisement designed to lure the reader to click on it and go to a Web page designed to make the sale. There is a growing amount of demand for writers of these latter pages.

- *Web advertisements*—Web advertising has recapitulated the history of a century of traditional advertising in a tenth of the time. Thus, as the Web became more valuable as a source of revenue (and users began to ignore banners), full-sized formal advertisements emerged. These were roughly the same as print ads (and indeed, often were), with the added advantage of, once again, being able to add links to almost infinitely scalable web sites. In addition, given the larger real estate of the ads, it is also possible to embed videos. Web advertisements, like their print counterparts, are typically created by ad agencies. Copywriting for these ads, or the scriptwriting for the embedded videos can be quite lucrative, and the opportunity to do so is often open to junior advertising people, who are assumed to be more in touch with the generation that spends the most time on the Web.

- *Web commercials*—Web commercials are the next evolutionary step in Web advertising. This form was not constrained by technology—they were possible almost from the earliest days of the Web—but by cultural resistance: most users weren't willing to accept elaborate video commercials (often expansions on television commercials) on existing sites. By 2010, as the Web and online shopping moved into a dominant role in the global economy, as the revenues advertisers could gain from popular sites grew sufficiently lucrative, and as hugely popular sites such as YouTube developed sufficient user loyalty, full-blown commercials began to appear. As with their Web predecessors, what these commercials offered was the appeal of television commercials with the scalability of links. Whereas, despite years of failed initiatives, television still required viewers to go to a store or on the Internet to make purchases of the offered goods and services, on the Web similar commercials empowered the viewer to go directly to in-depth product descriptions, demonstrations, user configuration, and purchase. They could even tour past commercials for the same item as an alternative entertainment. The Web also offers advertisers the ability to embed links in noncommercial content to act as doorways to these commercials.

  Career opportunities for writers in Web commercials are currently almost unlimited. In time, most advertising is likely to migrate to the Web, and that will present opportunities for everyone from entry-level copywriters to the most veteran top-end copywriters currently creating national TV advertising.

- *Logos and branding*—This is a very specialized field, one deeply interconnected with graphic arts. Logos are more closely related to graphics, as the client typically already has a company or product name and now wants it presented visually in the most compelling way. However, there are rare, and usually very high-paying, occasions when a new name and look are created at the same time. Experts in corporate name creation are very rare and specialized, as the work exists at the nexus of language (including ancient language roots), human psychology and trademark law. This can be hugely interesting work; but, understandably, it is not a profession that can hold many players. Branding work—coming up with corporate or product positioning statements—is a much more common activity. But because it tends to be one-off work, with months or even years between jobs for a particular client, it is usually bound up with other advertising work (or even handed off to the PR department). That said, a talent for brand writing—and the diplomacy of dealing with different client constituency—is valuable to any agency and can work wonders for job security.

- *Viral advertising*—This is the youngest form of advertising, and also the oldest. In its original form, it took the form of targeted gossip: that is, a business, or more often a political campaign, would create a rumor or whisper campaign for its own purposes in hope of having it proliferate across a community. In the modern wired world a similar effect is created using more scientific and systematic methods. One of the impressive (and sometimes disturbing) features of the Web is that it can perform the same proliferation at historically unprecedented speeds, sometimes reaching a billion people or more in a matter of days. Not surprisingly, small companies and the advertising agencies of large companies have jumped on this phenomenon in hope of having the same impact, and preferably without leaving their fingerprints on the process. Noted Silicon Valley marketing guru Tom Hayes created the term "beme," a portmanteau word combining "business" with "meme," the latter the basic unit of an idea or thought that is transmitted and evolves in the manner of a biological gene. In Hayes's formulation, a beme is a carefully crafted marketing/advertising message that is injected into the culture to self-perpetuate without leaving any record of its source. Thus, a beme is indistinguishable from a meme to the recipient, who passes it on without knowing it has a commercial purpose.

Bemes look like the ultimate form of advertising. But there is one problem: no one yet has figured out with any confidence how to create them. Nevertheless, their potential power makes them almost inevitable in the years to come, and anyone with a talent for creating them will become very wealthy.

Jobs in advertising

Advertising jobs can be found in two distinct venues: corporate executive offices and stand-alone advertising agencies. And though there is considerable duplication in the job descriptions found at each, the nature of those jobs can vary widely.

Agency—Ad agencies are private businesses that offer advertising services to corporate, nonprofit or government clients. Most agencies are independent enterprises. However, regular waves of consolidation have created a handful of national and international "super" agencies that often have scores of offices located in major cities and are treated as quasi-franchises. Stand-alone agencies can be quite small, managing perhaps a score of clients with all-purpose service. The big urban agencies—both independent and part of a larger firm—often have specialized departments ranging from consumer research to video production to ad space buys.

Copywriter—This is the primary job for professional writers in advertising agencies. Copywriting, which usually consists of writing the support copy in print ads or the script in radio and TV work, offers the opportunity for interesting creative work covering a wide array of subjects. That's the good news; the bad is that copywriters are usually second-class citizens in ad agencies. The real glory goes to the creative folks who come up with the client campaign themes. That said, veteran copywriters, after founders and partners, likely have the best job security in the gypsy-like world of ad agency life. For this job it is crucial to be able to write clear and succinct copy, often conveying complex messages in a simple style. It is crucial in this job to be flexible: you can't fall in love with your prose, because the client may demand you do a complete rewrite for its own purposes, and you will have to write that new copy with the same commitment and intensity. Veteran agency copywriters make good money, but not top money. In large agencies, copywriting operates as a separate department.

Account executive—The high priests of agency life, account executives manage all relations with individual clients. AE's often pitch prospective clients; then, if they land the account, direct all of the creative effort (including copywriting) for that client and serve as the sole point of contact with the client for the duration of the relationship. When you think of ad agency life in television and film, it is usually the life of the account executive you picture in your mind's eye. Being an account executive is not a writing career—though occasionally a copywriter will rise into such a role, especially in a smaller agency. However, account executives are the equivalent of managing editors, with the best exhibiting a real skill at editing copy and recognizing good prose. Unlike copywriters, account executives have almost no ceiling on salaries, as wages and bonuses are typically based upon the size of the client and the contract. By the same token, that salary can also go to zero—that is, they are fired—when a major client is lost.

Creative—Strictly speaking, "creative" at an ad agency is the art department, the graphic artists who come up with the design for an advertisement or visual storyboard for a commercial. Those folks will treat your well-crafted copy as a mere design element, one of the deflating experiences of being an ad copywriter. That said, there is one form of copywriting to which even the creative folks will defer: These are the brief phrases that are either attached to a campaign (*advertising slogans*) or product/service (*tagline*). Since these phrases define almost everything attached to a campaign or product introduction, they are of supreme importance to agency operations. And though they are typically a group effort by everyone involved with an account, they are usually devised by copywriters. Great phrase writers become famous, and are amply rewarded and, like rock stars, they aren't known for longevity.

Web—Most ad agencies employ one or more in-house specialists. The larger agencies have complete departments. At the turn of the twenty-first century, especially during the dot.com bubble, these specialists focused on creating and placing banners and other ads on the Web, as well as on helping clients create promotional and e-commerce sites. Much of that work has migrated to traditional agency departments, such as media, production and research. With the rise of social networks, agency Web specialists shifted to focus on Facebook, Twitter and other sites. This remains a largely hybrid activity—that is, most Web specialists combine copywriting, art and placement in their job descriptions, making it interesting and eclectic work for writers interested in independence and technology.

Principal/partner—In the traditional organization chart for an ad agency, this job is at the top. We've put it at the bottom because it is the least likely position for a professional writer. It is very rare that any copywriter ever becomes a partner in an established agency—it is far more likely for someone already in a management position, such as an account executive or business manager. That said, it is not unprecedented for a superstar phrase writer to spin off from a current employer and become the founder a new agency.

Corporate—Life in a corporate advertising department (or "marketing communications" if it also incorporates public relations and in-house publications) is very different from life in an advertising agency. For one thing, corporate advertising typically does very little creative; rather, it acts as the client for independent agencies, contracting them to create and place advertising, monitoring the process, and measuring the results. That makes corporate advertising rather dull creatively, but exciting in regard to the size of the budget and perquisites that come from holding the purse strings.

Copywriter—This job might be more properly called "copyediting," as the professional writer in a corporate advertising department is largely engaged in the process of providing the information needed by an agency copywriter to create text, editing that copy and fact-checking it thoroughly so the company cannot be accused of misrepresentation or fraud. That said, larger companies may create their own advertising targeted at their particular trade press, and department copywriters are often asked to prepare the copy for these ads, in part because they are likely to have considerable expertise on the subject and because the budgets for the creation of these ads are tight.

Product line ad director/MarCom—This is the corporate equivalent of the account executive. The fundamental difference is that this individual has as a "client" a manufacturing group or division of a company. For that reason, in a large corporation, this individual is just as likely to be employed by, and reside at, that division. Thus, a multinational corporation may have division or product ad directors scattered around the planet at scores of locations—reporting first to their product group and only secondarily to the corporate advertising department, the latter usually establishing design standards and protecting against overlap. How independently these individuals can operate depends upon whether or not they have their own ad-creation and media-buy budgets.

Corporate advertising director/VP—The counterpart of the agency director/ partner, the corporate advertising director is responsible for all the advertising produced by the company, including that generated by outside agencies, as well as for managing the budget for all corporate advertising in all its forms. Some companies, especially those in consumer products and other large advertising buyers, consider this position of sufficient important to give this individual a full company directorship or vice-president position (though never a senior or C-level title). In very large companies not all advertising professionals may directly report to the advertising director, but rather to their own operating groups. Nevertheless, all company advertising professionals are required to follow the content standards, messaging and campaign slogans as signed off by the director.

At this level, corporate advertising directors do little writing beyond reports (usually ghost-written by subordinates) and the occasional by-lined trade media article (also usually ghost-written). That said, unlike in an agency, it is possible for a corporate ad copywriter to move up through the ranks to a director's job.

Career: The good

Advertising as a career appeals to a certain type of individual, typically a creative person who is more interested in the process of artistic creation than the actual result or in who is credited for it. Aesthetically, advertising work is as demanding creatively as any of the literary fine arts and typically is much more eclectic and far-ranging in subject matter than, say, newspaper reporting or magazine writing.

Agency

It's exciting—When it comes to entertaining work environments and exciting venues, advertising is hard to top among writing careers. Agency life itself can be high-pressure, but it is also highly creative, respects eccentricity and is filled with smart and witty people.

Great work conditions—Ad agencies, especially in the art and copywriting departments, are like toy stores for adults. It is also work punctuated by high-level public events (such as launch parties), cocktail parties, trade shows and expense-account dinners—mostly for account executives, but sometimes for copywriters and other creative types as well.

Very creative—Did we mention that it is very creative work? You may not be writing deathless prose, but there is a chance that the words you write—especially a clever slogan that will be repeated by millions of people and may even outlive you. But short of that, you will likely find yourself perpetually challenged to learn about a brand-new product, service, non-profit campaign or company and then quickly convert that knowledge into precise, punchy and informative prose. Whatever envy you may have of your counterparts in journalism, you can take comfort in the fact that they are covering boring PTA meetings while you are introducing billion-dollar products to the world.

Access to the top (Corporate, Hollywood, DC)—As with speechwriting, and sometimes PR, advertising is a way to meet and work with some of the most powerful, interesting and creative people on the planet. If you are working with the movie or television industries, you may find yourself writing scripts for stars (and sitting in on the filming). If you are working for a corporate client, you may find yourself making a presentation to the CEO and board of directors. And, because you are a contracted professional rather than a subordinate employee, those encounters will be much more on equal terms. You will have some amazing stories to tell.

Good, even great, pay—When times are good, and clients are happy, advertising agency work can be a very good living. And though copywriters typically don't do as well as account executives, if you can reach the rarified position of writing slogans and taglines for giant clients, you can make a fortune: indeed, these superstars make as much as any form of professional writer.

Corporate

Job security—The single greatest advantage corporate advertising offers over agency is *longevity*. Agency work can be a gypsy existence, as you move from one job to the next as a major contract ends. By comparison, you can grow old in corporate advertising, filling a long career that ends with pensions, stock and a comfortable retirement. Companies don't fire their advertising people—they have their advertising people fire their ad agencies, and then have them try out new ones. Furthermore, corporate ad people don't have to assiduously keep up with the latest advertising trends—they just have to know enough to make sure their ad agencies do so.

Management opportunity—Want to run an ad agency? Quit and start your own. Want to make VP of Advertising or Marketing Communications in your company? Work hard, be ambitious, take on ever more responsibility and you may very well get there. Ad agencies resemble most PR agency and marking firms: that is (with the exception of the large global firms) they are organizationally flat and often never grow larger than the number of direct reports the founder(s) can handle. By comparison, corporate ad departments are typically vertical, with a defined hierarchy, including a professional management with its own upward and outward mobility. This establishes a well-marked pathway for copywriters to find their way into entry-level management roles and beyond, even to other jobs elsewhere in the company.

Power—Being one of the people who helps craft the public image of your company carries with it a considerable amount of influence in your organization, as well as with your professional peers in the advertising industry. Be part of a successful and/or clever campaign and you'll also enjoy the admiration of your friends, neighbors and other business people you meet.

Huge budget—Working in the ad department of a large corporation will often make you directly responsible for the distribution of a large budget—hundreds of millions of dollars if you become VP Advertising in a large consumer products company. Copywriters rarely have that level of responsibility, but they do often have a budget for hiring agency talent. So, just about any job you have in corporate advertising will have some financial responsibility, and it will multiply as you rise through the department. That can have its own appeal, as it will give you more control over your fate than you normally would have as an employee.

Access to the top—You may not be hobnobbing with movie and TV stars (unless you work for a studio or sit in on your agency's ad shoot), but you will be talking on a regular basis with the executive row of your company, and that will be a whole lot more important for your career.

Glamorous (with some limitations)—Corporate advertising isn't as exciting as agency work, but it does have its moments. As part of the team that creates campaigns and makes large ad buys, you will be invited to many of the glitzy events that are part of agency life. And there are advantages to be being the client's representative at these events rather than an agency's foot soldier. Moreover, you get the best of both worlds: the excitement of the advertising world with the sense of family and stability of corporate life.

Career: The bad

While some people are made for advertising—they love the excitement, the connection to interesting clients, the constant change in subject matter and so forth—for others, the experience can be frustrating, even excruciating. What's interesting is that it is almost impossible to know in advance how you will react. Some writers, who fear their work will be degraded by the experience, find to their surprise that they love advertising copywriting, often because of its sheer novelty. Others, who assume they will like the business side of the work, discover that they cannot bear either the anonymity or surrendering ultimate editorial control to others. The lesson is, don't assume you know how you will react to an advertising career until you try it, and certainly don't dismiss or disdain this work until you can speak from experience.

Agency

No job security; gypsy existence—In agency life you are only as good as your current client list. Last year's superstar can be this year's failure if one or more clients decide to take their business elsewhere. This is especially true for account executives, but even copywriters—who typically enjoy a bit more job security—can be victims. Disappoint a major client with your copy on a new campaign, and if you can't fix it quickly, you will likely be gone that day. And, since you are at the bottom of the food chain at most agencies, and since you don't bring in new business, and because you can be easily replaced by a freelancer, should revenues fall far enough you will also likely be the first to be laid off.

At the mercy of clients—Some clients have great taste and appreciate quality writing. Others have lousy taste and are fools. The problem with agency life is that you will have to deal with both types: as they say, anyone with money in their pocket is your boss. And as a writer you don't get the choice of which clients to work with. That will mean that some of your best ideas will be rejected in lieu of copy for which you want to have no public connection. The perversity of life is that the lousy clients usually have the most money and are the most loyal to you—so you are stuck with them forever, while the smart client moves on to another agency. Thus, a lot of being an ad agency copywriter involves swallowing hard and doing the work. And the only thing you can do about it is to try to educate stupid clients to be more discerning, and to save your best rejected ideas for good clients when they come along.

Creative frustration—Literary writers grow frustrated when their prose isn't as good as it can be. For advertising copywriters, the frustration is just the opposite when they can't get clients to buy into their best work. We noted the problem of being at the mercy of dumb clients, but there are times when that isn't an isolated event. Rather, you experience a run of vetoes on your copy from a series of clients. Usually this is just coincidence: your writing skills are as good as ever, but you just happen to have a group of clients with a different perspective. Of course, that doesn't make the experience any less painful. Nobody likes to have their skills, developed over many years, consistently devalued. Meanwhile, the agency itself will only have limited patience with a copywriter who can't satisfy one client after another and is growing increasingly bitter. The only solution is to not let the frustration overwhelm you, trust in your skills and keep doing your best. Of course, that is easier said than done, and you may find that you need a change of venue: finding another agency or going corporate.

A second source of creative frustration is that, unless you are a slogan writer, an awful lot of copywriting is repetitive. You are writing plain vanilla copy for an unsophisticated audience for products that are lot like each other. In other words, it can sometimes become boring and repetitive when you are just plugging specialty terms into a copy template. If your life dream was to become a poet or novelist, this type of work can be soul killing. You can sometimes alleviate this frustration by doing your own, more creative, work on the side. Another is to just be patient, in the hope that more interesting assignments will soon come along.

You can't grow old—Agency life is a young person's game. Given the nature of the work, youthful energy—that is, the ability to create tons of copy for multiple diverse clients—can be more important than well-crafted copy for a few similar clients. Some writers grow faster and more prolific as they age; most don't. In addition, language changes—and few writers evolve with it. So, what was seen as elegant prose at the beginning of your career may seem stiff and out-of-touch to readers (especially young ones, who are the most important targets of most advertising). What this means is that your ad copywriting career may grind to a halt even as you are becoming, by any objective measure, a better writer. You may also eventually find the entire experience of agency life exhausting—the endless crises, the last-minute all-nighters, the rewrites—especially after you have a family and your priorities change. Finally, though for legal reasons no agency will ever admit there is a bias in the advertising business towards youth—who are automatically (though not always accurately) assumed to be more in touch with the Zeitgeist and client customers.

Corporate

Insider/outsider—You may feel, that as an employee of a company, you are an insider—just like your counterparts in manufacturing, R&D and sales. But the reality is that most companies, and their executives, look upon advertising (even more than PR) as a supplementary activity and not a direct contributor to the bottom line. That, of course, isn't true, but it is easy to see where that impression comes from: you aren't designing, building or selling anything; you are merely raising the consciousness of potential buyers. Moreover, it's difficult to make any direct correlation between advertising and revenues.

On top of that, your dealings with your own company are necessarily limited. You may get briefed by product teams or get approval of your campaign strategy from senior management, but you will spend far more time dealing with your agency contractors.

As a result, your fellow employees, while they may recognize you as a member of the company "family," will also see you as an outsider to the organization. Ironically, the agency people you deal with will likely see you as an insider, their client's gatekeeper and paymaster. Thus, working in corporate advertising can feel a bit like living in limbo, neither one nor the other. That, of course, can have its advantages in terms of career flexibility; but if you are ambitious in either world, you may be frustrated.

Little creativity—Corporate advertising, for the most part, is not creative work; it is the management of creative work. If the challenge of being part of a successful advertising campaign—and supporting that effort with your writing talent—is what appeals to you most, then this is the job for you. But if what matters is the craft of writing itself, of sculpting powerful prose, then join an agency: a corporate advertising career will leave you frustrated, and your writing ambitions unfulfilled.

Scapegoat—Already noted is that corporate advertising has a lot of job security. That said, there is one real danger: a failed product launch. A great advertising campaign cannot save a bad product for long. And when sales at last collapse, the blame game will begin. Sales will blame manufacturing, manufacturing will blame R&D and everyone will blame the marketing department, particularly advertising. Why? For one thing, no one really understands advertising. To the outsider (that is, senior management and people in other departments of your company) what you do is both magical and frivolous. The sales folks don't think you've done enough to help them close deals; empirical engineers think you should have built your campaign around performance specifications; and executive row now feels confirmed in their hunch that advertising is, at best, a self-indulgent waste of money and, at its worst, actually drives customers away from buying company products. This is the cost of being an insider/outsider, as discussed above: you risk being scapegoated for outcomes that are beyond your control.

Of course, you can always fire your advertising agency. But the ultimate cost will be to you and your department. You aren't likely to be fired, but you will see your budget slashed, sometimes to the point that you won't want to work for the company anymore, and you will, essentially, fire yourself.

This, by the way, is a good reason for educating senior management on how advertising works, and what you can and cannot do. It is also an argument—especially if you are the company's advertising director, but even as an entry-level copywriter—for developing contacts throughout the company and erasing that image of being an overpaid (!) and artsy outsider with a company name badge.

Turning points

The turnings points in a career as an ad copywriter are similar to those in public relations and marketing communications although, because of the high-pressure nature of the profession, these events typically occur sooner and stronger.

Growing older—As already noted, ad agency life is such that it is hard to grow older there. It is a young person's business—not just because of the stress of the pressure-cooker work life, but because the target market for most products and services is young adults. At the start of the career, you likely will have a deep understanding of this market because you are part of it. As a young parent, you may have an even greater understanding of the more youthful end of this market. But as you approach middle age you inevitably will lose touch with this market. You may no longer understand the lifestyles of these consumers, their fads and values, even their vocabulary. You can maintain contact, but with each passing year it will require more and more effort—even as your younger workmates swim effortlessly in this marketplace. The question then may become whether you want to continue to make that, ultimately losing, effort, or find some other career where your talents are more valued.

One of those alternative careers is corporate advertising. It is slower-paced, and less youth-obsessed—if only because you can manage younger professionals, rather than try to be one of them. But there are limits even in corporate life: you are likely to hit your career ceiling at a younger age than in most departments in the company.

Lost mojo—Creative collapse, or just creative stasis, can happen at any age; but it is more likely as you grow older. In the fast-moving world of advertising copywriting, when you regularly have to come up with clever new ideas on demand and with a tight deadline—a pace often quicker than for a beat reporter on a breaking story, and usually with less information—you are always at risk of burning out, if only temporarily. "Temporarily" is the operative word here; it is rare when a professional writer simply loses his or her creative skills. A novelist may run out of plot ideas, but a novelist has to pull those plots out of thin air. As an ad copywriter, the information you need to construct a slogan or body copy for an ad is almost always in your hands. We will discuss so-called writer's block later in the book, but for now just remember that being blocked is often simply the belief that what you are writing isn't as good as you can do. If that is the case, just get over yourself. Write something, anything, and then edit it better.

That said, there are two very real forms of burnout:

1. *Exhaustion*—Your creative energies are not bottomless. There will be times in your career when maintaining an extended fast pace will simply leave you worn out. The mistake is to confuse this physical and mental exhaustion with the loss of your creative abilities. The reality is that you are just plain tired. Learn how to correctly identify this kind of exhaustion and then deal with it. Push yourself further and you really will collapse. Tell your boss and take a few days off and get as far away from a keyboard as you can. If the boss refuses

to give you the time or offers to give you added free time on the books, you should probably look for a new employer. Push too far past the point of exhaustion, and you will never work in that profession again.

2. *Losing the thread*—This kind of burnout is a very different matter. It almost never affects copywriters, but eventually it does hit those advertising superstars who specialize in writing slogans or taglines. This type of work carries very heavy responsibilities because the entire ad campaign rests on it, and it requires enormous facility with language, but—and most important—this work demands the writer be deeply immersed in the culture to the point that he or she can intuitively sense even the slightest shift in mood. Few individuals can do this for long.

   Not surprisingly, even the most talented and facile writers of this work can, with time, lose their grip on the culture. They achieve this high-paying/high-profile role during a sweet spot in their creative careers and, like professional athletes and musicians, that time at the top is almost always brief. The author's only suggestion is to know it won't last forever, enjoy it while you are at the top, save your money and don't be shocked when it ends.

Writing tips

There are a lot of commonalities in the tips for all professional writers, and especially so for professions in the business world. That said, most of these tips have particular nuances for the advertising world.

• *Listen to the client*—If you want to be an independent writer, producing work that follows your inner compass, get out of advertising. It is not for you (and don't kid yourself: even fiction and nonfiction writing at the highest levels are still done for readers). You are taking your employer's pay and your client's nickel. They call the tune. If their demands are unacceptable or their oversight too heavy, then you may want to look for replacements for both. But short of that, keep in mind that both—and especially the client—ultimately will have to sign off on your work. So, if you don't want to either re-do your hard work or get thrown off the account, it will pay to at least get within range of client acceptance the first time out. And the only way to assure that is to determine just what that client wants. That means asking a lot of questions upfront, trying out preliminary ideas on your clients and divining their expectations. If you want to try anything new or unorthodox, run it by them first. You may be surprised: some clients will be more adventurous than you expected.

- *Know the audience for the ad*—There is one more important line of questioning: Who does the client believe are the potential customers being targeted by the planned ad? Very likely they've held some focus groups or surveys on that topic and can provide them to you. It doesn't hurt to ask. And if they don't have that information, you may want to ask your account executive to propose gathering it for them. This will both help you with your work and be a revenue source for your agency. If you are corporate, you need to demand this information for the sake of your employer; your market-research people haven't done their job.

- *Educate the client first, the audience second*—Whether you know it or not, education is the heart of your job. Good ad copywriting teaches. It teaches potential consumers to become customers (for example, why they need your product or service), and then it teaches them to become successful customers (for example, they get the most out of that product or service). But, before you can successfully teach the marketplace, you must first teach your clients: about that market, about how advertising works (and how it doesn't) and about what makes good copy. Most of all, you must manage expectations. Ironically, your clients may have more faith in advertising than you do, and what you consider to be a successful campaign could be seen by them as failure. Teach them, beforehand, the realities of your profession.

- *Know the purpose of the ad*—This is the ultimate purpose of your questions and research: to understand what the ad is supposed to do. At whom is it targeted? What story is it supposed to tell? What key messages should it convey? What visual and narrative style will appeal most to prospective customers? How should it make its appeal: What modality—emotional, empirical, specifications, utility? What action is it supposed to induce? Until you know those things, you cannot proceed with any confidence of success.

- *Ad copy is subtraction, ad slogans are geometry*—Great ad copy is economical, succinct, and it makes the best choice of words. It never uses two words when one is sufficient. It also is almost impossible to write in one or two drafts. Rather, it is the result of intense editing, subtracting everything that isn't necessary to drive the message home to the targeted reader. Ad slogans and taglines are on a whole different level of writing; they are more akin to poetry, even to haiku. Sometimes it isn't enough to remove everything superfluous. Many great slogans ("Coke is It") even strip out important, seemingly necessary, details and depend upon customers to fill in the blanks. This is incredibly difficult writing, not least because what works one year may be an utter failure the next. Because of that, you need to be ruthless with your writing and editing and, even then, test it on audiences first. With slogans, your intuition may be your best guide, and your gut your best friend.

- *Every picture tells a story*—So why tell that story twice? Whenever possible, get a look at the mock-ups the proposed ads. Study the imagery: whatever you eventually write, it should either complement (that is, complete the visual message) or supplement (add new material to) the visuals. If you merely say the same thing as the images, albeit in print form, you have rendered your text superfluous. And if that's the case, who needs you?
- *Support the slogan*—Just as copywriting is designed to back up any imagery without duplicating it, copywriting needs to fill in the blanks created by the shorthand of the overall slogan. This can be accomplished several ways. One is to continue the tone of the slogan in the copy in order to establish a mood (think of a perfume ad). Another is to counter an emotional slogan and/or tagline with a more concrete and detailed explanation (think of an automobile ad). And, less often, to establish a storyline to give emotional support or real-life applications for a plain-vanilla slogan (think appliances, electronics, homes, food ingredients, and so forth). Since it is almost impossible to predict which of these clients will want, this is yet another subject you should address with them before you begin. Don't be surprised if client doesn't know, either, and will order one of each.
- *Love the process, not the result*—We mentioned this earlier but will repeat it for emphasis: do not fall in love with your creation, or you will be disappointed. Clients can be fickle, and not always in a good way. If you create something great, and the client vetoes it, put it aside in the hope you can modify it some day for a different client. Meanwhile, take pride in your skills, and in your work—the process of creation, not its eventual fate. That attitude will lead to a long and rewarding career. And if it proves insufficient, do your own writing—for yourself—on the side.
- *Edit most adjectives, kill all adverbs*—This is not a hard and fast rule. If your copy is too long, look first to cut out all adverbs, as they are the most expendable. After that, look to editing out adjectives. Keep only those necessary to define the subject. After that, try to put verbs in the present tense. Look at replacing multiple redundantly structured sentences with a bulleted list describing the same subject. If all of that still leaves you with too-long copy, then prioritize the points being made and start cutting away at the bottom.
- *Write fast, edit slow*—If you are sweating over the first draft of your copy you are probably doing it wrong. Great ad copy is bright and breathless, carrying the reader along with its enthusiasm. The best way

to achieve that is to write the same way: pound it out in a single session in a white heat. Leave blanks or TKs if you don't have facts and figures immediately at hand. Use strong verbs and don't worry about leaving in adjectives and adverbs. Just get it down. *Then* go back and take your time editing that copy, whittling it down as tight as you can get it. The mistake amateurs make is to do just the opposite: they write slowly and carefully, usually leaving dead copy on the page, then following that with a desultory edit. The inevitable result is the worst possible scenario: badly written, badly edited writing.

- *Know your subject*—It is a natural tendency for writers to hurry to get to what they do best: writing. And the previous tip underscores this, by suggesting that you write when you are especially inspired. But don't jump into writing *too* fast—first learn at least something about your subject. Why? Because the nature of the subject you are writing about may shape not just the content, but the *form* of the copy. A second reason is that if you are not focused on the content, you will likely fall into your standard writing tropes, and that will almost always lead to lazy writing. Content first, style second.

- *Write for your audience*—This is a corollary of the tip about knowing your audience. Your job is to create copy that will have the most impact on potential customers for your client's product or service. It is not to create prose that personally pleases you. If your audience is surgeons, then you will want to write for highly educated, highly trained but not necessarily culturally hip, readers. If you are writing for a high-school-age audience, you should not write at the university level or reference topics only appreciated by middle-aged adults. Market research should give you an idea of the nature of your audience and, while writing, you should try to keep that profile in mind—certainly do so when you are editing that copy.

- *Think upside down*—The "inverted pyramid" is a literary style usually associated with journalism. It's the proven strategy that you should heavily front-load your copy so that the lede paragraph contains all the reader needs to understand the gist of the story being told; that half of the information should be covered within the first few paragraphs; and that all of the necessary information should be delivered before the story jumps to a later page. We explore this in much greater detail in the journalism chapters of this book. For now, it is important to appreciate that, in advertising copy, this inverted pyramid is even more exaggerated—think a mile wide and an inch deep. The reality is that, for most advertisements, the slogan and tagline—with the imagery—should capture *all* the emotion and information of the pitch being made to prospective customers. The copy itself should only support this opening pitch; you should never introduce any important new material in the ad copy.

- *The prettier the images, the more concrete the copy*—When you think about it, the reason for this should be obvious. If the images in an ad are purely emotional or nebulous or mystical, then to complete that ad you must almost always provide some empirical content in the copy. Otherwise, the ad will seem incomplete to the reader. At the very minimum, you must use the copy to direct the reader to a retailer or a Web site where all the reader's questions will be answered or a purchase made. Conversely, if the ad simply shows a product, then the copy should "sing," eliciting an emotional response from the reader. This is the main reason why you need to see the layouts (or script) and slogan/ tagline of an advertisement or commercial before you start writing: your job is not just to provide information, but also a counterbalance to complete reader/viewer/listener experience.

- *Precise nouns; active verbs*—As you train and apprentice to become a professional writer, you will often hear that what distinguishes good writers from poor ones is that the former consistently use strong "active" verbs, while the latter—often because they fear making a definitive statement—use weak, "passive" verbs. Thus, while an amateur might choose "went," a pro would be more specific, using "ran," "walked," "drove," "flew," and so forth. True enough. But a second characteristic of good writers—and advertising copywriters in particular because there is such a premium on words—is that they use precise nouns. Thus, where in normal speech you might say "car," the ad copywriter will say "the 1965 Ford Mustang 289 convertible." Why? Two reasons. First, if the subject of the ad is that "car," you want to be precise enough that the potential customer knows what to ask for at a dealership, or to search for on the Web. Second, given the premium placed on every word you write because of the limited available real estate in an ad, or the time available in a radio or TV commercial, you want to compress as much useful information as possible into your copy—and that calls for the right words: that is, 40" 1080p 60MHz LCD flat screen. For a potential customer, that provides a vast amount of information that can't be conveyed in, say, "full-color flat-screen television." Similarly, "collagen" provides much more precision than "bone byproduct." Of course, this creates a contradiction: you want every word to contain as much weight as possible, while at the same time keeping the message simple enough to be understood by the average person. And that is why you are a paid professional.

EXAMPLE: A PR/advertising agency advertisement for itself. Note the amount of copy, which is more than most modern ads—that's because this is designed to be an informational ad to corporate clients, not a consumer pitch. Nevertheless, the copy was edited numerous times to make it as tight as possible.

Speechwriter

Speechwriting is among the oldest of writing professions, likely dating at least as far back as the birth of written language. Indeed, it's quite possible that some Neolithic chief or priest memorized his speeches—or had someone create them for him—in strictly pre-writing verbal form.

More than any other form of language, speeches have changed the course of history. We remember the words of great figures millennia after they were spoken, and more than any other form of writing those words still have the ability to thrill us today. Think of Cicero in the Roman Senate, Leonidas at Thermopylae, Lincoln at Gettysburg, Chief Joseph as he surrendered to the US Cavalry, Winston Churchill standing before Parliament in 1940, Martin Luther King on the National Mall. Even many of the greatest moments in other literary forms appear as speeches: the St. Crispin's Day speech in Shakespeare's *Henry V* and Hamlet's soliloquy, the Nantucket minister's sermon in *Moby Dick* and Tom Joad's exit in the movie version of *The Grapes of Wrath*.

Great speeches can turn certain defeat into victory. They can galvanize people to act or to steel themselves for an impending challenge. They can explain, appeal to duty, draw upon the conscience—and, in a few words ("Carthagio delenta est"; "Mr. Gorbachev, tear down this wall!"; "that government of the people, by the people, and for the people shall not perish from this earth"), bring inchoate thoughts into a tight focus that everyone can instantly understand.

For all these reasons, the speech is often considered the queen of writing, and thus the profession of speechwriting an exalted one. But it also comes with sacrifices, especially in our age. In an older, slower time great and powerful men and women wrote their own speeches. One can picture Cicero walking slowly through a temple, using it as his memory theater as, in his mind, he attaches vivid images to every statue and fixture while composing his next speech to the Senate. Or Lincoln, sitting in the guest bedroom of a Gettysburg house, composing the famous last paragraph of his Address.

But the demands of our fast-moving and increasingly complex world have changed all that. These days, it is the rarest of the powerful who have the time, knowledge, or even the ability to write their own speeches. Instead these important men and women are served by *speechwriters*—a single person or a team—who typically assume the task of interviewing the speaker to determine the message and objectives of the speech, researching the subject, drafting the speech in a simulation of the speaker's voice and then editing that speech according to the speaker's specifications.

The nature of speeches, too, have changed. An Athenian oration could last most of a day; a Restoration sermon an entire afternoon. Attendees broke for dinner during the Lincoln–Douglas debates. But the rise of modern media changed all that. FDR understood that he had to keep his fireside chats to less than 30 minutes. And over the last half-century clips of speeches broadcast on television news have shrunk from an already-truncated 10 seconds to just three seconds—long enough for less than ten words. Smart political speechwriters know this and embed just such "newsbites" into their longer addresses. Meanwhile, in an age of short attention spans and fast information transfer, most speeches abjure not only florid descriptions, no matter how beautiful, but also extended logical chains and syllogisms—listeners are just too impatient for the former and too distracted for the latter.

The schism between screenwriter and speaker that has characterized the last century has had both advantages and disadvantages. Bringing professionals to the process of speech preparation has saved many an audience from a dreary hour: you only have to attend a few small-town Chamber of Commerce or Rotary luncheons to appreciate what we mean. This schism has also created a nice livelihood for writers, one that pays well, connects them with important and influential people and puts them right next to the center of action. But it has also so separated the message from its deliverer that it can be impossible to discern where the soul of the speech resides. Is this really how the speaker thinks and speaks, or is he or she merely verbalizing the ideas and words of the speechwriter? Who is really the man behind the curtain?

The result has been a growing contradiction. On the one hand, professional speechwriters are more popular, and more in demand, than they've ever been. What used to be mostly work with elected officials and corporate CEOs now extends to gigs with middle managers, entrepreneurs, professionals and authors. Yet, at the same time, professional speechwriting may be less celebrated than ever.

Some of this anonymity goes with the job. Precisely because speeches are delivered verbally—and when done well appear to be extemporaneous—the profession of speechwriting is often overlooked by listeners. And since speeches are naturally equated with those who deliver the speech (especially successful speeches), speakers are motivated to *not* credit the speechwriter. Indeed, and unfortunately, too often you learn the name of a speechwriter only when the speech fails, and the speaker is looking for someone to blame.

But another force, less obvious, is at work as well. It may just be that the existence of speechwriters (still a novelty in the 1980s, when President Reagan's speechwriters Peter Robinson and Peggy Noonan were celebrated figures in their own right) has become such a common feature of public life that we take their presence for granted. After all, can you name an important figure in the twenty-first century who actually writes his or her own speeches?

The result is that speechwriters, at least for now, seem destined to enjoy steady work and good pay, albeit while laboring in obscurity. Most veteran speechwriters are content with that arrangement, as their work has always been designed to be behind the scenes, and the brief interval of recognition for celebrity speechwriters an exception to the rule. However, newcomers to the field should be forewarned not to look back for career models, but around them at their current professional peers.

Why speechwriting?

Because public figures are either too busy, too stupid, or too ineloquent to write their own speeches. Also, because public address, in this multi-media world, is readily reduced to sound bites, each of which requires considerable craftsmanship to be effective.

Who gives speeches?

Almost anybody, from Junior League members to the president of the United States. All of us in our careers will be called upon to give speeches, even if they are only toasts at weddings. Even speechwriters themselves are regularly called upon to give speeches.

Every one of these speeches presents a potential business opportunity to a speechwriter. Though at the lower end, these opportunities may be mostly for community service or to help a friend, even that work can help build one's reputation, which in turn can lead to the call for more remunerative speechwriting jobs.

Speakers typically fall into a handful of categories.

Professional speakers—These are people who make their livings giving speeches. Typically, this work is connected with a parallel career, such as book authorship, consulting jobs, or personal development (or some combination of the three). Thus, a business journalist may write a book and go out on a speaking/publicity tour to support that product. Should the book prove highly successful and the demand for public appearances strong, that author might well embark on a program of regular, high-paying speeches around the country or the world. Because these programs have a limited lifespan, that author is likely to write a quick follow-up book—and start the speaking tour all over again.

Conversely, self-improvement speakers often begin with a low-paying speaking tour, slowly building both audiences and speaking fees. Only then is this established audience used as a target market for a subsequent book, which is then sold at the speaking events.

Either way, if everything works as planned, the books and the speeches are designed to create a virtuous cycle in which each component—book, speeches, eventually consulting contracts—builds upon the other, making it possible for the professional speaker to enjoy higher speaking fees, expensive consulting contracts and guaranteed bestsellers. If, in fact, as a speechwriter you discover a talent for public speaking and self-promotion, you should probably consider this lucrative path by writing your own speeches and books.

Professional speakers, because they are likely to be writers themselves, usually write their own speeches. Thus, outside speechwriter opportunities with these individuals are rare. That said, there are still occasional (and high-paying) opportunities to either

1. Write the basic "stump" speech that the professional will modify for each speaking occasion or, conversely,
2. Take the professional's existing stump speech and modify it for the venue, event topic or audience. This latter job is likely to be as much research as actual writing.

Speaking professionals—These are individuals for whom public speaking is not their full-time job, yet being successful at it may be critical to their careers. The list of these speakers includes elected officials, corporate executives, professionals, scientists and heads of government organizations and NGOs, heads of nonprofit organizations and foundations, university presidents, clergy, military officers and celebrities. And the number of speeches they give can range from one or two per year to that many per week.

These individuals are the prime source of writing gigs for speechwriters, and the potential contractual commitments can include

- Editing or updating an existing speech;
- Writing a specialized one-off speech;

- Preparing (researching, writing and editing) a standardized stump speech;
- A monthly retainer to "doctor" or create multiple speeches;
- A full-time position as speechwriter to create any sort of content as needed.

Needless to say, the remuneration for this work varies with the importance of the speeches—that is, length, audience, occasion, and so forth—of the speaker and of the speaker's employer. Thus, a major speech before shareholders by the chairman of the Fortune 50 company is going to pay many times more than the speech by a start-up entrepreneur to potential customers at a middling industry trade show. The same is true for extended contracts: you are likely not to get such a contract, but rather be paid per job, by a congressman or small-business owner, while you can probably make a very comfortable living on the staff of the Secretary of the Interior.

The two big categories of speeches

In the broadest sense, speechwriting takes two forms: those you write for yourself and those you write for others.

Speeches you write for yourself—If you are a member of one of the many writing professions described in this text—author, novelist, academic or editor, among others—you may well find yourself in that category we just described of Speaking Professionals. That is, to help sell your work, or improve your professional standing, or attract advertisers and readers, you may be required to spend some portion of your time giving speeches. But even if you are not in that category, chances are that you will still be regularly asked to give speeches at the local Chamber of Commerce, service club chapter or industry group. Writers are constant targets of those invitations because people assume—rightly or wrongly—that people who write well can talk well, too.

The biggest challenge to writing a speech for yourself is that it has to exhibit what *you* think. At first blush, that may seem liberating—you finally get to speak your own words, rather than putting them into someone else's mouth. It's only when you walk up to the podium for the first time that you realize that there is a wide gulf between writing a speech and *delivering* it. That's when you often discover that while you know how someone else speaks—their vocabulary, cadence, personality and mannerisms—you don't necessarily know your own.

Moreover, it is one thing to sit in a comfortable chair at home writing a speech for someone else, secure in the knowledge that they will ultimately have to take responsibility for both its content and its delivery, and you standing in front of five hundred or a thousand people taking that responsibility yourself. That is when you make another discovery—one you long ago made about your clients, but never realized about yourself: *you don't speak the way you write.* That veteran-speaker client of yours may have enough breath discipline to get through your long, loping sentences without running out of gas, but you probably don't. And your client probably knows how to enunciate those multisyllabic words you love so much, and doesn't whistle saying sibilants, and knows better than to laugh at his own witty lines.

That's why, even more that you do for your clients' speeches, you need to spend a lot of time reading your speech out loud, in front of a mirror, with a stopwatch in your hand. Even better, test out your speech in front of someone you both trust and who cares enough about you to be ruthless in their criticism. Have them stop you every time you stumble, and make you edit the text into something with which you are more comfortable. Listen carefully to your own rhythms and cadences.

Most of all, prepare yourself for your actual presentation of the speech in front of a live audience. Recognize that you are going to make mistakes, stumble, perhaps even lose your place. Forgive yourself ahead of time and then prepare for these potholes. If you need reading glasses, take along two pair. Blow up the font size. As you speak, track your words with a finger on the text. Remind yourself to look at the audience. When you arrive at the venue, have someone walk you through your steps to the podium (especially stairsteps). Don't eat much beforehand—and never, never have wine or alcohol (save that for when you get home with the check). Try to enjoy yourself.

Not only will these preparations help improve the odds of your speech going over well, but just the experience of giving your own speech can be a salutary one in other ways. It will help you better understand what your client must go through, often with consequences for an error—stock crash or suspended trading, a lost job or reputation, falling employee morale, becoming a pariah in one's profession—infinitely greater than you face with your speech. It should motivate you to give that client the best work you can.

Speeches you write for others—For most speechwriters, this is 99 percent of their work.

In one respect, writing speeches for others is much easier than writing speeches for yourself. As noted, you bear none of the burden of responsibility for the speech's content and delivery. That doesn't mean that the work is risk-free: as we said at the beginning of this chapter, if your client really, really screws up, he or she is going to look around for scapegoats and one of them is likely to be you. But even a small disaster with a speech can lead your client to lose faith or trust in you. Either way, you are going to get fired—and if it is one of the big screw-ups you will also likely be blackballed in that corner of the world. It may not be fair; but that's the nature of the profession—and the gamble you take being merely a scribe to the rich and powerful.

Still, the chances of that happening are pretty slim. So, the reality is that when writing a speech for someone else you get a lot of freedom to apply your craft and carry little burden of responsibility in doing so, other than to do the best writing you can. Compared to many jobs described in this textbook, that's a very good deal.

But in saying that speechwriting for others is philosophically easy, we don't mean to say that it is not a lot of in-the-trenches work. In particular, you have to learn to *embody* your client and then deal with the vagaries of shepherding your draft through the gauntlet of approval cycles to get it to the point where your words actually come out of your client's mouth. Here, in detail, is what we mean:

1. In the speech, you must capture what your client thinks about the subject; what he or she wants to convey in the speech; and what goals he or she has for the speech. The last can range from "keep the audience entertained" to "find potential new customers" to "impact current legislation."
2. To understand the speaker's needs and capture relevant information, you typically need at least one interview (in-person is best, over the phone second best, via email the worst).
3. The speech must also not only reflect the current views of the speaker, but also his or her past history—so as not to accidentally give the appearance of hypocrisy. Learn of any scandals or bad publicity in your speaker's past so that you don't inadvertently remind the audience of them.
4. The speech must sound like the speaker—that is, it should capture the cadences, vocabulary, areas of expertise and so forth in his or her normal, everyday speech. If you make your speaker sound like an expert in a subject he or she knows little about, you may be setting them up for disaster during the question period or off-stage afterwards. Make a speaker sound too "street" or "down home" during a speech and they'll sound like a phony afterwards when they revert to their usual patois; conversely make them sound too smart (that is, obscure polysyllabic words, classical references and so forth) and they may face unreasonable expectations afterwards.
5. The speech must be readable by the speaker in terms of phrase length, sounds, stresses and accents. As an extreme example, don't give a

person with a small lisp a lot of sibilant sounds in the speech. By the same token, too many run-on sentences will leave the speaker panting for breath; while too many fragments will make them sound aggressive and abrupt. And make sure that your client can pronounce properly every word you give him.

6. You must deliver a rough draft of the speech to your client and have him or her mark it up. You may have to go through multiple iterations of this step before you get approval to move on.

7. Once you get approval, you can then produce the polished, final draft of the speech.

8. You must physically prepare the speech as much as possible. That is, lay out the text in the way you want it read, with words marked for emphasis and pronunciation, breaks to enable the speaker to breathe, and a readable typeface. If you cannot deliver a hard copy to your client, then at least make sure that the hardcopy he or she will use will be printed out with the right font size (the older the speaker the bigger the letters) and appropriate page numbers. You can support this by sending instructions to the speaker or an assistant.

9. You must be prepared—and available—to make last-minute edits and changes. There is no shortage of anecdotes of speakers calling their speechwriters from backstage to rework a phrase or two. Some of these fixes will be at the behest of your client, but others may come as the result of recent news events or even special demands by the sponsor or venue (that is, the slide projector is broken, or the length of the speech must be cut by one-third because of rescheduling). At these moments, you must be prepared to drop everything and scramble to make the necessary changes.

Types of speeches

As you no doubt have noticed by now, almost every type of professional writing is delivered via multiple—even scores—of vehicles. Speechwriting is no exception. Here are some examples, and how they are used. We've listed them in order of complexity (and typical length). The speeches at the top of the list, because of their brevity and lack of time for preparation, are sometimes improvised on the spot, from perhaps a few notes or an outline. The speeches at the bottom of the list almost always must be prepared and practiced repeatedly ahead of their actual delivery.

Public statement—These are the very short, unornamented and fact-driven speeches you typically see on the evening news. An event has occurred—a crime, a disaster, an arrest, a victory, an award, a death, a sudden retirement and so forth—that, to stave off an onslaught of questions from reporters, is answered by a spokesperson who steps in front of the microphones and cameras and offers up the basic facts of the matter. Sometimes this speaker takes questions, sometimes not, usually depending upon whether it is good or bad news.

Public statements are typically made by the subject of the news, a person in authority (such as a police officer) and occasionally by an official public relations person on staff (such as the press secretary of the president of the United States). Because of that, a professional speechwriter is rarely involved. But when they are called in, the time horizon for writing copy can be a matter of minutes. In this brief interval it is important to keep one's head, don't try to be clever in the copy, and make sure the facts are complete and accurate.

Mea Culpa—This form of speech is much like the public statement, but it is almost always a job for a speechwriter. Mea culpa speeches are a form of public expression that admits guilt or culpability, while at the same time minimizes its impact. This combination, done right, can be hugely important: it may be the difference between your client having his or her career destroyed or their living on to fight another day.

Great mea culpa speeches are among the highest form of theater in public life. The guilty party stands on the steps of the US Capitol, or in front of a courtroom, or at a podium, usually flanked by a noble spouse, loving children and well-wishers and supporters (the more famous the better) and admits his or her crime. The goal is to have the audience there or watching at home either forgive them or at least psychologically minimize their crime. Classic examples range from the Nixon "Checkers speech" (where the vice president of the United States talked about his dog and his wife's cheap cloth coat and turned disaster into a path to the White House) and televangelist Jimmy Swaggert's tearful "I have sinned" speech, which maintained his career, damaged, but ultimately intact.

Mea culpa speeches present a real challenge to speechwriters: They must be carefully written to minimize the bad news, while at the same time providing the proper platform for the client to take responsibility, appear chastened and changed, look noble—and pull out all the emotional stops. It helps that, more than a Public Statement, a mea culpa speech usually offers a little time for writing, and veteran speechwriters know to start the first draft well before the client admits, even to himself, that he is guilty.

Introduction—Done right, introductions are the easiest, most fun, and potentially most rewarding, of speech forms. They are easy because they are short, and the audience rarely remembers them. They are fun because you are allowed to play with your comments and tease the speaker being introduced. And rewarding, at least for your client, because the very fact that he or she has been tapped to make the introduction puts them at a higher level than the audience, and sometimes even higher than the main speaker. They can also be rewarding for you: writing a few witty lines that make your client look clever can be a quick and regular source of cash or a retainer that can go on for years.

There are basically two types of introduction speeches, and each takes two forms: *formal* and *informal.* Formal introductions typically take place at proper, solemn occasions: investitures, graduations, funerals, shareholder meetings and so forth. These introductions are typically brief and list the speaker's credentials.

Informal introductions, by comparison, are typically given at luncheons and dinners, award ceremonies, reunions and social gatherings. These are the speeches where your client will want to have fun—in particular, to find the right balance between getting through the necessary details about the main speaker, while at the same time being both witty and worldly.

So, the two forms of introduction speeches are *impersonal* and *personal.* That is, the introduction is either about someone, usually important, that you don't know; or it is about someone you—and likely the audience— personally know, such as a former or current member, someone who lives in the community or a past or present acquaintance or workmate.

The result is a 2x2 matrix of the four possible combinations. Thus, at the most rigid corner is the impersonal formal introduction, wherein you help your client essentially list the achievements and credentials of the great person and then get out of the way. And, at the opposite corner is the informal personal introduction, wherein your client tells funny and warm anecdotes about his or her old friend in order to humanize them to the audience.

When writing introductions it is important before you begin to know the nature of the event and the relationship between your client and the person he or she will introduce. If you get it wrong, you client will, at best (formal at an informal event) look like a stuffed shirt; and at worst (informal at a formal event, or personal with someone they don't really know) like a thoughtless idiot.

The Toast—The toast is essentially an introduction that is short and places wit over content.

By definition, toasts take place when people either have drinks in their hands (such as cocktail parties, post-prandial celebrations, funerary wakes, graduations and wedding receptions) or near at hand (formal dinners, reunion dinners, regimental dinners, bar mitzvahs, and so forth). The ancient nature of toasting, and because so much depends upon their being done right, adds to their heightened sense—and because the toasting is usually done with an alcoholic beverage, the first successful toast is usually a mark of adulthood.

Toasts generally take two forms:

- *The targeted toast*—This is most often found at a wedding, where some sibling or friend of the groom is asked to stand at the reception and make remarks about the newlyweds. This type of toast is done well so rarely that when it is performed properly, the audience remembers it for years.

  There are a number of reasons why targeted toasts usually fail so miserably, but mostly it comes down to alcohol, sentiment, crudeness and a lack of understanding about the purpose of the act. The embarrassing, obscene, endless maudlin wedding toast scene is a cliché of comedy films. Such moments are far worse in real life, because they lack the comedy: endless, discursive, filled with inside comments no one understands, and ending with a weepy, incoherent finish.

  That's why smart (and usually wealthy) people, when asked to prepare a targeted toast hire the services of someone who can prepare the words for them. For a few hundred dollars, it's not a bad investment, especially if it saves the client's reputation.

  The key to writing a targeted toast is to keep it short and witty. The client should tell one or two amusing anecdotes about their common past, how the couple met, (if appropriate) welcome the bride or groom to the family, say how the pair were meant for each, predict great things for their future, and wish them bon voyage on their marriage. Anything over five minutes is too long. Never, ever mention embarrassing (especially sexual) moments about either the bride (especially the bride) or groom. As the writer, you can typically gain what you need in a brief interview with your client. Make sure your client practices the speech until it is entirely memorized—or nearly so—such that it can be given not only without notes, but with an air of spontaneity.

- *The untargeted toast*—It may surprise you how often, at a formal dinner, the individual standing to make a clever toast has either hired someone to write those words or copied them out of an old collection of famous toasts.

  Untargeted toasts are, as the name suggests, toasts made without a target, but rather are designed to encompass everyone in the room—that is, "Ladies and Gentlemen, the Queen!" or "May she always be right, but my Country right or wrong" (Stephen Decatur). Like an introduction, an untargeted toast can be formal and solemn, or informal and fun. Indeed, formal toasts can be of stunning solemnity, wherein the toasters honor the dead, rededicate themselves to king and country, or swear mutual loyalty. Informal toasts are among the wittiest utterances in daily life— and great toasts are remembered and repeated for centuries. They are the haikus of elegant society.

The mistake most toasters make is to either assume (once again, usually thanks to alcohol) that they can improvise a brilliant line on the spot, or that because others seem to make toasts so easily and casually that they carry little impact beyond the moment. The truth is that many of those casual and clever bon mots are in fact the product of paid professionals (like you) and the result of endless practice.

Why do these toast makers go to such trouble? Because they understand that those few words can signal to powerful figures in attendance the intelligence, the cleverness and creativity, and the comfort in rarified surroundings of the speaker—often far more than any resume or CV. What appears as merely a witty one-off among inebriated celebrants may in fact be a job interview for a higher position. That's what you need to impress upon your client, and that's why you must edit and polish their toast copy to a lapidary sheen.

Practically speaking, a good untargeted toast should be no more than a sentence or two. If solemn, it should be of elevated tone, and you will need to research any established phrasing or ritual. If clever, be witty and not cruel, risqué but not vulgar, always taking advantage of memorable turns of phrase and clever plays on language. In other words, it's not easy, so you should probably go buy one of those old books of great toasts, study its contents, and not be afraid to steal as needed.

Master of ceremonies—Serving as a master of ceremonies (and writing the script for one) is a complicated duty. On the one hand, you are expected to be casual, engaging and spontaneous. On the other, this style is expected to operate within a very rigid schedule that, likely as not, will run on a clock. Thus, the required stage-setting happy talk will have to be brief and limited to the opening and closing of the event, as well as during a few short 'interstitials' (fillers between segments).

Once again, the mistake many speakers make is to assume they can just make this stuff up. The result is often an emcee who stalls the presentation by taking too long to tell an anecdote or wrecks the mood by interjecting a comment that is either inappropriate or unrelated to the action at hand. Again, the key to looking spontaneous, while still hitting your marks, is to prepare extensively ahead of time. And because most masters of ceremonies have their own busy careers, the smart ones will come to you, the writer.

The key to being a successful emcee lies in that word *master*. Great emcees take control of the event from the very first moment and then serve as a knowledgeable and welcome guide to the end, where they cap the event with a summary of its proceedings and its place in the larger world. This is not a simple task: look how many famous entertainers have failed as hosts of the Oscars—a job Hollywood once took for granted because Bob Hope made it look easy for quarter century.

Some of the success of great emcees is a matter of personality and charisma. You can't do much about that. Nor can you do much about the actual schedule of the event. But you *can* help in two ways:

1. Write the opening, closing and interstitials in a manner that is warm, engaging, and brief. For the opening, you want to set the stage by having your client introduce the event, explain its importance, lay out the schedule for the evening, and make a few witty remarks about himself or herself. For the interstitial, write brief one-line comments on the proceedings, especially trying to amplify what is going on (that is "past awardees include _____" or "Now we come to the highlight of the evening," and so forth).

2. Help your client through the rest of the presentation. In particular, if he or she is going to be announcing a number of names as award recipients, and so forth, you can help by putting the phonetic pronunciations in the script. You should also try to learn everything you can about the venue, so you can add stage instructions that might be missing ("Stay onstage to the right rear of the podium during the acceptance speech. When someone else is speaking, don't move.").

One of the biggest dangers for masters of ceremonies is ego. Given their central role, some emcees assume that they are the real stars of the evening. There is not much you can do about that, though you might put in a few self-effacing remarks into the script to keep your client's image in check, if only for the audience's sake.

The acceptance speech—Acceptance speeches are fun; but they can also be, at the very moment of celebration, disastrous.

We have all watched the Academy Awards or Grammys or other high-level award ceremony in which an honoree, after being cheered by the audience for their achievement, throw it all away by getting up and giving an acceptance speech that is too long, too pompous, to insider, too maudlin, too vulgar—or all of the above. Astoundingly, after all the bad examples of what not to do, some awardees still attempt to get up in front of hundreds of millions of people around the world and improvise. The cringe-worthy results are predictable.

A wise person will write a thoughtful acceptance speech beforehand. An even wiser person will hire someone like you to write the speech for them. Here are some tricks:

1. Find out how long the honoree is allowed to talk before the walk-off music begins. Write to that length.
2. Be witty, but not funny—even if the award is for a professional comedian. If they wanted to tell a joke they wouldn't have hired you.
3. Be inclusive, but not detailed. Thanking a laundry-list of people from an index card is tacky and boring—especially if your client starts naming agents and relatives. Instead, just thank everyone who helped your client in a single sweeping gesture, perhaps prefaced with a comment about there being "too many people to name."
4. Thank no more than three people. If your client has to name names, keep the list two or three or less—and make sure there is a good reason for each of them.
5. Anecdotes work. If your awardee/client has a story that can be told in less than 15 seconds use it ("I want to thank my high school drama teacher who told me that my future was in chemistry, because I had no chance in theater. He was right."). Note that sad stories usually play well, as do funny ones—but never be cruel, self-pitying or vengeful.
6. Have your client practice the acceptance speech to the point that he or she has it memorized. And don't take long odds as an excuse: think of how many unexpected, and unprepared, winners you've seen over the years. If there is even the slightest chance, *prepare*.

Formal address—Now we get to the big guns. A formal address is essentially any speech that

- Is of sufficient length—typically 30 minutes or more;
- Stands alone in its presentation—that is, it may be part of a series of events, and even one of several speeches—but still is independent and typically requires its own separate introduction;
- Is scheduled ahead, usually no less than two weeks, and sometimes as much as a year; and
- Is promoted separately—that is, it has its own venue, or is listed as a featured event in a program or distinctly advertised in promotions for the event and covered separately by the media.

A formal address is almost always written in advance and delivered from a printed text, electronic display or teleprompter. It has a beginning, middle and end. And whatever entertainment value it may offer, the content is always intermixed with the presentation of some useful knowledge, whether it is news, empirical data or just the speaker's experience and acquired wisdom.

Formal addresses come in multiple forms:

1. *The press conference*—Press conferences are highly organized events designed to convey important news to the media (and thus the public) en masse. There are several reasons for holding a press conference. One is to give all the media the information simultaneously, so that no one gets a time advantage (a "scoop'). Another is that it saves time and effort: rather than giving dozens of interviews, the speaker can get the message out to everyone at once. Finally, there are regulatory reasons: for example, financial and other announcements by public corporations that can potentially impact stock values must be delivered concurrently to all relevant media so that one group of investors cannot have an advantage over another.

   Anyone who has ever watched television news knows that press conferences, while sometimes relatively informal in tone, are highly structured events that begin with a welcome, followed by an introduction of the main speaker—who speaks to media briefly, offering the key highlights of the news event—and then, if the speaker wishes, a usually chaotic question-and-answer session with reporters, during which the speaker may choose whether to answer specific questions or pass them off to other experts at hand in the room.

   If you are hired to be the speechwriter for the speaker at a press conference, the scenario will likely take two forms:

   1. It is an announcement, usually corporate, that has been planned well in advance.
   2. It is a breaking news story, and you will have minutes to compose something, sometimes by hand on a sheet of scrap paper.

      The whole point of a press conference is *control*. In many cases you will have only a few moments to get the message before all hell breaks loose as reporters begin shouting questions. The key then is to be very brief and very factual—be sure to check every fact and number beforehand—and keep your client's personal views out of the speech. Other stuff will likely come out during the Q&A, which is beyond your control.

2. *Policy address*—This is typically the province of politicians, though this genre of speech can also be used by corporate and nonprofit CEOs, university presidents and even military leaders. The purpose of a policy address is to present an organization's long-term strategy to its members. The goal is to offer a well-defined path to achieving

that strategy, provide some limited rational for the plan and enlist the various stakeholders in implementing that plan.

Policy addresses can be very tricky because of one inevitable contradiction: the speaker wants to present the new policy as inevitable, a fait accompli, while at the same time is still trying to enlist the organization's support. Thus, in writing such a speech, you must walk a fine line between having your client come across as confident, competent and decisive to the point of being autocratic ("the program is already under way"), while at the same time making your client appear open to alternative views (even when the client is not), democratic in asking employees or subordinates for their endorsements, and as someone who needs the support of the rank and file.

In writing a policy address always keep in mind that everyone else involved in this announcement probably has a greater stake in it than you. You need to understand the strong opinions on either side of the matter and be prepared for the ones against your client's position. You can also do your client and the organization a real service by using the address to not only announce changes, but to explain them in the simplest and most transparent writing you can muster.

Don't get bogged down in details. The minutiae of the new policy will unfold in the days and weeks ahead. Your goal is to get the audience of stakeholders to—if not adopt the new policy—at least understand it well enough to give it thoughtful consideration.

3. *The lecture*—A lecture is a formal speech designed to convey a specific piece of information to a captive audience, sometimes with some sort of measurement of the audience's attention afterwards (test, quiz). Lectures are most often found in an academic setting, as they are the most commonly used pedagogical tool, especially at the high school and university levels. But lectures can also be found in professional settings, such as in continuing education, certification programs and training seminars.

The lecture exists in private life as well. Get a speeding ticket and, if you do not want to pay a fine, you will most likely have to sit through a day-long safety lecture. Your local hardware store likely presents Saturday morning lectures on everything from weather-stripping to solar-panel installation. And, seen from a certain perspective, even the Sunday morning sermon at church is a form of lecture.

The reason most lectures are dreary, even those with compelling content, is that they are usually written by the speakers themselves. There is a good reason for that: they have been asked to speak because of their singular expertise. But great knowledge is not synonymous with good presentation, so the odds of getting both a useful and entertaining lecture are pretty low. Just ask any college student.

However, it is possible to have both, and one of the best ways to do so is for the expert lecturer to pass the talk by a professional speechwriter, like yourself. On the rare occasions when that happens, here's how you can help:

a. Brighten—Assuming that the useful content is already in place, try to shape the presentation by breaking it into sections and themes and then give each of those a clever, memorable title. Replace bland verbs with strong ones, add powerful adjectives and adverbs.

b. Tighten—Break up all long-winded sentences and paragraphs into shorter versions. Look to see where there are redundancies or time-consuming digressions and cut them out.

c. Lighten—Don't force the audience to keep track of long, complicated logical threads. Stop at various points and remind them where they are—and even where you are going.

d. Declare—Show the bones of the lecture by using a lot of subheads, bullet points, even mnemonics when possible. The purpose is to have the audience know exactly where you are in the lecture at any moment.

e. Prepare—Start the speech by telling the audience where it is going to end and the key points you are going to make along the way.

f. Compare—Insert real-life anecdotes as examples wherever you can. If some of those examples are from the lecturer's own life, you will make him or her more human to the audience.

4. *Honorary address*—The honorary address is, as the name suggests, a speech delivered after the speaker has received some kind of honor or award. This differs from the acceptance speech, because the former is supposed to be brief and largely consist of thank-yous, while the latter is expected to be attenuated and tackle larger issues revolving around the award. In particular, the speech usually is expected to focus on some special expertise for which the speaker is being awarded in the first place. The classic honorary address is the high school or university graduation speech. Whether given by the class valedictorian or the famous individual receiving an honorary doctorate, graduation speeches follow a standardized formula—and one should be wary of diverting too far from that format, as has been proven over thousands of occasions over the last hundred years

There are other kinds of honorary addresses as well—notably those given by the recipient of a major industry award, at the retirement of a notable figure and during recognition of lifetime achievements.

Honorary addresses are often written by speechwriters, and if hired to do so, one of the biggest challenges you may face is a divergence in views between you and the honoree over the tone and length of the speech: you may want the speaker to be triumphant, when he or she wants to be humble, or vice versa; and you may want to keep the speech short and strong, while the speaker wants to use this singular occasion to use the address as a soapbox. You will do yourself a service by working out these differences at the start (and sometimes even politely walk away) rather than in the middle as the deadline date approaches.

The key to a good honorary address is to make the speaker gracious and self-effacing, but also proud and deeply honored. Personalize the speech with insider references, but don't go too far (see below). Be amusing with turns of phrases, but stay away from obvious jokes. Understand—especially at a graduation—that this moment isn't just for you, but also for the graduates, so don't wander off (as many politicians do) into policy statements that have nothing to do with the event at hand. Also, beware of the usual clichés spouted at these events, but be uplifting without being obvious, warm without being maudlin and honor the audience even as it is honoring the awardee.

5. *Monologue/stand-up routine*—We put in this exotic form because it, too, is in the end a kind of formal speech. A stand-up comedy routine can be seen as a speech that is polished to the point of poetry, in which every word is weighed and chosen for its precise subjective impact, and the sentences themselves are recited with a very carefully orchestrated beat and meter to create the maximum emotional effect at the punchline.

If you are writing a comedy routine, you need to remember the following:

- Momentum is everything—The best routines aren't collections of individual jokes, but a narrative that ties the jokes together in a continuous story.
- Transitions keep the audience attached—Organize your jokes in such a way that you can smoothly segue from one to the next without forcing the audience to make a sharp turn.
- Have a beginning, middle and end—Comedy routines are like novels: they have a rising action, climax and conclusion. Don't peak too early and leave the audience exhausted and waiting for the end.
- Edit, edit, edit—Pare the routine down until there are no excess words; and make sure those words that remain are the best at maintaining the highest level of audience amusement.

- Practice, practice, practice—This is your client's (or your) career: Why would you not give the audience the very best he or she (or you) can give?

6. *Industry speech*—Outside of academic lectures and perhaps political speeches during election season, industry speeches are the most common form of speech in modern life. Thousands are delivered every day in the industrialized world and are the bread-and-butter income source of most speechwriters. Though they may seem monolithic—that is, a man or woman in business attire standing in front of a hall filled with professionals and pointing at a graph on a glowing projection screen—industry speeches actually take three different forms. As a speechwriter, it is important to understand those differences or risk creating an unfriendly audience and an unhappy client:

   —The scheduled speech—These are what might be described as "content-driven" speeches. They are typically part of a larger industry event, such as a trade show, conference or convention. They also typically take two forms. One is a smaller, focused and more vertically oriented speech that is usually given before an audience of less than 50 and is part of a string of such speeches on one of many content tracks for different audiences. The other is the "keynote" speech that usually opens or closes a large industry event. These can be given in front of an audience of thousands and typically involve a well-known industry leader.

   As a speechwriter, you need to know the difference between the two. The "tracked" speech needs to be more intimate (your client will be looking each audience member in the eye) and yet also more technical (the audience will expect your client to burrow down into the topic, not skim the surface). If you don't share a deep knowledge of the subject, get help either from your client or someone they recommend. Keep the actual speech short—no more than two-thirds of the allotted time—and leave the rest open for questions and dialog.

   The "large" keynote speech, because it is addressed to a diverse audience—even if they are from the same industry—should stay away from fine details and technical subjects and instead should almost always be about larger and more sweeping topics: industry policy, government regulation, the future of the industry or its technology, the state of competition and so forth. A common problem for speechwriters is that the keynote speaker wants to use the time to promote his or her company, new products or latest cause. Unless that was the specific reason for the speaker's intention, you should do your best to pull them away from this inevitable mistake.

   Because Q&As are difficult to coordinate in very large gatherings, they should be kept at a minimum, or not offered at all. That means the speech itself must be 80 percent to 90 percent of the allotted time. To keep that length from boring the audience, it always helps to have visuals (charts and graphs, photographs, movies and a PowerPoint presentation) to provide a break.

—Luncheon speech—One of the most common mistakes speakers (and their speechwriters) make is to treat a luncheon speech as a scheduled speech. They are very different. In a scheduled speech, the goal is to educate and inform the audience. Any entertainment value is incidental, and sometimes even unwelcome. A luncheon speech is just the opposite: whatever takeaways the audience leaves with are subordinate to the fact they enjoyed themselves.

For that reason, luncheon speeches should be amusing, emotional, witty, trenchant—indeed, any emotion evoked from the audience that leaves them satisfied by the experience. Remember: the audience is composed of people who are usually coming off a busy morning that has demanded their attention and participation; and soon they will be heading into an afternoon filled with the same thing. They've just eaten a meal, they are chatting amongst themselves or checking their phones for messages, and now they are being asked to spend an interval of time politely listening to your client. They want to laugh or cry or be called to arms—they don't want to have to learn a lesson or take their medicine.

The trick is to have a funny opening (again, not a joke), several anecdotes and some surprising facts, and all at the service of one key point or message the audience will remember. Keep the speech short: anything over 20 minutes and people will start digesting their meals and drift off. Take a few questions, but not many, and leave them wanting more.

—After dinner speech—The after dinner speech is the luncheon speech in a tuxedo. It has much the same structure as its midday counterpart, but with the added factor of alcohol. That, plus the fact that it comes at the end of a long day and a heavy meal, will make the audience more philosophical, but also more sleepy. If the goal of the luncheon speech is to entertain, for the after dinner speech it is to enlighten. For the former it is to leave the audience with one new idea or concept; for the latter it is to synthesize multiple concepts into a single, higher vision.

That doesn't mean you shouldn't be amusing—on the contrary. But, unlike a lunch, the goal is not to amuse, but rather, engage. In the best after dinner speeches, the audience members come away feeling like they have a deeper understanding of their industry, their careers or their lives—all given by your client as one smart person to another.

None of this means that the after dinner speech should be any longer than the luncheon speech. But the open-ended nature of its scheduling usually means that the Q&A session can risk going on forever. One way to deal with this is to teach your client to say, "One more question, please, otherwise we can talk afterwards in the bar," or something like that.

Structuring a speech

1. Ground the speech in the event or location, but be careful because the audience will know those details better than your speaker. Present your speaker as worldly and knowledgeable, but not as an insider. Audiences can sniff out frauds.

2. Use humor but pretend not to. Be funny but don't wait around for laughter. And no dirty or sexist jokes—ever. The author once attended a press conference given for Silicon Valley executives by a big, old East Coast corporation. The first speaker began his talk with a joke that managed to be vulgar, sexist and, worst of all, not funny. No one laughed but him. The reporter from the *Los Angeles Times* sitting next to me whispered, "Thirty seconds in and they are already dead." In the age of the Internet, your client will not only be dead, but buried.

3. That said, if your client can make an audience chuckle twice, they will like him or her and give the speaker a good review. If they can make that audience laugh twice, they will love your client and recommend him or her to their friends.

4. Show the bones. There is nothing wrong with announcing at the beginning how you plan to structure the speech—and then remind them where you are in that structure as you go along, for example, "My third point ..." The old line that you should "tell your audience what are going to say, then tell them, then tell them what you just told them," may be a cliché, but it is absolutely correct.

5. Look for memorable titles and phrases. After you've written a speech, go back and look for ways to say things more cleverly or more memorably. Acronyms help, but even better are clever titles and phrases. Great speechwriters will spend more time on these phrases than the entire rest of the speech.

6. Less is more—Never leave the audience fully satisfied—or worse, wishing the speech had been just a little bit shorter. As the old vaudeville line goes, "Leave 'em panting for more."

7. Close at the climax. Rather than fading out at the end, finish hard at the peak of the speech. Use the subsequent question period as the aftermath and conclusion.

8. Beware PowerPoint. There is nothing wrong with using slides, but if you do use them, assume the audience knows how to read, and just amplify the words on the slide; not read them verbatim. Also, don't overdo graphics: there are cases of speakers, overenthusiastic about PP, who have actually made audiences physically sick from the spinning and bouncing slide content.

9. Know the room. Will there be a stage or dais? A lectern? Will there be a light on the lectern? Will you be speaking into a fixed microphone or lavalier? Is the hall wide and shallow or long and narrow? Will there be cameras (it will affect lighting)? Try to get your client to come early for the speech and check out the hall for these factors, so that there are no surprises.

Delivering a speech

1. Read as little as possible—If your client has read the speech enough times, he or she can likely glance down at the beginning of each sentence, then look up as he or she completes it. If you maintain eye contact with your audience members, they will do the same with you.

2. Spare the notes. This follows from number 1. Get your client, if possible, to know as much of the speech as they can—to the point that they can even improvise without the notes.

3. Don't trust technology. Teleprompters break, lectern lights burn out, remotes controlling the slide projector run out of batteries. Your client should be prepared to make the speech without any external help.

4. Practice and time the speech with your client. What looks long on the page can prove short when spoken, and vice versa. Moreover, don't clock your own reading, but that of your client, the actual speaker, because there are great divergences in speaking pace. Never delude yourself that your client can hit the required time length by either talking faster or slower. Cut or pad the speech instead.

5. Train your client to talk forcefully, with his or her chin up (not easy to do when reading) and to enunciate. Warn them to keep their eyes open—you'd be amazed how many speakers talk with their eyes closed out of fear of the audience.

6. Underline or italicize stressed phrases and words in the speech. Show your client, during rehearsals, how to come down with emphasis on those words and phrases, raising their voices, moving up a note or two and carefully pronouncing every syllable.

7. Stay in command. Audiences can smell fear in a speaker. Train your client to finish every sentence strongly and not fade off; to focus their eyes on the audience at regular intervals; and to end the speech

stronger than they began, particularly the final sentences. Tell your client that no matter what happens—the microphone goes dead, the slide show crashes, and so forth—remain calm and unflappable and the audience will be on their side.

Types of speechwriting jobs

Speechwriting can pay well, though mostly only at the highest levels. And, even there, salaries are a fraction of that made at the top in other professions. Often the best and most secure speechwriting jobs are those hidden behind other titles, such as VP Marketing Communications or Director of Public Relations.

Part-time PR speechwriter—This is often how you start, as a public-relations specialist (sometimes agency, but usually corporate) who is asked to write or edit the occasional speech for a senior executive. There won't be any additional pay or bonus for the work—but do it well and you may get asked again and again until it becomes a major part of your job, and one that gets you much more access to, and attention from, the very people who will decide your future at the company.

Corporate communications part-time speechwriter—Same as above, but this time you are working in corporate communications on a company publication. Writing speeches for senior management, especially the CEO or chairman, often leads (because you know their style and positions) to jobs writing bylined articles, shareholder letters and other written productions for them. Both of the previous jobs can eventually lead to:

Corporate speechwriter—Most large corporations have a full-time speechwriter for at least the CEO. Once they have found a speechwriter with whom they are comfortable, top executives rarely change them, so this job is seldom open except when that CEO moves on. So, at least in mature companies, the best chance of getting this job is to be the part-time speechwriter for another C–Level executive fast-tracked for the CEO slot. There are much better odds with young, fast-growing companies, where the part-time speechwriter is invited to take over the brand-new head speechwriter job. And, since these individuals are often offered stock options, this is one of the few ways to get rich as a speechwriter.

Government speechwriter/Political speechwriter—These are the best-known speechwriters, though it is important to note that at the level of a presidential speechwriter you are almost always part of a writing team. That means, if you really care about your prose, you'd better be prepared to swallow your pride in your craft when you are edited out in lieu of someone's else's deathless phrasing. That said, you are at the center of power, with access to the greatest figures of the era—imagine what you will tell your grandchildren. And sometimes you just may get the chance to write that one phrase that rings through history; which is as close to immortality as you can get as a writer.

Author/touring speaker—At any given moment there are hundreds of people travelling around the country giving speeches and making often very comfortable incomes. Many are authors, others are professional (often motivational speakers) and most are both. There is a singular symbiosis between speaking and nonfiction writing: that is, many authors write books in order to attract big money ($10K-plus) speaking fees; and many professional speakers write books to sell them at their speeches. Done properly—a book every couple of years, 20 or more speeches per year—and a critical mass can be reached. This virtuous cycle can ultimately result in bestsellers and six-figure speaking fees. Properly done (and if you have the right combination of talents) this strategy can be maintained for decades.

Stand-up comic—As noted earlier, we usually don't think of stand-up comedy as public speaking. But it is a very close relation. And though it is rare that a comedian depends entirely upon writers (Bob Hope is a famous example), many of the most successful ones do have a stable of freelancers to help them). This can be very high-paying, but unpredictable, work. Writing your own stand-up routine is a different matter, and your success and failure will largely depend upon your native talents.

Hired-gun speechwriter—There are contract speechwriters, but their numbers are few, at least full-time. Most have other work and are either brought in as one-off consultants or are put on a small retainer to be accessible when needed. At the highest level, these hired guns are the equivalent to "script doctors," brought in to save a project and able to charge very large fees. More often, this work is occasional and good for a little cash on the side.

Career: The good

It's real writing—Great speeches contain some of the most lyrical prose ever written. And, unlike most other corporate work, you will be pushed to the limits of your talent—and there's nothing better for a writer than that.

It can help sell books—If you have just published a book, supporting it with a speaking tour can multiply sales (and royalties).

It can be for the ages—"Four score and seven years ago ..." Great speeches are among the most enduring creations of mankind.

You can change the world—A great speech can be more powerful than an army. You may get very few opportunities to write such a speech, but most people never get such a chance.

You'll have close access to the very top—Look at the memoirs of speechwriters. If you want to be around the great and near-great, learn their deepest thoughts, and help them make history: there is no better place to be.

It's an entrée into other writing fields—Who is better to write the biography of the great man or woman than the person who wrote their words, and was at their side during good times and bad? Or, conversely, who better understands policy—and thus is the perfect candidate for a fellowship at a think tank or a job as a newspaper/magazine columnist—than the person who helped formulate and explain that policy to the world?

It's a way into politics—This is a tricky one. Many speechwriters underestimate the other factors, besides policy and speechmaking, that make for a successful politician: these factors include dealmaking, fundraising, charisma and compromise. However, if you can cross that divide, a background in making speeches and explaining policy to the public can be enormously useful.

Career: The bad

Ultimately, you are putting your words into other people's mouths—and they are getting credit for it. If you can't check your ego and live without a byline, this is probably not the career for you. And keep in mind: you may be willing to give up credit at 25 because you figure you'll get it eventually; but not at 45 when you are running out of time to build your legacy.

You are unappreciated by the audience, sometimes even by your own client—Imagine what it is like writing that brilliant speech the whole world is talking about and no one knows you wrote it. Worse, you watch your client taking credit on CNN for his or her genius. If you can't live with that, you probably shouldn't get into speechwriting. If you can, more power to you—the world always needs great speeches.

It's a chance to die in public—If you are giving your own speech, you may discover there's a reason people rank public speaking just after dying as their greatest fear. As you write your speech, you'll imagine your audience on its feet and cheering, but sometimes in real life, they only stand to boo louder—or walk out. As for your clients, if that disaster befalls them, they will scapegoat you—end of that contract.

It suffers from volatile job security—Speechwriting can be the most secure of jobs until your client retires, loses the election, or gets fired. Then, often well into your career, you may find yourself looking for work.

Turning points

"I just can't go out there anymore"—If you are giving your own speeches or doing stand-up you may find over time that it is getting harder and harder to walk out on stage and experience the pressure of live performance. Even Laurence Olivier, arguably the greatest actor of the twentieth century admitted to a debilitating stage fright in his later years. It may never happen to you; but, then again, it may sneak up on you when you are least prepared for it. If that happens, find alternative work until it passes (if it does). Keep in mind that your personal speechwriting skills can be transferred to others—consider contract work.

"I'm tired of that stupid fool getting credit for my brilliant words."—This is the age-old "valet" problem: as the saying goes, no man is a hero to his valet. There is something particularly frustrating about putting your great words into the mouth of someone who doesn't deserve them—or worse, gets all the credit for them. Sometimes this can be solved by finding a better client, but at other times you must simply swallow your pride and start exploring a different line of work.

EXAMPLE: Here is the opening of a speech given to the Phi Beta Kappa graduates and their parents on the eve of their graduation from Santa Clara. Note the scene setting at the beginning of the speech, a bit of self-effacing humor (not told as a joke) and the statement of the speech's purpose. The rest of the speech is an enumeration of the opportunities/threats announced in the last sentence.

Speech to Phi Beta Kappa Graduates (2017)

Good evening. It is a very great honor to be here before you on this special night. And speaking as both an alumnus and a faculty member I can say with certainty that this university has been honored to have you here at Santa Clara University. You have already achieved great things—and we will be following your even greater achievements in the years and decades to come.

I assume that I have been asked to speak tonight not because of my teaching skills; certainly not for my undergraduate GPA—or even, like Phi Beta Kappa itself, because I too got my start in a tavern—but because I've spent the last forty years outside these walls, as a journalist, author, and entrepreneur in Silicon Valley. The assumption is that I have seen things out there—perhaps even a glimpse of the future—that I can convey to you at this moment when you are about to launch into your own careers.

Well, I wish I could give you specific facts and trends about that future—that I could just say, as the businessman said to the Graduate in that movie of the same name: "Plastics' . . . and make you all rich and famous. But there is no simple answer. The only real truth is Moore's Law, society's metronome for the last six decades. This law of semiconductors has become the rule of innovation, one that ticks away, doubling performance every three years or so, each time opening a new world of innovation and opportunity. Stunningly, about the time you entered Santa Clara, the curve of Moore's Law essentially went vertical—meaning that each year now see leaps as great as entire decades a half-century ago.

The implication of this is that the incredible pace of change that has characterized the modern world—and all of your lives—is just a prologue of what is to come. That's why we can no longer predict the future—what lies ahead is one long minefield of radical discontinuities, one that may very well characterize your entire careers. You will never be able to be complacent, to coast, but rather you will have to be always vigilant, ready to zig or zig with the next sudden change, with the death of one industry and sudden birth of another. And always prepared to abandon where you are to leap onto the next great opportunity.

What will be those opportunities? Where will be those threats? [etc.]

Technical Writer

What is technical writing?

Technical writing is the careful use of language to make the complexities of technology and science—especially the application of the former and the understanding of the latter—comprehensible to users, students, professional peers and other interested parties. The applications of this writing discipline include explaining the operation and repair of products and devices, instruction in the use of a service or application and, in the case of technical and scientific papers, the sharing of new knowledge.

What makes technical writing different?

More than most other forms of corporate writing, and certainly more than writing for media, technical writing gives priority to clarity of communication over art and style. And whereas accuracy is vital for all forms of media writing—especially for all forms of journalism—for technical writing absolute accuracy is nearly an obsession. And for good reason: make a mistake in instructions for, say, the repair of an airplane engine, and the results can be catastrophic.

Therefore, those individuals who gravitate to technical writing are different from their counterparts in the writing professions, even from those in other corporate writing jobs. Indeed, technical writers seem to exist in a different reality from those counterparts, with their own training (there are far more technical writing programs than there for all other professional writing careers combined), professional organizations, conferences and seminars.

Because the priorities of technical writing are so different, potential professional writers who care most about writing, rather than content; or about style over clarity, would be well advised to steer clear of the technical writing profession or they will be doomed to unhappy careers. Conversely, writers who give priority to explanation, and to helping others understand, may find a comfortable home in this profession.

Types of technical writing

As a rule of thumb, technical writing takes as its province those tasks that involve a complex process or a difficult topic that must be *transformed* into a linear and highly organized narrative or series of steps that are explained in plain language mixed with accurate terminology. Thus, the most common vehicles for technical writing are texts that deal with the operation of complex systems (how to fly an airplane, how to operate a gas chromatograph), the repair of such systems (diesel engine repair) or procedures for working with a complex methodology (computer programming, surgery).

A second application of technical writing revolves around the *cataloging of information* that requires great accuracy and precision, such as a listing of product specifications or prices, or a catalog of goods for sales. A variant of this is a record of results, such as the output of lab experiments.

Finally, a third common application of technical writing is in the *creation of scientific or technical papers*, where the most advanced ideas must be presented in a cogent and precise manner that can be understood by peers in that profession. Variants of this are research reports that have to be presented in a manner understandable by corporate executives, government agencies and other non-technical enterprises and institutions.

Here are some sample applications of technical writing:

Operator manuals	Catalogs
Instruction manuals	Specification sheets
Repair guides	Performance records
Rule books	Technical reports
Textbooks	Tech product advertising copy
Trade magazine articles	Technical articles
Scientific papers	Rulebooks
Guidebooks	Handbooks
Product warranties	Product guides

Key tenets of technical writing

Get trained—Unlike most professional writing careers, the technical writing profession has developed its own infrastructure of training programs, certifications, ethical guidelines, quality control and associations. It isn't necessary to do any of this to start a career in technical writing, but it certainly makes progress in that career easier and opens the prospect, later in your career, of becoming an instructor yourself or being entrepreneurial and starting your own technical writing firm. If you choose to go corporate, certification also increases your job prospects. But most of all, training will teach you skills at the beginning of your career that otherwise might take you decades to learn.

Know the subject—It isn't necessary to be an expert on what you are writing about, but it sure helps. That's why many technical writers stick to one or two areas of interest in which they can maintain high levels of expertise and stay on the leading edge of innovation. No one expects you, as a technical writer, to be an actual scientist or engineer, but you will be expected to have sufficient knowledge of the subject about which you are writing to be able to talk to those scientists and engineers, to be able to take their work and understand it enough to explain it to others in a comparatively simple way, and to be able to edit their work, if not for small data errors, then at least for larger errors in logic and fact.

Organize, organize, organize—Because much of technical writing is designed to walk inexperienced people through a series of steps to a predetermined and successful end (restoring a house, tuning an engine, troubleshooting a procedure, writing a program), it is vital that the nature of these steps and the trajectory of the process be carefully determined beforehand. A missed or confused step—even too far a step—will lose the reader and render the experience a failure. Therefore, it is absolutely crucial that the project be carefully outlined and that the outline be fine-tuned and tested. Indeed, the outline of a technical writing project should be the equivalent of the lede in a news story: that is, it should consume as much as half of your time and energy. Ideally, your outline should provide every detail and turn of your final narrative such that the actual writing is little more than fleshing out its entries.

Accuracy is everything—As a reporter, an error in your copy can lead to the embarrassment of having to publish a correction. As a novelist or screenwriter, an error can leave your readers or audience scratching their heads about a failure in continuity. But an error in a repair manual can lead to millions of dollars in damage to expensive machinery—or even to deaths.

For that reason, technical writing needs to be an obsession. You need to check and double check that every word you have written is the correct one. And after you have checked your writing enough times to be certain there are no errors, *then* you need to check it again using someone else who understands the subject, most likely another expert than the one who gave you the assignment.

Think in multiple media—Being a successful technical writer in the twenty-first century means understanding that words and numbers aren't the only way to convey information. In years past, your ability to use photographs, illustrations and certainly video, were seriously constrained by the cost of production.

No more. And that means that part of your preparation for a technical writing project is determining what is the best presentational format for the job. It may still be a written manual, but just as likely that manual will be filled with photographs or illustrations to show the actual physical action at every step of the way, demonstrating the use of tools and identifying the parts and components involved.

By the same token, you may also determine that the best way to convey the necessary information is to video the entire process and put it on YouTube or in the Cloud for easy access. This doesn't mean you won't still be writing, but it will now take the form of a script, with a narrator.

From all of this, it should be obvious that the nature of technical writing is evolving faster than many other forms of professional writing— and that if you want to have a long and successful career you need to regularly upgrade your proficiency with the latest tools, as well as become competent in other writing forms, notably screenwriting.

Clarity always trumps artistry—A well-wrought sentence—a dynamic verb, perfectly chosen adjectives and adverbs, multiple clauses hung onto the end to precisely place the subject in the natural world—can be a beautiful thing. But it has no place in technical writing. Here you need a different esthetic, one that celebrates simplicity, clarity and efficiency. Save your poetic writing for your personal life. On the job, your goal is to convey the maximum amount of information in the fewest and simplest words, taking the typical, untrained reader and, by the end of the text, having them fully prepared to tackle the task at hand. That requires very careful writing, in particular:

Define your objects and tools—Don't assume your reader knows anything. Whenever you introduce a new device, part, procedure or tool, you must explain them: what to call them, how they are used, and what are the proper terms to describe their purpose or application.

Contextualize actions—Users want to know how the procedure they are performing fits into the big picture of the overall project. This can be done quickly and easily ("the clutch conveys the rotational power of the engine to the transmission, and from there to the differential and rear axle").

Control adjectives and adverbs—Unless the modifier is of direct purpose to the instruction, leave it out. Thus, "look for the red wire" stays, but "closing the case should be accompanied by a healthy plastic click" doesn't need those two adjectives. They are distracting and should be removed.

Don't get distracted by peripheral knowledge—The airplane wing repair person doesn't need to know that the original Wright flyer had neither flaps nor ailerons. Stick to the business at hand.

Make the bones show—Make full use of chapter titles, subheads, bullet points and other techniques to show the organization of the text and as guide posts to help users navigate through the text. Even consider specialty tools, such as colored tabs, to help with the process.

Harmonize text and imagery—There's nothing worse than reading about an action and not finding the accompanying imagery on the same page. Work with your publisher to make sure the layout of your text not only puts the right words adjacent to the right images, but that the captions of those images reinforce the text. In technical writing, unlike some other forms of writing, the imagery should never advance the text—rather it should reinforce the text.

Expand both ends of the text—Many writers treat the table of contents and index with relative indifference. That should never be the case with technical writing. Anything you can do to help the reader navigate the text is valuable, and few features are more important than an expanded table of contents (not just chapter titles, but all subheads) and a complete index (if you don't want to do it, put it in your contract to hire someone who will).

Follow the format—Technical papers and reports often have very specific guidelines regarding content, charts and graphs, and the formatting of sections. If you are writing one of these items, don't be creative with style—writing exactly to the format required. Otherwise, with a technical paper, you risk having it turned down; with the report, you may create more questions than you answer. Neither will go over well with a client.

Follow the style—If you are writing a manual or product handbook, don't assume your usual style is best. It may well be, but the publication still must be congruent in style with the other productions of your client—and your different style will stand out. Before you begin, obtain and study other company publications—study their style and imitate it.

Edit, edit, edit—All professional writing needs editing. It is an inescapable part of the craft. But the editing of technical writing differs in important ways from most other writing forms. Once again, the emphasis should not be on better writing, but *clearer* writing. And that kind of editing can be much more difficult because you are not just trying to improve the quality of the prose but more precisely relate it to actions in the real world. This can be difficult enough if you are writing a manual and working from a description of how something works (without ever having done it yourself), but it is even harder if you are editing a scientific paper about a topic only a handful of people in the world as yet understand. There are several approaches for doing this:

Tighten up—When the author was a teenager he was contracted by NASA to edit scientific papers by its astronomers and astrophysicists. I had almost no idea what I was reading in those papers, and I was even more intimidated because several of them were written by Carl Sagan and his team. But it turned out that it didn't really matter—the biggest contribution I could make was to break up run-on sentences, fix redundancies, replace passive verbs, remove unnecessary phrases and clauses and correct spelling mistakes. In other words, even with such arcane topics my job still came down to the usual blocking-and-tackling of cleaning up messy sentences.

Break it up—Smart people who are also bad writers (and their numbers are legion) tend to produce exceptionally murky prose. Not only are the sentences often indecipherable patchworks of obscure terms, passive verbs and pretentious grammar, but their paragraphs are endless.

The result, more often than not, is a solid slab of text run a page or more per paragraph, filled with dense, airless sentences. The result is off-putting: the mind just doesn't want to enter that black hole for fear of never getting out alive. The simplest strategy is just to wade in and start breaking up the text into paragraphs of two or three sentences each.

Where you break up these paragraphs, because the text usually has little narrative thrust, can be almost arbitrary. Just look at the copy to see where the breaks should be, and then look for a likely space nearby.

Educated people also have a tendency to use Latinate words whenever a simple Anglo-Saxon term works far better—thus, *face*

rather than *visage*, Sometimes, you must use the technical term—
"bolus" instead of "injection" for example—but for nontechnical
nouns and most verbs, always go for the simpler form. The same is
true for endlessly long sentences: cut them up.

Mark it up—Technical writing is all about precision. So is the
editing of technical writing. Learn the basic editing marks and use
them. Be consistent in your editing all the way through the text. If
editing by hand, keep your red pencil sharp and make precise marks;
if using editing software, use the comment function regularly to
explain what you have done. Don't hesitate to make the copy bleed
with your edits; ironically, it will make you look more professional.
Also use the search-and-replace function heavily.

Since you likely don't know the meanings of all of the technical
terms being used, you'll want to note each time one of those terms
appears in the text, understand its context and make sure the spelling
and capitalization are consistent. You may well discover that your
author doesn't quite know the definition of the term either. If you do
find the definition of a term, as used, varies in the text, look it up, post
the definition in one of your editing comments, and ask the author
whether he or she is comfortable with those differences.

Stand up—You are probably not surprised to learn that scientists
and engineers can be exceptionally arrogant people. Professionally,
much of that arrogance is earned (if unnecessary); unfortunately, that
arrogance often also extends to other parts of their lives, not least their
writing abilities. Few people look at a great artist and automatically
assume they can do just as well themselves. Most people know they
can't draw. But most people do know how to write, and many believe
they know at least as much about creating prose as do professionals.
Thus, it will not be an uncommon occurrence in your career as a
technical writer to encounter that author who simply ignores your
edits or, worse, edits your edits—badly.

The risks associated with this are obvious. The author may tell your
employer that you are incompetent and in so doing damage your
reputation. Or, the author may say nothing and go ahead and publish
his or her version, and the world thinks you are responsible for this
piece of lousy writing.

You have two recourses. One is to simply stand up to the author.
Remind the author that you are the professional and privately (not
publicly, because that turns a mess into a catastrophe) show him or
her the manifold grammatical and content mistakes they've made.

If the author still refuses to use your edits, go to the person who
hired you and explain the situation. Bring along both drafts to make

your case. At this point, you are not going to win with the author, but you can at least salvage your own reputation. Get your employer's agreement that you are in the right (that will likely get you hired again in the future) and politely ask to bow out of working with the author ever again. With luck, your position will be reinforced by the next poor editor tasked to work with that author. If you've got the nerve, or are obviously the aggrieved victim—or if you don't want to work with this company ever again—ask for a kill fee. You deserve it.

Career paths

Much like PR and advertising—but with some interesting differences—technical writing careers have two basic paths: corporate and freelance. Plus, there is a third, hybrid, path growing in popularity that might be called a contractor confederation, or writing shop.

Corporate

In-house technical writer jobs are a luxury usually enjoyed only by the largest corporations, or by smaller firms with a heavy output of technical material. This type of employment enjoys all the advantages (and disadvantages) of working for a large company, including:

Job security—Since no one else in the company, especially management, really understands how you do what you do, but only sees the results, your chances of being laid off are pretty slim. And if your employer does get into trouble and you are let go, the odds are good that you will immediately be hired back as a freelancer.

Specialization—Working on a single technology at a single employer really gives you the opportunity to make yourself an expert. And the company will likely pay to keep you up-to-date on that technology by attending training programs and seminars. And that will only make you more irreplaceable. Being an acknowledged expert in your field will open side freelance opportunities to write books and manuals.

Insider knowledge—Continuous work on a single technology or product family in a company will give you unequalled access to both research and product-development people. That in turn will give you a forward look into products and technologies to come—something that, for a technically oriented writer, can be particularly rewarding.

Management opportunities—More than public relations or advertising, and especially corporate communications, technical writing departments at the corporate level tend to be small, and at the division level rarely have more than one or two individuals. Sometimes they are even merged into those other departments. That said, there is still an opportunity to move up into a supervisory or even a management role.

Teamwork—As with any corporate job—and unlike freelancing—corporate technical writing offers the chance to be part of something bigger than yourself, to work with others in different lines of work and to share your company's successes. Moreover, if you put in the years, there also may be the opportunity for stock options, stock purchases, profit sharing and a pension. This may seem a secondary matter at the beginning of your career, but it looms large as you approach retirement.

Freelance—Because of the intermittent nature of the work, most companies have neither the money nor the inclination to retain in-house technical writers. For that reason, most technical writers operate as freelancers, taking gigs at different companies as projects present themselves. Sometimes this can lead to extended periods without work, but at other times it presents an opportunity to double, or even, triple up on work and enjoy a considerable payday.

Freedom—The biggest advantage to being a freelance technical writer is the independence it offers. You can take on work when you choose and turn it down when you want to take a break (or perhaps try your hand at other writing). Of course, you don't want to turn down too much work—or you might lose that client—but certainly the flexibility is far greater than in the corporate world.

Range of experience—Unlike corporate work, where you are typically assigned to one topic for long stretches of your career, as a freelancer you will likely take on lots of different jobs on many different topics. This can certainly make your working life a lot more interesting. The trade-off, of course, is you will likely never develop the expertise in a single subject like you would working for a single employer.

Entrepreneurship—One might assume that working as a freelancer forecloses the opportunity to obtain the perquisites of a corporate job, including stock and a pension. Perhaps surprising to outsiders, freelance technical writing actually offers a different opportunity to earn far more—in particular, founder's stock in new start-up companies. Needless to say, a lot of those shares will turn out worthless, but one or two successful start-ups can set you financially for life. Thus, freelance technical writers should always dedicate some portion of their time to working for stock, not money, speculating on interesting new companies.

Business

Freelancing means self-employment, and that in turn means control over the business side of your career. Being good at business and finance can make being a freelancer not only easier, but actually more lucrative. Rather than leaving withholding in the hands of an employer, and foregoing deductions because those items are provided, a financially astute freelancer can maximize revenues—they charge their clients as much as 30 percent more—and minimize taxes, thus earning a higher income.

Needless to say, and this cannot be repeated enough, if you are going to be a freelance writer in any form, you need to run your career as a real businessperson, and that means immediate invoicing and careful record-keeping.

Writing shop

If you want the advantages of both freelancing and corporate life, one solution that has attracted many technical writers is to form a kind of confederation of professional peers. The comparables are a doctor's office or a law firm, in which essentially independent operators share facilities and services (such as bookkeeping, billing, marketing, and so forth) to enjoy economies of scale.

Technical writing shops are typically organized around a veteran writer who also has management and organizational skills. This individual typically exchanges these skills for a director's salary composed of some fraction (usually 5 to 10 percent) of the fees charged by the other partners. This frees the director to do less technical writing and instead focus upon the challenge of building and running the enterprise. For many freelance technical writers, the writing shop represents the best of both worlds, combining work independence with business support. Others, especially those with business skills, often still prefer to go on their own and keep all their revenues.

Technical-writing shops typically succeed if they share the following traits:

Comparable skill levels—While these shops may include interns and neophyte writers, the actual partners—that is, those who share earnings on projects—need to be of comparable experience and skill. Otherwise, there is liable to be resentment when one hard-working partner comes to feel he or she is carrying another slow-moving partner.

Complementary partner skills—If all of the partners in a shop have identical talents and knowledge there is liable to be competition for the available work. It is far better if the partners have skills that dovetail—for example, one is experienced with manuals, another with marketing documents, still another with instructional videos. Such a combination will enable the shop to pitch potential customers with a complete line of services and thus improve its odds of landing a full-service contract.

A business director and team—As they say in the law, the most successful legal firms have "a finder, a minder, and a grinder"—that is, someone to land clients, a second person to run the business, and a third person to do the actual legal research. This is also the case with a technical writing shop: you need someone to serve as the manager or owner and actually run the business. And you need someone (it may be the same person) who markets the team and signs customers. And everyone else needs to do the actual working of writing according to their skills. For the shop to remain healthy, the manager must fairly distribute the available work to the partners so that there are no recriminations, which will tear the shop apart.

Management of facilities and services—Successful technical-writing shops act as the representatives for their members in all non-writing activities. These activities include locating, negotiating and managing facilities and support staff; obtaining discounts on equipment, furniture and supplies; billing clients; managing bank accounts and distributing payment; and negotiating with and managing service providers, including bookkeeping and tax accountants.

Career: The good

Job security—More than just about any other form of writing, technical writing confers the best job security. You can start young as a freelancer, jump to corporate life a few years later and, after you retire, join a writing shop. And it is the kind of career in which you can enjoy steady work well into old age.

Certification—Technical writing is one of the only writing careers where you can receive actual college-level training and, often, certification in your craft at almost every level of experience. This rationalizes the profession and makes competing for work more efficient.

Independence—Especially if you are freelancer, but even if you work in the corporate world, you will enjoy a considerable amount of work freedom. Many companies won't require you to be on-scene but will let you work at home. And because your work is so specialized, few will look over your shoulder as you write (though they will scrutinize your results).

Available work—As the modern economy becomes increasingly defined by science and technology, its need for technical writing only grows, and because of the unique skills and temperament involved there will likely never be enough good technical writers to meet that demand.

Reward—Not only can technical writing be satisfying work—teaching people to use equipment and tools properly not only can increase productivity but even reduce injuries and save lives—but the work not only pays well (if not great) and, of particular interest to freelancers, consistently.

Career: The bad

It's not creative writing—If your temperament is correct for the work, and your priorities are for precision and communication over emotional impact and art, then technical writing can be very satisfactory. But if your priorities are of the latter type—that is, you are what most people think of as a "writer"—a technical writing career can be a living hell, and you will likely either quit or fail.

Lack of respect—As the above suggests, creative writers don't understand technical writing and give it little respect. In fact, most other writers don't even think of technical writing as being part of the writing profession (A confession: I forgot to include this chapter in the first draft of the book). What that means is that if you want to feel part of the great guild of writers, you are likely to be disappointed—rather, you will spend your time with other technical writers. Meanwhile, working as closely as you will with scientists and engineers, you will find many of them will treat you not as writers, but as mediocre members of their profession. And because they know little about writing, they won't give you much credit for that either.

Ghettoization—If you dream of starting out as a technical writer, then using the credibility you've gained there to bridge to another type of writing career, forget it. Because other writers don't really consider technical writing to be "real" writing, even the most distinguished technical writing career won't do much if you want to subsequently become, say, a novelist. On the other hand, the skills you learn as a technical writer—including clarity, simplicity and organization—will stand you in good stead. The noted novelist Amy Tan (*The Joy Luck Club*) began her career as a Silicon Valley technical writer.

Turning points

Wrong Place—There aren't many turning points in a technical writing career. The big one usually takes place at the beginning: you enter the profession confused about its nature and expecting something very different, such as creative writing. It doesn't take long to realize that this isn't the work for you. The best recommendation is to be honest with yourself and get out—it won't get any better.

Go it alone, get it together—It is not unusual, at the midpoint of a technical writing career, to either get out of corporate life and enjoy the independence of freelancing or, conversely, to leave freelancing for the safe harbor of a corporate job.

Losing your edge—Technology moves fast, and science nearly as fast; and if you don't keep up with those changes—or your particular field goes obsolete—you may find yourself without work. Depending upon where you are in your career, you may at this point choose to retire, get more training, or move to a different industry.

Part Three

Writing Careers in Media

As we have just seen, corporate writing careers are characterized as much by the job of being an employee of a larger enterprise as they are by the actual writing work itself.

By comparison, writing jobs in the media typically put the writing work first. If you consider the creative writing process to be of prime importance in your career, this second type of work may prove more appealing, and satisfying to you.

You will also notice that this part is the biggest of this book. Writing for the media is by far the largest source of employment for professional writers—ranging from a blogger sitting at a computer in a spare bedroom and writing for a loyal audience of a few dozen readers, to writing the screenplay of blockbuster movie that costs a half-billion dollars to make and destined to be seen by 100 million viewers. Media writing careers also range from the most precise and formalized nonfiction to the most obscure experimental fiction.

In fact, there is almost no kind of media-oriented writing that has sparked your interest that does not present at least a small chance of your earning a living from pursuing it. What that means is that you should not just scrutinize one of these chapters to learn more about the tricks of your own current trade, but perhaps should look through the other chapters as well to see if another type of writing captures your imagination. It may be a side, or even second, career to which you can aspire.

Note that several of these chapters include additional sections that take a closer look at specialty careers within these professions. In those cases, such as investigative reporter in the news-reporting chapter, the main chapter is the typical gateway into the specialty career, while the added section is devoted to a top practitioner in the field.

Finally, personal experience has shown that while you may need to pay more dues—and get paid less money—to be successful in these careers than in corporate life, these kinds of jobs are uniquely emotionally rewarding. A creative life can be a very satisfying life.

Blogger

"Blog" is a neologism created from the phrase "web log." Strictly
speaking, a blog is a web site on which an individual or group of users
record opinions, information, interesting links, solicited comments and,
more rarely, conduct traditional field reporting, on a regular basis. There
are an estimated 200 million bloggers currently active in the world. The
universe of bloggers is usually called the Blogosphere. While it is possible
to earn a living as a blogger, the number of those who do so is extremely
small, as the competition for readers is high, and the business model itself
not particularly lucrative.

Why blog?

Blogging sits at the nexus of the natural human desire to share our
thoughts and beliefs with others, with the hope that our words will live
forever, and with the speed and infinite scalability of modern digital
technology. Most bloggers get into the profession because of its very low-
cost ease of entry (most blogging software is either cheap or free), and
they stay in despite the limited financial return because they enjoy both
the platform for their writing and opinions and the interaction with loyal
and equally opinionated readers.

A brief history of blogs

Blogs began as extended diaries entries (hence "log") and essays on
the pioneering sites of the Internet, such as the Well, Compuserve, BBS
sites, and so forth. Successful diarists—usually the most colorful and
opinionated writers and experts in tech-related fields—found they were
gaining loyal, even obsessive, followers and continued because they
enjoyed the response.

Archival data suggests that the first real blogs appeared in 1994–1995
at Swarthmore College by a student named Justin Hall—and by other
pioneers such as science-fiction writer and essayist Jerry Pournelle, who

moved his *Byte* magazine column "Chaos Manor" (founded in 1980) to the Web.

The transformative event in the history of blogging was the September 11, 2001 terrorist attack and the perceived failure of traditional media to keep up with the pace of news. The events of 9/11 made the reputation of Matt Drudge, and his news portal, "The Drudge Report," which would soon have millions of visitors each day, became a model of how much influence a single individual could have using the Web. Ev Williams, who went on to found Twitter and Medium, devised Blogger, which provided the first tools for blogging, and made becoming a blogger easy even for non-techies.

The size of the Blogosphere likely peaked around 2010, and for two reasons. First, a lot of first-generation bloggers discovered just how difficult it was to maintain a regular blog over the course of months or years, especially when it was never financially rewarding, nor did it attract a lot of readers. The numbers of bloggers leaving the field eventually exceeded those entering. Second, the rise of Twitter offered a quicker, shorter alternative for self-expression on the Web. Even professional journalists found Twitter a more appealing way to speak to their readers.

Nevertheless, the blog is still the vehicle of choice for millions of writers. Why? Because it is the simplest, easiest and least expensive way to become a writer, to write about what you love and have the potential to reach a vast global audience—or at least a group of loyal readers anxious to talk about what you've written. And, with luck, you may even make an income doing it. Some bloggers have made history by exposing stories the traditional media refuses to touch. That's why blogs are likely to be around for a long time.

Types of blogs

Blogs basically come in three forms:

1. *Thumbsuck*—Thumbsucks are the most common form of blog. Thumbsuck blogs are essentially a series of journal entries and commentaries. The term comes from newspapers, where a top feature writer would be promoted to writing a personal column about anything that interested them at a given moment. And, like those predecessors, thumbsuck blogs are written by a single individual, though they can be written by groups of like-minded individuals. In terms of style, they can range from the intensely personal to comparatively detached opinions on larger topics and events. Thumbsuck columns have certain comparative advantages, including:

the author enjoys complete editorial control, intense relationships can be created with readers and, in the case of a successful blog, revenues do not have to be shared with others. The downside of thumbsuck blogs is that they are hard to maintain: the author must meet regular and frequent deadlines to maintain a readership and, when a blog is especially personal and tightly focused, the blogger can simply run out of interesting content.

2. *Shared knowledge*—These are sites dedicated to sharing expertise or ideas, typically around a single theme. The topics of shared-knowledge blogs can range from professional skills (law, politics, management, engineering, architecture and countless other professions) to hobbies (photography, vacations, collecting, film, books and an almost endless number of fashion blogs). Needless to say, it helps the blogger's credibility if he or she is actually knowledgeable on the subject (though good reporting can make up for a lack of expertise), but being a good, precise and entertaining writer is even more important. The advantage of shared-knowledge blogging is that it comes with a built-in audience and provides a venue by which otherwise unknown professionals and experts can reach a national, even global, audience and burnish their reputations. That said, nearly every one of these target markets was long ago saturated by other bloggers, many with world-class credentials—so the big challenge is finding a way to break through the noise and establish one's own market niche.

3. *Portal*—The most successful form in terms of audience, but also the most demanding, is the portal blog. These sites, almost always managed by multiple editors, are typically composed of short set-up entries, often in the form of commentary, featuring a link to another site. In the United States, perhaps the most successful one-person portal blog editor (though he has lately added other contributors) is University of Tennessee law professor and author Glenn Reynolds, whose *Instapundit*blog offers as many as twenty such entries and links per day. Portal blogs have the advantage of being easy to start and an almost unmatched potential for audience building (especially if they are eclectic in their coverage). That said, they are a tremendous amount of work to maintain—as they are usually updated many times each day, as opposed to once every few days with most other blogs. And that doesn't count the enormous amount of reading and Web searching required just to find link sources and to be knowledgeable enough for the eclectic commentary.

4. *Astro-turf*—These problematic sites are the one type of blogging in which it is possible to earn a living, or at least a sizable fraction of one. Astro-turf blogs are those in which the blogger is employed by

a corporation, institution or politician to tell its story, report its news, and advocate its interests. Most of these entities operate transparently on such matters, but some try to camouflage their advocacy.

Working for the former is an acceptable career choice, so long as you understand that it may compromise any plans you may have for future employment in journalism (though in the twenty-first century, for good or bad, those boundaries are not as rigid as they used to be). If you take such a job, you should try to make it a condition of full employment instead of a contract position—that way you'll enjoy all of the benefits.

If, on the other hand, a company or other employer/contractor wants to hire you to write this type of advocacy blog while keeping your business relationship secret—or worse, wants to hire you to write comments on other blogs and web sites while keeping your paymaster hidden—walk away. This is unethical and unprofessional and if found out will wreck your career as a writer; and even if it is not found out it will rot your soul, and no salary (and this work doesn't pay much) is worth that.

Meta-blogs

Related to blogs, and often outgrowths of them, meta-blogs operate at a much larger scale and can even be multi-million-dollar enterprises. Meta-blogs are all but indistinguishable to readers from Web magazines—the fundamental difference being that the editorial content of meta-blogs is usually created by multiple contributors, often unpaid, while the magazines, usually the Web wing of print publications, feature a large percentage of staffers. Moreover, meta-blogs can take submissions from a small army, even hundreds, of contributors, while Web magazines are more likely to work from a smaller collection of contributors.

Make no mistake, meta-blogs are real *businesses.* Unlike simple blogs, they have business managers, advertising directors, salespeople, an editing staff, and investors. And even if they are built on the backs of unpaid contributors, they still require large amounts of capital to get underway and to operate. Unless you have access to millions in venture money, you probably won't be able to start a successful meta-blog; and unless you still live at home, have another source of income and are only looking to pad your resume, you probably won't want to write for one other either.

Meta-blogs take two primary forms:

1. *Neo-magazines*—These are the equivalent of traditional news, commentary and literary magazines for the Internet Age. On these

sites you'll see reporting, reviews and commentary, almost all of them bylined. What fundamentally distinguishes Web magazines from their print predecessors is the crucial role played by commenters: whereas the older model never had more than a couple of dozen letters to the editor, Webmags are as much defined by their comments sections— which may have hundreds of entries and lively debates—as the articles themselves. Examples include Huffington Post, Salon, Slate and Ricochet. They include bylined articles, features and criticism, with an added blog/commenter factor.

2. *Uber-bulletin boards*—This type of meta-blog is an evolution of the bulletin boards (such as the Well) that characterized the Internet before the advent of the Web. These sites, which can have hundreds of thousands of loyal users, are characterized by content created by those users (often linking to outside sources) and immense chains of commenters that can sometimes exceed more than a thousand messages over the course of months. The most popular of these sites, such as the liberal Democrat Underground and the conservative Free Republic, are characterized by their intense ("rabid," each would say of the other side) political opinions and calls to action. These sites do not pay contributors and largely survive on donations.

Blog topics

As you may imagine, with a couple of hundred million bloggers out there in the world, blog subjects cover just about everything under the sun. But, that said, blogs do seem to fall into a finite number of general categories. Here are some of the broadest of those categories. Among them you are likely to find the blog you'd love to write:

- *Politics*—These blogs approach politics from the top down (party leaders, government insiders), the bottom up (get out the vote volunteers, precinct walkers, local officials), the inside (party professionals) and the outside (think-tank experts, political scientists and academics); and from left, right and center and every form of fringe. Political blogs also address everything from the mechanics of governance to the most outrageous conspiracy theories.
- *Religion*—Religious blogs range from personal witnessing all the way to the most obscure theological thinking in all the world's great and lesser religions, and in almost every sect.
- *Daily Diary*—These can be among the most appealing (and conversely, among the most insular and boring) of blogs. Because Internet records are likely to be all but immortal, history is likely to treat these diary blogs

with great respect as unvarnished accounts of daily life in the twenty-first century. In the shorter term, even if no one else ever reads them, these blogs represent a unique family scrapbook for future generations.

- *Sports*—Professional athletes typically don't have the time, inclination or talent to blog, though some teams will keep a blogger on staff. So, sports blogging is largely the province of amateurs—true fans, fantasy-league players, university alumni, and so forth. Most of these bloggers write for a relatively limited audience, but they can enjoy considerable range as they often swap links with their peers. Sports blogging is challenging work: you have to find a new angle to differentiate yourself from competitors; you have to write quickly and assuredly after (and often before) each game; and you have to come up with creative content during the long months of the off-season.

- *Response to news events*—More than any other, news blogs have the potential to blow up into a national readership numbering in the millions. The key is to stay on top of breaking news stories and then post smart, thoughtful and clever commentary. Everybody has opinions, especially about politics, but when faced with writing down those opinions in a logical way and backing them up with considerable research and erudition, the task gets much, much harder. Then, doing all of this under a tight deadline (usually just a few hours, before the news cycle moves on) it is understandable why there are so few really enduring and influential political bloggers. Still, if this interests you, it is worth a try: if you have the aptitude for it, there is almost no easier way to get your views heard by the people who run your country.

- *Hobbies and expertise*—Most people are experts at *something*. Historically, the challenge has been to share that expertise with other like-minded people, especially when they are geographically scattered around the country, and around the world. Blogging, combined with research, turns the Internet into a vehicle by which they can connect, share knowledge and news and improve their skills. On top of that, it traditionally took credentials to earn a reputation as a leader in your field, but now anyone who can maintain a blog and write with adequate skills can build a similar reputation. This democratization of merit is one of the most important, and exciting, features of the Internet Age.

- *Local and community*—There are different-sized audiences, and anyone who is willing to play in a smaller pond—their neighborhood, or community, or region—can write a blog that will give them outsized influence on everything from school curricula to local zoning to politics. Local and community bloggers often become celebrities among their neighbors and can develop ardent readerships that depend upon them to learn everything from the topics of the next city council meetings, this week's school lunch meals, high school sports scores and the work of local nonprofit groups. In the longer run, many of these local and community blogs will be cherished as capturing their era better than any other record.

- *Travel*—There is an endless number of travel-related blogs, yet most survive because they not only serve an audience of interested travelers, but also act as a kind of virtual scrapbook of one's own journeys that is far more flexible and richer than social media, such as Facebook. This dual-purpose application—especially when enhanced by the added satisfaction of communication with other world travelers—makes this type of blogging especially appealing.

- *Collections*—A quarter century ago, there were two main ways to share one's collections (and expertise about those collections) with others: (a) join a local club, with all of its limitations; and (b) subscribe to a collectors' magazine in the field. There was also another way, (c) attend a collectors' convention or show, but that was expensive, so few people could attend even once per year. The Web has created its own version of these three experiences in one, and for free. Smart bloggers who focus upon collecting have learned to not only write blog entries that cover their own expertise and comment on related news stories (such as auction prices), mutually link with other bloggers, and sell (often in conjunction with the same listings on eBay) and buy items related to their collections.

- *Surveys*—This kind of blog, similar to a portal but more narrative driven, regularly looks at the state of a vertical industry or topic by analyzing trends, polling readers and offering summaries of academic papers and other articles related to the blog's theme. Successful survey bloggers often become leading lights and opinion makers in their fields.

- *Lifestyle choices*—This genre covers perhaps the widest range of blog topics, from sexual orientation to parenting to health and nutrition, to age cohorts and self-improvement programs. One of the great advantages offered by the Web is that while the number of people who may share your niche lifestyle in your community may be extremely small, the number of people who do so around the world almost always amounts to millions of like-minded individuals.

- *Owner/user*—Own a Porsche 356C? Building a crossbow? Repairing your obsolete stove? Want to know how to de-pill a wool sweater? How about washing your new jeans? This type of blog overlaps collecting, hobbies and lifestyle blogs, but features a much greater attention to the actual operation and repair of physical items. The type of individual who operates this type of blog is typically adept at filming or photographing these activities, and knows where to find, and how to install, replacement parts, upgrades, and after-market equipment. Particularly popular versions of this type of blog also include classified ads for reader/owners who want to sell items and have lively advice sections to help readers.

Career: The good

Blogging is easy to do. It can be done on any imaginable subject. And, in theory, it is almost infinitely scalable; in terms of production it is no harder to reach a million readers than to reach one. It is also incredibly cheap: you can start a blog on the Web using free software and post your first entry today. Best of all, you are free to write about anything you choose, write about it as often as you like, and prepare your prose in any style you choose. Want it to consist almost entirely of photos with short captions? Fine. Only post short science-fiction stories? No problem? Make it your ambition to create a blog solely about the bioluminescent fungi of New Guinea? Knock yourself out—though you'll probably discover that someone has already beat you to it.

Career: The bad

For all the advantages of blogging, there is one big problem: *Noise*. With 200 million bloggers out there, it is almost impossible to get noticed. That's why the average blog never sees more than a couple comments per month, nor traffic of more than a few hundred visitors—most of them via Google. It may be possible to earn a living blogging, but the odds against you doing so are astronomical. More likely, you will make a few bucks per month from the banner ads that ad brokers place on your site—and you still need hundreds of regular readers to get that.

Turning points

Starting a blog can be exciting. Seeing your comments page filling up is even more exciting. But if you can't make real money being a blogger, and it consumes hours per week that you could otherwise use more productively and lucratively, how long will you keep doing it? Six months? A year? Five years? Ironically, your biggest challenge will likely not be that you can't come up with enough good content (though it can be tough with thumbsuck blogs) or build an audience of loyal readers, or even that you won't make any money—but that you will do just well enough in each category so that you don't want to quit but can't justify going on indefinitely. The most painful blog retirement entries are those in which the blogger finally says goodbye to his or her loyal readers in order to spend more time with family or a job or just to get some relief from endless exhausting deadlines.

Tips to successful blogging

1. *It's a business*—The first thing is to understand that successful blogging is a form of *entrepreneurship*. In other words, whatever the subject of your blog, it is a business and needs to be run as a business using business techniques and methodology. Some of these techniques are described in this book, notably in PR and marketing communications. You must also be comfortable with self-promotion, marketing, graphic art and design.

2. *Your product*—Recognize that you have a product—your content. You need not only to produce a high-quality product (edit!) but increase your churn rate (that is, regularly add new entries) to bring your customers back. New entries twice per week should be your minimum; daily is best. Most of all, you need to capture the reader's interest (strong writing, topical, timely). That's why veteran bloggers tend to write shorter and more often.

3. *Tools*—There are a lot of diagnostic software tools out there to help you understand the operation of your blog: rates of traffic at different hours and in relation to your postings, geographic locations of your readers and commenters, and so forth. Use them. Try different content and timing and see how it changes your traffic. Use what works.

4. *Durability*—You should be in the business of producing your blog for the long haul. Too many bloggers start out as sprinters and burn themselves out quickly, which is why at any given moment almost as many bloggers are quitting the field as joining it. Get a rhythm and pace going that isn't too burdensome; then keep it up until you've turned that pattern into a habit. This combination of rhythm (it's not tiring) and habit (you feel the need to get it done on a regular basis) is the most powerful tool a writer has. It will not only keep your blog fun and fresh, but as an added benefit will also train you to write books.

5. *Differentiation*—In a typical blog, what distinguishes you from your competition is your narrative style, your *voice*. Blogs are supposed to be intensely personal, so don't be afraid to state your feelings, your opinions, and so forth. Stronger voices tend to attract larger audiences. This is true even if the topic of your blog is empirical—such as a tax blog.

6. *Marketing*—This is where most blogs fail. Most good bloggers aren't necessarily good businesspeople. But the reality is that with all that

noise out there, the only blogs that succeed—including those with great content—are those in which the bloggers work hard to add readers. There are three primary ways to do that:

a. Get your entries picked up either by scores of other low-traffic blogs, or by one big one. This means developing relationships, sending links to the owners of other sites, explaining why their readers might be interested in your latest entry, and carrying other bloggers' links to get them to carry you (via links to their stories, blogrolls, and so forth.)

b. Send your most interesting blogs to publications and web sites you admire in hope they will pick up the story, run with it, and credit you. This can get you in front of huge audiences.

c. Team up with other bloggers you like to create a group blogging site. This not only combines your readers, but also reduces your frequency demands. Or, write a blog for a big neo-magazine or an aggregator site like the Huffington Post and use it as a lure to readers to come to your site (it also means more work).

7. *Sales*—Once you get up to a traffic level of several hundred readers per week you should begin looking into revenue sources: banner and other ads, Amazon reseller, and eventually retailing blog-oriented items. Again, it is almost impossible to make a living as a blogger, but you may be able to offset your time and effort with a few hundred dollars per month. That may be enough to keep you going.

8. *Customer service*—Solicit comments from your readers, and then try to reply to everyone. The more you can develop a relationship with your readers the more loyal they will become. A lively comments section can be even more valuable than the blog itself.

9. *Strategy*—Writing for love usually isn't enough over the long term: eventually, you just fall out of love. But if there are other, compelling, incentives then you can keep on pursuing them. So, determine what you want to be the end result of your blogging: better writing skills, a book deal, speaking gigs, a job as a full-time journalist, to be recognized as an expert in your field of interest, to network with famous and influential people, to stay in contact with your friends and peers, or to leave a permanent record for your descendants. Decide which of those things matter deeply to you and write and market your blog toward them.

News Reporter

What is news reporting?

Reporting the news is the heart of journalism, which is why it has always constituted the front page of newspapers, is the primary work of wire services and is the cornerstone of journalism education. News reporters make up the plurality of nearly all newsrooms. All other types of reporting are second in priority to the news.

What is news?

It is in the word itself. "News" is made up of events of importance to the reader that have either just occurred or are still unfolding. Reporting on these events typically requires the reporter to be on the scene (if possible), gathering facts and quotes and preparing a story under a tight deadline. In television and radio this reporting often is done live, with the reporter standing before a camera or microphone and improvising the story from rough notes.

Types of news reporting

In terms of format, all news reporting is basically the same—as we shall see. Where news reporting is differentiated is by *beat*; that is, by the particular area of daily life where news stories are most likely to be generated. Here is a list of some of the most common beats for news reporters:

General Assignment—This is often the first job of the neophyte reporter. As the name suggests, general assignment reporters arrive on the job each day and are told by the assignment editor what story they are to cover. The stories can come from any one of the various beats, even from one of the other departments of the publication or station. For newcomers, general-assignment reporting is sort of a test by fire: every day is something new and often unpredictable. One day you can be interviewing a famous figure visiting your town, the next covering the horror of a plane crash.

For veteran reporters, general assignment offers both novelty and a kind of completeness. The author used to work in a newspaper newsroom across from two women, both veteran reporters who had chosen to stay in general assignment work. Because I was a business reporter, my desk was perpetually buried in press releases and briefing documents related to ongoing stories. By comparison, when the two ladies finished their work day and filed their stories, they would just sweep all the paperwork off their desks into a nearby waste basket and go home without a worry. I often envied them.

Metro—This is the traditional newspaper term for *metropolitan* (that is, city, suburbs and immediate outlying districts where the majority of the newspaper, television or radio's readership/viewership are found). Typically, all the news stories from this area are gathered together in a separate, usually second, section in a newspaper, and presented immediately after national and international news in all three media (as well as on the Web). That said, the biggest metro area stories, if sufficiently important, can move to the front page of the paper and the lede in radio and TV newscasts. In terms of raw numbers, the number of metro reporters likely exceeds any other type of news reporter. Typical metro reporting beats include:

- *City hall*—This coverage focuses on news coming out of city government, notably the office of the mayor or city manager, plus all administrative offices. Many reporters on this beat, particularly in big cities, have offices in city hall and rarely go to their own newsrooms.
- *City council*—This reporting work, especially in smaller cities and towns, is often done by the city hall reporter. But because city councils typically meet at night, meeting coverage is more often handled by a separate reporter, often a general-assignment person on the night beat.
- *Crime*—This reporter, who often has an affinity for the police (sometimes too much), either sits in an office at police headquarters or by a radio in the newsroom, and upon hearing a report of a breaking crime or fire rushes out to cover it. This is some of the most exciting reporting work— the stories are often composed in real time over the phone to a copy editor—and as such is not for the elderly or faint of heart.
- *Local politics*—Depending on the range of a paper or station, local news may cover more than one city government as well as a county board of

supervisors or some other form of governance. Because they may have major importance to their lives, readers expect coverage of these entities.

State coverage—Coverage of news around the state is often bundled into a separate section in the paper or a distinct segment on a news broadcast. Usually this coverage takes two forms:

- *State politics*—Unless the paper or station is located in the state capitol, it typically either has a bureau there covering state government or contracts regular coverage from a freelancer or a reporter at a news operation there. Most of this reporting involves votes by the legislature or press conferences held by the governor's office.
- *Statewide news*—Usually this is a round-up of stories from around the state as reported by other publications. A general-assignment reporter is often asked to search through a pile of these stories, convert them into short summaries, and compile them. This is the grunt work of general reporting and often given to rookies or even to interns.

National and international coverage—Only the very largest newspapers and radio/TV stations are capable of maintaining news bureaus and paying correspondents to cover news at the national and international levels, and even they are cutting back on those operations. Thus, almost all national and international coverage is purchased from other sources, especially wire services and newspaper story syndicators. If you are interested in pursuing this type of work, applying for a job at one of these services, such as Reuters or the Associated Press, can be a very interesting way to start your career. In the author's experience, however. a sizable portion of wire-service reporters eventually grow tired of the pace and comparatively low pay and move on (with impressive portfolios) to other venues.

Other beats—There are many more venues for news reporting than just general interest, traditional news. All the other sections of the newspaper, web news sites or departments of TV and radio stations have, to some degree, an element of breaking news. The skills required for this reporting are identical to those of the front sections/segments. The difference is that the reporters involved may be required to mix these breaking news stories with the writing of extended, longer-term features. Here are some examples:

- *Traffic*—Radio and TV stations are the venues of choice for traffic coverage because of their timeliness. The standard daily coverage of commute times and accidents is one form of news reporting and is usually created from multiple reports. But there are occasions—notably major accidents—when a reporter will need to race to the scene to give live coverage.

- *Weather*—The coverage of weather is pretty standardized, with a reporter taking news feeds from the national weather service and turning it into a narrative. But, when severe weather hits—hurricanes, tornados, blizzards, heavy rains accompanied by flooding or landslides, and so forth—reporters will usually be sent to the field to provide extended on-scene reporting.

- *Education*—The education beat is normally pretty staid, with comparatively long lead times on features about local programs, graduations, teacher awards, and so forth. However, this beat can sometimes become exciting when stories break about protests, scandals and other features of modern educational life. Most of these breaking stories are covered by general-assignment reporters—but education writers are often asked to help because of their unique knowledge and access.

- *Sports*—The coverage in the sports section or segment is bimodal almost every day. Part of the staff of a sports department spends much of its time writing analysis of teams, conducting interviews of sports stars, making predictions of outcomes, and so forth. But the other half attends games, providing (especially on the Web) real-time coverage and box scores. Of all the forms of news coverage, sports reporting has some of the tightest deadlines.

- *Business*—Financial reporting resembles sports reporting, in that one part of the job involves feature writing with its longer lead times, extended length and analysis, while the other part—sales and earnings announcements, new-product introductions, lay-offs and so forth—are pure news reporting, with the stories written under the pressure of deadlines.

- *Arts and entertainment*—Most coverage of Hollywood, the fine arts and television consists of feature stories, notably profiles of celebrities, reviews of various productions and gossip items. Still, a lot of breaking news—awards, announcement of new productions and their stars, weekly box office results and many other topics—emerges from this world, and a lot of readers care deeply about that information. Most publications, stations and websites dedicated to arts and entertainment combine wire stories (which they rewrite for their readership) with in-house reporting. Typically, they send their reporters to Hollywood several times each year on meet-and-greet junkets to interview studio heads and stars, or to New York or Paris fashion weeks to cover the latest styles.

- *Technology*—The pace of technological innovation guarantees a constant supply of new-product innovations and upgrades. Meanwhile, the basics of digital electronics—such as silicon gate technology—are so complex as to be of only limited interest to the general reader. Thus, technology reporting tends towards news coverage. The chief requirements of a good tech news reporter are, first, to stay on top of the state-of-the-art in the key technology markets (especially consumer) and, second, be able to translate arcane tech topics into everyday language. Technology reporters are in great demand during tech booms and bubbles, but they may find themselves unneeded and unwanted during busts.

- *Science and medicine*—These two types of reporting are closely related and are heavily influenced by public relations, especially in the case of television news. Indeed, much of the "news" you learn about regarding the latest breakthroughs in medicine or discoveries in science are the creation of PR agencies that (unlike most television stations) have the money to create all the graphics and wide-ranging field reporting to tell the story. These video news releases are put up on the satellite, where they can be downloaded without fee by any news program that wants them. Some of these stations will use their own science and medicine reporters to edit the VNR with local footage and interviews; others will run the program verbatim, or at most record their own voice-overs for release.

Secrets of news reporting

Prioritize your writing—You should be thinking about the lede even as you gather information on a story, modifying the lede as you go. Research has found that most newspaper and web news readers, television news watchers and radio news listeners almost universally pay attention to the headline and the lede paragraph. But by the time they get a few seconds beyond that into the story—or to the "jump" of the story to another page deeper in the newspaper—half have dropped off and continue dropping off after every additional paragraph or second of coverage, until less than 10 percent of readers, watchers and listeners who began remain at the end.

Your priorities in writing your story should be the same: put your main attention on the start of the piece, and less as you go along. There is more than a little truth in those movie scenes where the reporter telephones in the story by carefully enunciating the lede and making sure the initial quote is precisely recorded and then ends by saying to the editor, "Et cetera, et cetera [...] just fill in the rest." Obviously, you can't quite do that in real life, but the idea is the same.

Let the 5 W's be your guide—Who? What? When? Where? and Why? may be a cliché, but no one has come up with a better guide for the questions that need to be answered in a typical news story. Moreover, the goal should be not only to answer these questions, but to move those answers as close to the top of the story as you possibly can. The sixth news question, How?, can be left until later in the piece because it usually requires a longer answer.

Veteran reporters often make it a personal challenge to see how many five W's they can answer in the first two paragraphs of a story and still do it with clarity and style. That's not a bad habit to get into, and one you can roll around in your mind as you cover an event and prepare to write and file.

Answering the How? is more difficult. Here, the challenge is to take what may be a long and complicated series of events and present them in a short, coherent manner that nevertheless gives the reader or viewer a comparatively complete understanding. If this is not possible, and the explanation will be too long and complex, you should discuss with your editor whether to write a second explanatory article or sidebar (or get someone else to do it) either that day or in the days ahead if the story still has strength.

Get the money quote, and get it right—The classic news story begins with a strong lede or one or two paragraphs, followed immediately by a quote. As noted at the beginning of this text, we are all hard-wired to attend to the human voice. We crave it. And it personifies the subject of the story by giving us someone with whom to identify. That's why veteran news reporters, whether on the telephone or at the scene of a news event, make an extra effort to find a person to interview who is an eyewitness—or better yet a participant. Watching these reporters in action you'll notice that, while they may ask a lot of questions, they will focus on no more than one or two, and for those answers they almost always ask the subject to repeat them, writing them down or recording them very carefully, and usually repeating those answers to the interviewee to confirm they got them just right. Those are the "money quotes," the ones you will see at the start of a story.

Spell their names right—The great nineteenth-century showman P. T. Barnum reportedly said, "I don't care what you say about me, so long as you spell my name right." Ever been part of a newspaper story, or been interviewed for television or radio? What was the first thing you looked for? No doubt it was your name first, and your title second. Now, imagine if the reporter on that story got either one of those things wrong. How would you feel? And at that point how much would you care about the rest of the story? Well, *every* person you write about as a reporter in the course of your career feels exactly the same way, and if you get their names or titles wrong they will be motivated to contact your editor and demand a very public correction. You don't need that career embarrassment.

Make your notes retrievable—Some of the most impressive reporters you will ever meet (though their numbers have all but disappeared) are those who take their notes on a story in traditional shorthand. You don't have to go that far. But if you do take your notes by hand, there are several things you should do.

First, get the right notebook. There is a reason why many reporters carry a long, thin spiral-bound notebook: it is small enough and flexible enough to stick in your pocket; you can flip over the cover to the back of the pad, and if you bend it slightly along its length it becomes a rigid surface you can hold in one hand while writing with the other. Conversely, you can get yourself a full-sized binder that holds pads of paper. They are bulkier, but they do provide a large, rigid platform. But only get one with a cover that can be folded behind or it will be ungainly.

Carry several pens with you at all times; if you only carry one it will inevitably run dry halfway through the interview.

Most important, write neatly and as fast as you can. There is a tendency, when interviewing someone, to scratch down notes as fast as the person is speaking for fear of missing something. The author can't tell you how many times I've gone back to a newsroom and spent hours trying to decipher my illegible chicken scratching. Overcome that tendency: slow down the interview, and whenever the subject says something important that you know you are going to use, have that person repeat what they said, slowly, until you know you've got it right. As for name and title: don't write them, block-print them. And if you have any doubts, turn the notebook around and show the spelling to the subject.

If, on the other hand, you choose to digitally record your interviews, be careful. If you screw up the recording, you have no back-up. And beware of ambient noise, even if you have a directional microphone, stick that recorder or smartphone right up into the subject's face. And as soon as possible, download that file somewhere safe for security.

Keep your eye on the clock—More than most other types of journalism, news reporting operates on very tight deadlines. Some days you'll have hours to polish your story, but on other days you'll have no more than minutes to pound out a quick report. If the latter is the case, get your lede down fast, as well as the first quote. Just use standard form, don't try to be creative—you don't have time. Then just get the rest of the facts down, add a second quote, preferably from another source, and finish out the piece as quickly as you can. Don't worry about rereading and editing the piece—there's no time for that either—just send it to the editor assigned to the story and let him or her do a quick edit and send the story off to composing and the back shop. Delay this process, and you may delay the entire paper—layout, printing, even delivery. Or, if you are doing a television or radio news story you may throw off the entire broadcast.

When I was first starting out as a newspaperman I found myself in the unusual position, as a business reporter, of writing a front-page news story. I wrote as fast as I could, but I wasn't used to that torrid pace, and so I found myself in the humiliating position of typing away while my editor, from the far side of the newsroom shouted "Malone! You've got ten seconds. Nine. Eight. Seven [...]" as the entire editorial staff turned in their chairs and stared. I managed to hit the "send" button with two seconds left.

Then, to my horror, I realized I'd put an inaccurate piece of data on the last line of the story. So, without telling anyone, I made the correction, adding a half-dozen words—that is, another line to the story. What I didn't know was the editor had already copyedited my story, and the line I had just appended now made the piece too long for the front page.

Ten minutes later, the managing editor pulled me out of my chair by the collar and, calling me various obscenities, dragged me down the hallway to the composing room and, waving an Exacto knife in front of my face, demanded to know where to make the cut. Then, visibly shaking with anger, he told me to get back to work and, to paraphrase, "Never do anything that stupid again."

News reporting means always working with very little margin for error.

Keep a tickler file—One of the biggest challenges to completing a news story on time is getting quotes from "experts"—individuals with particular knowledge or a set of skills that enables them to speak with authority about the topic of a story. These can be academics, industry analysts, government officials, legends in their field, and so forth.

The problem is that you may know who these people are, but reaching them is another matter. And if you do manage to get through their filters and get them on the phone or by text, there is still no guarantee that they will be able to provide an intelligent comment on the subject.

For that reason, most news reporters keep a "tickler" file. This is a list of individuals who have proven to be good sources of quotes in the past, and who will either answer your calls immediately or get back to you well before your deadline. When you create a tickler file, the standard procedure is to include not only their contact information, but also their area of expertise. Often, PR people will solicit you to include the name of their client on your list. Whether you do so is your choice, but even if you do, those individuals are usually given one chance to deliver.

Over time you will interview these folks so many times that you will not only not have to look up their expertise, but you will have memorized some of their contact numbers. The trick, however, is not to get into a rut because using the same sources again and again can become obvious to readers. And you don't want to become too dependent upon the opinions of just a few people; rather, you should mix it up: when you aren't on a tight deadline you should search for new sources. If you find yourself going back to the same person on several stories in a row, try somebody else on your list.

Finally, you will find that some sources who have been dependable in the past suddenly begin to take their role for granted and become increasingly inaccessible. You don't have time for games: take them off the list and find new sources.

Get to know people in authority—If you are covering downtown politics, get to know people in the mayor's office, including the mayor. If you are covering the crime beat, get to know the police chief. And so forth. These individuals are uniquely positioned to help you obtain access, give you credentials (such as a press pass), and sometimes even give you a heads-up on a breaking story.

Don't assume that these people in authority are only the ones at the top. That desk sergeant in the sheriff's office can be particularly useful in getting you an interview with an arresting officer; the elderly clerk in the county records office can help you find that one escrow document you need, and her counterpart in the courthouse can let you see that legal brief.

Ask a veteran—The one person who can help you the most when you start a new beat is the reporter who had the job before you. He or she may have retired, or been promoted, or switched to a different beat. In almost every case they will not only be willing, but even anxious, to share their acquired wisdom, their connections and their bag of tricks with you. They may be initially gruff and crusty—that's the nature of old news reporters—but once you get past that (often after a few drinks) you'll likely find them warm and willing to help. Cultivate that help. Ask for permission to call them whenever you get stuck, and promise yourself that you'll one day do the same thing for your replacement.

Career: The good

It's exciting work—Being a news reporter will likely be among the most exciting and engrossing work of your professional career. When something newsworthy happens, you are there in the thick of it. You will end up with a body of experiences and stories that will keep you, your family and acquaintances entertained for the rest of your life.

At the center of history—It is a cliché that news reporters write "the first draft of history," but it is nonetheless true. Future generations will use your reporting as original documents as they interpret and reinterpret the story of your times. At the highest levels of national and international reporting, your words or broadcasts will survive almost forever—in some cases even more than celebrated book authors and historians.

You define the message—As a news journalist you have a particular responsibility to get the story right, because it will be how the general public begins to interpret events. Your lede will become, at least at first, the received view of what actually happens; and the words of the people you choose to quote will be the first analysis of an event—as well as the eyewitness reports that will be used by future authors and academics.

Access to the famous and powerful—Particularly if you are covering news for a specialty beat—for example, business or sports—you will enjoy unequalled access to the key figures in that beat. Thus, as a business reporter, you will talk directly (typically at a press conference or other public event) with the most powerful CEOs in the world. As a sports reporter, you will do the same with famous athletes, typically in the locker room after a game. Those experiences will be priceless in years to come.

Start anew every day—Remember those two lady reporters who sat across from the author? While I had to come into the newsroom each workday morning facing the legacy of unfinished stories, they got to sit down to an empty desktop, get their assignments and know that at day's end—clear the decks and go home.

Never know what will happen next—Because every day is brand new for a news reporter, every day is also fresh. You may occasionally know of a scheduled event you need to cover that day, but you never know how it will turn out or whether you may get pulled from that story and sent off in pursuit of some other breaking story.

Help people—People read the news not just for its entertainment value, but also to make their lives better. Your breaking television story about a new medical discovery may save the lives of some of your viewers. That story about an automobile recall may do the same for your readers. And that radio story about a family left homeless by a house fire may convince listeners to step in and help. We tend to diminish the importance of our daily work, but for news reporters that impact is very real and very visible.

Career: The bad

It's short-lived—As the saying goes, "today's news is tomorrow's fish wrap." By definition, news has a very short life before it is replaced in the public's mind by the next breaking story. Feature stories are often read and set aside for future reference, giving that kind of work a durability and extended impact. That's rare for news stories The best reporting you've ever done will likely be forgotten in a matter of days—while that recipe in the back pages of your same publication will be cut out and used for generations.

High-stress career—Being a news reporter is a lot like being a cop or firefighter: all are work lives punctuated by extreme and unpredictable spikes of high excitement. That kind of life is hard on the body—and so, not surprisingly, news reporters seem to have a higher risk for many of the health-related problems associated with extremely demanding careers, including smoking, alcoholism and heart disease. These problems can start early, so if you pursue a career as a news reporter you should take care to live a healthy lifestyle.

Negative career trajectory—Because it is less writing than access and is energy driven, you get better as a news reporter over time, but not that much better—not like you do as, say, a columnist or critic. What you do get is more expensive as raises and seniority increase your salary; and, thus, your overhead to your employer. What this means is that at a certain point, usually a couple of decades into your news reporting career, it becomes more cost-effective to replace you with a younger reporter who will chase stories with a whole lot more energy for a whole lot less money. At that point you will need to either move up into management, which is unlikely given your professional skills, or face the prospect of slowly being shunted off an exciting beat and onto one—such as school board coverage, obituaries or night police radio monitoring—that is not only less appealing, but is ultimately designed to convince you quit or retire. The ugly fact is that, unlike feature writers, news reporting careers often don't have particularly happy endings. Know that is coming and plan for it.

Few secondary careers—News reporting skills are also not particularly transferrable to other jobs. A business reporter can go into corporate public relations. A technology reporter can freelance to electronics magazines. A sportswriter can work for a professional sports team. But a news reporter's options are limited. The good news is that those options are better than they used to be—ranging from reporting for an in-house corporate newspaper to blogging.

Turning points

There are two turning points in being a news reporter, and they take place at opposite ends of your career. The first is when you are promoted from being a general-assignment news reporter (or even an intern) to getting your first real beat. That is when you can finally settle in, get to know the players, and start developing your expertise. For now, and for years to come, you are the journalist synonymous with that beat and you will enjoy considerable job security and power.

The second turning point takes place years later when you are taken off that beat—the stated reason is usually that the publication or station wants to bring in some "new blood," but you know the real reason is that you are no longer cost-effective—and offered a lesser job. This is the moment when you need to decide if you want to look for a new career or to stick around, even if it means ever more demeaning jobs, in order to get your pension.

Investigative reporting

Investigative reporting is the most celebrated form of news reporting. Much of that reputation is deserved.

On the one hand, investigative reporting is still news reporting and follows most of the rules and advice listed above. But on the other hand, it is very different and for the following reasons:

The team—Most news stories are reported and written by a single reporter, perhaps with contributions by one or two others. Most investigative stories, and particularly series, are reported and written by teams of reporters and editors, often chosen for their distinct skills.

The stakes—Investigative stories often deal with high crimes and
   corruption. They also uncover these crimes, rather than simply report
   upon them.

The scope—These stories are often multiple-part series published over
   several days, with main stories, sidebars, charts and graphs.

The time—Regular news stories are typically one day productions.
   Investigative stories can take weeks, even months, to report.

The risk—An error in a news story can require a public correction. An error
   in an investigative story or series can lead to devastating lawsuits. That's
   why almost every important investigative story is picked over by libel
   attorneys.

The impact—An investigative story is often designed to lead to changes
   in laws and regulations. It also can lead to imprisonment of targeted
   subjects.

The honors—While a typical news story is forgotten the next day,
   investigative stories and series not only can lead to permanent change
   in a community or nation, but the reporters themselves have a strong
   chance of earning their profession's highest awards.

Secrets of investigative reporting

In many ways, investigative reporting is the highest calling of the
news journalist. Because the stakes and risks are so high, only the best
reporters are given the opportunity to do this kind of work (though less
experienced reporters sometimes do get the chance, if they have unique
knowledge or first uncovered the story). It is hugely exciting work, but
also hugely challenging. And the responsibilities can be enormous: as
the result of your work, people may go to prison, laws rewritten and
lives saved. The reporters themselves may even find their own lives
at risk.

Needless to say, this is not work that can be taken lightly, and it can
have a heavy emotional toll. Few news reporters ever become, or remain,
full-time investigative reporters. But while you have the opportunity, there
is no greater use for your professional skills.

Here are some tips to help you be a successful, effective and safe
investigative reporter. The list is necessarily incomplete, but it does reflect
the wisdom gained by the author from his own successes and failures.

Establish the scope of the project—Before you get underway, determine
exactly what this investigation will cover and, just as important, what
it will not. Investigative stories have a tendency to go off on tangents
following paths of least resistance. Because of that, they also tend to be

open-ended: you just keep reporting until someone tells you to stop. You can save yourself a lot of trouble—and stay in the good graces of your editors—by establishing goals and deadlines from the start. And, painful as it may be, it usually pays to have a tough-minded editor with the power to keep you on track.

Double your back-up—In the news reporting section above, we discuss the need to have a reliable means of capturing your interviews, and the value of having a back-up system. In investigative reporting you need to doubly insure that you've got this information, because you may never get a second chance. Once, while working on a story about drugs in Silicon Valley companies, my partner and I interviewed a young woman in a halfway house, where she had been sent for rehabilitation. She had a wealth of knowledge on the subject—so much so that several times during the interview I checked the tape recorder to make sure the VU meter needle was bouncing to confirm that the microphone was working.

It wasn't until we were back in the newsroom, congratulating each other over capturing such a great interview that we discovered to our horror that the recorder's pause button had been on the whole time. Luckily, the woman was willing to repeat the interview.

The lesson for you is to never trust your tools That doesn't mean you should handwrite your interview notes—on the contrary, using pen and paper makes it difficult to get accurate quotes and can intimidate the subject. But, if you are using a digital recorder or smartphone, use two, even three, and make sure that each is fully charged and you have a good directional microphone.

Don't be bound by arbitrary rules—On another investigative story, this time looking into toxic chemicals used by the tech industry, the author and another partner found themselves inside a large corporation requesting access to official health and safety records on that company. We were told we could look at the documents, but only for a few moments, and could not take notes. We asked if at least could have a private office to look at the papers. The company agreed. So, we picked a room that just happened to have a copier. While I stood watch at the door, my partner copied the documents as quickly as possible.

That information was crucial to setting off a transformation in how Silicon Valley handled its dangerous chemicals that continues to this day. The lesson? Get the story. You have a higher calling.

Trace your sources—On still another investigation, this one into sweatshops, my partner and I started out struggling. Though we had heard rumors, we just couldn't find any proof that these illegal operations actually existed in our community. We asked every contact we had—nothing, at least not initially.

Then, amazingly, after a couple weeks of frustration, we suddenly began to hear from the latest round of sources that they had heard, quite recently in fact, reports of sweatshops throughout Silicon Valley. Excited, we redoubled our efforts and, incredibly, we started hearing more and more of these reports. Finally, we were on to something.

But something was wrong. Unlike most such investigations, these rumors remained just that—nothing ever was substantiated, no evidence emerged. It was then that the truth hit us: the rumors we were hearing were just our questions going full circle through several intermediaries and coming back to meet us from a different direction. The lesson? Don't just get information from your sources, find out where *they* got it.

Work with law enforcement—As it happens, we did find those sweatshops, and my partner and I decided to see if we could conduct a sting: meet a shop operator and negotiate some illegal work. We used the home of a friend of mine to hold our sting. As we waited for the man to show up, we considered locking him in the house with us and threatening to call the police if he didn't give us information.

Lucky for us, the operator was happy to talk. Because if we had trapped him the house we would have been in more trouble than him—for kidnapping. We would have known that if we had talked to the police first.

On another occasion, when the author was running a magazine, I gave one of my editors the assignment of looking into online child pornography. Shrewdly, he suggested we talk with the FBI before we started and let them know our plans. The resulting story, which won several major awards and led to numerous arrests, proved emotionally devastating to that editor. He was truly heroic in his efforts, but all would have ended badly, even prison, if we hadn't cleared it with the authorities in advance.

And on a third occasion, when the author was investigating a criminal—terrorist group conducting robberies at local corporations, authorities warned me that I should hide my notes at all times and take a different route each day to and from work. I followed their advice. Did it save my life? I'll never know. But the lesson I learned from these experiences is that, if there is any doubt, keep law enforcement constantly updated on what you are doing. Investigative reporting often puts you above the rules, but never above the law.

Back up with legal paper—Among the best skills you can have as an investigative reporter is facility with court records, deeds and other legal documents—and good relationships with those bureaucrats who can help you find them. As we'll see with the next tip, anything in your story that isn't backed by some sort of official support is vulnerable to being edited out of your story. It is a heck of lot easier to start with that legal paper than it is to try to find that kind of support after writing your story.

This may sound like needless work. But that same partner who worked with me on the sweatshop story is the same reporter mentioned earlier who won a Pulitzer Prize by finding the trove of real estate filings in an obscure courthouse on the other side of the country. As it turned out, those papers documented the hidden wealth of a foreign dictator, and my partner got to watch on the news as a half-million people marched in a distant capital, many of them waving his story. The dictator stepped down a few days later. It was the once-in-a-lifetime story every investigative reporter dreams about. And it was because he found the incriminating legal paper.

Expect to be edited to death—Every publication or station that regularly pursues investigative stories keeps on retainer a libel lawyer or two. These professionals are paid first to protect the publication from being sued; and only second, to help get the story into print or on the air. What that means is that they will be ruthless with your copy. Being an investigative reporter can be exciting and romantic, but it also means sitting in a small room with your editor and the attorney going over every sentence in the story. Every claim and every fact in the article will be challenged, and if you can't back it up with legal documents or published statements, you will get to watch the attorney make a big red X and cut it out. And there goes a week of hard work.

There is no easy way through this experience. Just expect to have a sizable portion of your work cut—and to have no recourse. Just look on the bright side: at least you won't get sued. Well, probably not.

Know the law—You don't need to be an attorney to be an investigative reporter, but it sure doesn't hurt to know something about the possible crimes being committed by your story subject(s) and about libel law. One answer for the first is to talk with a criminal attorney or the local district attorney. For the latter, you can choose to depend upon your employer's attorney—the one who will edit your copy—but it sure helps to know enough to keep from committing libel in the first place and not raising any more doubts in your employer about your reporting skills.

Tap your sources—Investigative story subjects will sometimes drop in your lap. The author knew a reporter who would occasionally find secret documents in his mailbox at the newspaper office. He never knew how they got there, or even how the source got into the building. But most investigative stories are uncovered by the reporter's work. And since, by definition, someone has hidden them, your best chance of finding them is to regularly poll your sources—especially those who inhabit the gray market and other borderline criminal activities—to see what they've heard. Of course, never fully trust those sources—check everything—but they can often be a good place to start.

Recharge your batteries—As will be discussed further below, there are some severe occupational hazards to being an investigative reporter. If you don't give yourself a break after each story, your career will be short. So, after the story or series is published, give yourself some time off. Go somewhere where the skies are sunny and the food good and people don't commit crimes (that you know of or care about) and heal your soul. Only get back into the game when you are ready. And if your superiors don't understand that, it's time to update your resume.

Remember the victims—Finally, keep in mind that even if the cause of your investigation is righteous, and that your target is indeed guilty, that there are figures on the periphery who may be caught in the blast as well. That bad person may have a wife or, worse, children who are entirely innocent, and when your story appears, they too will have to encounter their relatives and friends, neighbors and schoolmates.

That doesn't mean you shouldn't pursue your investigation with everything you've got, or that the subject is any less guilty. But the knowledge of those others, the innocent bystanders, should at least temper any exultation you may feel in successfully completing your story. When you are out at that celebratory luncheon or preparing to receive an award for your work, at least give them a moment's thought. It will make you a better person.

Career: The good

As a journalist and writer, this will likely be the most important thing you do in your life. You will help find justice for the afflicted, bring down the bad guys and perhaps even change life for the better for millions of people—and your reporting and writing talents will be tested like never before. Every day you will know that what you are doing matters. What more can you ask for?

Career: The bad

Investigative reporting can take a heavy physical and psychic toll. And sometimes, even a vacation can't entirely heal the wounds. You should look for the following symptoms in yourself, and if you find one or more of them, either get help or go back to the life of a regular reporter:

The avenging angel—Not every bad person you pursue will you successfully take down. That corrupt official or businessperson may have the money to put up a wall of lawyers that you can never breach. Or, your libel attorney may say you just don't have enough legal proof to make your case. Whatever the reason, sometimes there are people you just know are guilty but can't touch.

When that happens—or even when you've had a long and successful career as an investigative reporter—you can find yourself operating beyond the law, serving as judge and jury to your erstwhile opponent. The author knew one great reporter who, when he failed to take down a figure he was convinced was a criminal, took to calling him late at night to whisper that he would get the man someday.

But, you are not the legal system; you are a reporter. And never forget it.

Risk aversion—Most investigative reporters start out full of energy, ambition and bravado. But, over time, a few failed investigations, some errors and even physically threatening situations can make them less willing to put themselves on the line and to take on riskier stories. They slowly drift, sometimes unconsciously, toward stories that are safer, that don't have as much at stake, that don't produce real change.

If you find this is happening to you, celebrate the end of a great career and step aside for a younger replacement who still has the fire in his or her belly.

Cop's disease—In the midst of one of the darker story investigations of my career, I found myself growing increasingly cynical about mankind. I remember driving home one evening and looking at the drivers in the cars around me on the freeway and thinking, "All of them! Every one of them is guilty. I'll get them all."

Happily, my father, who had been an intelligence agent and a criminal investigator, noticed the change in my personality. He sat me down and gave me some advice. Yes, he told me, everyone has something to hide; everyone has a skeleton in his or her past—even you. But the glory of humanity, he said, is that nearly everyone rises above those mistakes, puts them in their past, and tries their best to live good and decent lives, and you should honor them for it. Don't be like those policemen who increasingly come to loathe human beings for their weaknesses. Instead, celebrate people for their strengths.

It may have been the best advice anyone ever gave me. Thanks, Dad.

EXAMPLE: Written for *Fortune Magazine*'s website. It's an analysis of a news item that had broken a few days before.

Intel's New Bug

We've heard this story before. But for all the similarities in tone regarding the latest Intel scandal and the notorious Intel bug of a generation ago, almost all of the details of the story, large and small, are very different. And though the new bug is vastly more dangerous, the public's reaction has been comparatively muted.

In particular, the world has radically changed. In 1994, Intel was on top of the semiconductor world. It held a virtual monopoly in the supreme chip type, the microprocessor. And it was in the midst of the most successful marketing campaign in tech history—*Intel Inside*—which taught consumers to think past the PC box to the chips within. And with the Internet ramping up, it seemed like nothing could stop Intel.

Then, in June of that year, an obscure college professor from Lynchburg, Virginia used his computer to perform an arithmetic calculation—and got the wrong answer. Within weeks, the world had learned about this Pentium chip 'bug' . . . and panicked. The Internet had recently set off a personal computer boom—and now millions of new users now thought those machines might be *lying* to them.

Panic ensued. By mid-November, lawsuits were being filed against Intel. The *Wall Street Journal* was covering the story almost daily. People feared planes falling out the sky, missiles firing spontaneously, the electrical grid shutting down. There was talk of a Congressional investigation. IBM publicly announced it was suspending shipment of its Pentium-based computers. The Pentium Bug was now a full-on panic. It was even the subject of popular jokes and late-night monologues.

Intel had been blind-sided. Bugs had always been part of the semiconductor industry. But until now it had mostly sold its chips to engineers and scientists—who knew the game, and installed fixes. But with *Intel Inside,* Intel had entered into a social contract with *consumers*, whose expectations were different. Rattled, Intel, especially its fiery CEO Andy Grove, responded with one publicity blunder after another, all-but suggesting they were idiots for being concerned about the problem.

Then, remarkably, after a weekend of soul-searching, Grove did the unimaginable: he reversed himself. On Monday, December 21st, 1994, Intel announced that it would replace the bugged chips. The Pentium Bug Crisis was over. Very few chips were actually returned by users.

Now Intel finds itself in another scandal—the 'Kernel Krisis' of Meltdown and Spectre is much more widespread and dangerous. Intel is no longer as dominant in semiconductors as it once was. And though this crisis is shared by its competitors, notably Advance Micro Devices and ARM. their problem is a software fix (hence their stock jump on the news). As the defining architecture, Intel's problem lies in hardware, and is much tougher.

Whereas the Pentium Bug was very much an anomaly, this time the problem is very real: it potentially opens a back door for hackers to access operations of the processor itself. And it is not just one Intel chip model, but dates back at least a decade. That's billions of computers and other devices, some of them embedded in *very* sensitive applications and in the Cloud.

Critic

What is criticism?

Criticism is the application of a deep understanding of a topic or field to the newest creations of that field. Criticism can also place past works of art or creation into a current context by challenging icons, rediscovering lost achievements or redirecting the viewer, reader or participant to new modes of understanding. Individuals who make their living in the field are typically known as *critics*; those who do it part-time are usually called *reviewers*.

Why criticism?

Because all fields of human endeavor, in order to advance, need critical judgment to recognize genius, determine quality and otherwise set standards. Criticism should be subordinate to the works themselves, yet should hold equal weight in terms of value to society.

Types of criticism—Criticism can be distinguished, not just by subject matter, but also by venue. Thus, some are created under tight deadlines while others can take years to prepare. By the same token, the majority of reviews deal with a single book, musical or dramatic performance, television show, movie, or recording. But there is also a genre of criticism that looks at the entire oeuvre of an artist, placing him or her in the larger context of an entire era or creative school.

Here is a partial list of types of criticism:

Newspaper reviews—These have the tightest deadlines of any form of criticism. And they run the gamut from books to opera, plays and musical, musical performances, television and movies, audio recordings, video games, and so forth. It is the nature of newspaper publishing—the need to make the next day's edition—that creates the time pressure. Writing newspaper reviews typically involves attending an afternoon or evening performance then returning to the newsroom (or remotely filing via email) to write the story in the hours (or minutes) before the morning edition "goes to bed" (that is, sent for printing). At best—perhaps for a weekend book review section—reviewers may have a few days to prepare their copy. Though there has been some great newspaper reviewing over the last two centuries, it is definitely work in which erudition and strong opinions take precedent over elegant writing. Newspapers that serve large metropolitan readerships typically have full-time staffers as reviewers (though with the decline of newspapers, that is changing), while smaller-circulation papers usually hire freelancers.

Internet reviews—Web criticism written for Web sites (usually for blogs, web magazines, and the on-line operation of print publications) are, in terms of process, largely indistinguishable from newspaper reviewing. The fundamental difference is in deadlines: as there are no distinct editions on the Web, stories can be filed and posted at any time day or night. In practice, however, this doesn't add much time to the process, as most public artistic events—movie premieres, concerts, play and musical openings, and so forth—have a time value, and must reach a hungry readership as quickly as possible. In fact, Internet deadlines can sometimes be even *tighter* than newspapers, as there is no need to wait for the next edition and they can be filed immediately. Internet-based reviewers are almost always freelancers—or, even more often, work for free.

Magazine reviews—Magazines usually have monthly deadlines, especially with the death of the weekly news magazine (though there are still some important weekly magazines noted for their reviews, such as *The New Yorker*). This allows for much more time to write a review, but also places upon the reviewer the duty to produce more thoughtful copy, a piece that typically exhibits greater research and more in-depth contextualization. Magazines usually have reviewers on staff.

Social commentary/cultural criticism—One of the highest forms of criticism, this involves writing about current events and cultural trends in a way that analyzes them, judges their value and places them in a larger historical context. The best cultural critics play an important role in society, are typically masters of the essay form and are wonderful prose stylists. Interestingly, many of these writers actually use as a launch pad one of the other forms of criticism and then take it to a new level. Thus, Isaiah Berlin was a historian and philosopher, G. K. Chesterton a novelist and mystery writer, Walter Lippmann a political columnist and Emile Zola a novelist—and all became hugely influential cultural and social critics. Not surprisingly, this type of critic is older, has another career (such as an academic or as a fellow at a think tank), and publishes only rarely. Thus, their most common role is as a contributor to a quality publication.

Product reviews—Reviewing products that could be anything from new model automobiles to appliances to the latest consumer technology, is its own genre and most often found in consumer rating publications, trade magazines or their Web counterparts (for example, CNet for electronics). Top-flight reviewers can have an enormous impact on product sales, even on the stock price of the manufacturer. That's why the best of them, such as Walter Mossberg at the *Wall Street Journal*, have been among the world's best-paid journalists. Good product reviewers don't have to be great writers, but they have to be extremely knowledgeable about the subject, have a consistent methodology, and have a reputation for rock-solid integrity. Ultimately, they are only as influential as their reputations.

Literary essays—For the purposes of this chapter, "literary" means a form of criticism that might be seen as more complex, researched and sweeping in its subject matter. Because they are usually not written to a tight deadline, they are also likely to feature superior prose. Thus, where a standard book review for a newspaper or web site might look at a single newly published book, a comparable literary essay for, say, the *Atlantic Monthly* or the (London) *Times Review of Books*, might look at five new books that exhibit a growing trend such as "Women Attorneys in Danger," or look at the entire oeuvre of an author and how it has changed over the course of 20 books and 40 years. Similar essays might be written about movies ("Reassessing the Films of Stanley Kubrick"), other arts ("Balanchine at 100"), politics ("The Changing Face of Neoliberalism"), and culture ("The Star Wars Generation Hits Its Twilight Years"). This type of essay is typically a one-off creation, as opposed to a regular feature (though there are exceptions, usually reserved for the most veteran and esteemed critics)— and, because it demands a lot of editorial space, is found only in a limited number of publications, notably literary journals, many of them expressly created for this type of content. This type of writing sometimes can pay quite well, though even when written without financial compensation, still pay highly in terms of professional and cultural cachet.

Art monographs—These are publications, rather than articles, and represent an extended investigation into the work of a single artist or school. Monographs often begin as scholarly papers, especially doctoral dissertations. And though they have a limited readership, the audience is extremely influential, so much so that a single much-admired monograph can make an art critic's or art historian's career. In the past, these publications were often strictly prose, given the cost of high-quality color reproduction. Nowadays, cost is no longer a challenge; so monographs are typically as richly illustrated (though often less readable by the general public) as mainstream art books.

Satires—You may not think of satirical writing as criticism, but rather as comedy. Still, satire has a long and noble history as social criticism, dating back to the ancient Greeks, notably the playwright Aristophanes. And no one would accuse Jonathon Swift or Mark Twain or Voltaire as writing strictly for laughs. So incisive can the criticism of satire be that in many countries today it can get its authors killed or imprisoned. Good satire requires tremendous wit and superior writing skills—which is why only a small number of writers in each generation can make a living from it, usually beginning as columnists or feature writers, then turning it into book authorship. For every P. J. O'Rourke or Dave Barry, there are thousands of budding comic writers today who attempt satire, fail, and retreat into stand-up comedy or sitcom writing or other less-demanding forms of humor. That said, if you can do it, satire can change the world and make the its author wealthy and all but immortal.

Appraisals and critical biographies—This type of criticism is a genre of nonfiction writing, one in which the tools of criticism are applied, in an extended format, to the life and work of a notable (or soon-to-be notable, as a result of the book) figure. This type of writing typically serves as a reappraisal of, or introduction to, that historic figure for a new generation of readers. Another reason for this type of writing is to take advantage of the appearance of newly discovered (or newly available to the public) information on the subject, or to cast the subject in a new light based upon larger cultural changes. These types of books are mostly of limited potential sales, which is why they are typically published by university presses. That said, sometimes one of these books will break out and become a mass market bestseller. One place where such books are well represented are as recipients of literary prizes.

Critical analysis—This type of criticism is usually targeted at trends in the arts, in government and foreign policy, and in cultural movements. Think of it as an expanded version of literary essays and cultural criticism. This type of writing takes two forms: extended articles by experts for targeted publications (such as *Foreign Policy*, *Commentary* and *New Criterion*) and books usually published by a university press or a think tank. Books of this type are designed to influence policy or, like Alan Bloom's *Closing of the*

American Mind and *Samuel Huntington's Clash of Civilization*, to establish thought leadership by exposing the weaknesses or dangers in the status quo. Successful critics in this genre often find themselves nominated for government posts and distinguished professorships.

Critical subjects

The various types of criticism and reviewing represent but one axis of this world. The other axis involves the subjects of this type of work. Here is an abbreviated list of topics, and in what venues they typically appear. The emphasis here is on how professional writers can earn an income, if not often a living, writing on these different topics:

Movies—Movie criticism can range from single paragraph mini-reviews to extended blog entries and magazine essays. At its most influential, movie reviewing can materially impact a movie's revenues (Siskel and Ebert); and at its finest (James Agee, Pauline Kael) it can approach the best of literary art.

Books—Book reviewing can be done by amateurs. But they are usually written by veteran reviewers writing in every form, from short reviews in magazines and Sunday newspapers to ten-thousand-word essays in literary supplements. Many famous writers (including George Orwell and John Updike) have also been notable book reviewers. Other than in extended essays, almost all book reviews are about new books and appear within one month of the publication date.

Television—Because of the nature of the medium, television reviewing is mostly done under an extremely tight deadline, literally within hours of a show's broadcast. Networks try to mitigate this when possible by sending (nowadays via the Web, but sometimes still on DVD for security) advance copies to reviewers. A growing phenomenon on entertainment magazine sites is to run a simple summary of an episode and solicit—"crowd sourced"—viewers' comments. This often yields excellent results but isn't a positive trend for professional writers.

Radio—Reviewing radio programming is a comparatively small field, particularly so now that radio is dominated by music programming and talk shows. However, NPR in the United States and BBC radio in the UK are examples of radio networks with traditional feature content and thus are occasional subjects of newspaper stories and reviews. But this small amount of programming is insufficient to employ anyone as a full-time radio critic. Rather, this work is usually handled on occasion by other types of reviewers.

Popular Music—Pop, rock, hip-hop and other forms of contemporary popular music have always been the subject of a healthy market in reviews, survey features and even literary essays. The Web has only further proliferated this work. The good news is that popular music reviewing is a field that is easy to enter (just create your own web site or blog) and lends itself to young, neophyte, writers. That said, it is also true that music criticism rarely pays well—even major publications such as *Rolling Stone* and *Spin* pay only small sums for music reviews, of both recorded and live concerts. It is also a profession in which, after a few years, it becomes a struggle to stay current on the latest trends. That said, a few individuals—Dave Marsh, Robert Christgau and Greil Marcus—have managed to enjoy long careers by moving to writing books and taking employment at mainstream publications.

Classical Music—Classical music reviewing (both recorded and in concert) has a century-old history. Perhaps not surprisingly, some of the finest classical music critics have also been superior composers or performers—most famously Virgil Thompson in the middle of the twentieth century. As newspapers slowly fade away—and as the audience for classical music turns increasingly into a niche—that traditional venue for this type of writing has all-but disappeared. The advent of the Web has not changed this situation—at least for professional reviewers—because most of this new reviewing is performed by users on retail sites such as Amazon. That said, there are blogs and review sites that specialize in classical music, but most are authored by their creators, usually fans writing to other fans, and they produce almost no revenues. Nevertheless, there remain a few publications—from major newspapers and magazines to intellectual journals—that still carry extensive writing on classical music. Better yet, most of this writing is of the extended essay format.

Jazz—Jazz criticism has largely gone the route of jazz music itself: from a widespread and popular genre in the years after World War II to a very narrow niche today. A few jazz critics endured into the new century—notably Stanley Crouch and the late Nate Hentoff—writing extended essays for the likes of the *Village Voice*. But even that has largely disappeared. Yet, jazz criticism does survive on the Web, in specialized blogs for limited audiences. Income from this writing is virtually nil.

Art—Art criticism has a long, long history. Examples of this kind of writing can be found as early as the works of Plato and, surprisingly, the Roman

Christian theologian St. Augustine. Modern art criticism is generally considered to have begun in the early eighteenth century, almost simultaneously in France and England. By mid-century, it achieved its first peak in the writings of the legendary French encyclopedist Denis Diderot. By the nineteenth century art criticism was being produced by some of the world's leading writers, essayists and poets, including John Ruskin, William Hazlitt, Charles Baudelaire and Oscar Wilde. Writing about art ranges from gallery and museum shows to profiles of new and established artists. In the twentieth century, abstraction found support from the Bloomsbury Circle (in particular Roger Fry); while after World War II abstract expressionism was championed by Americans Clement Greenberg and Harold Rosenberg, both of whom were often more influential than the painters they wrote about. The most important art critic of the final years of the century was Australian Robert Hughes of *Time Magazine*. Art criticism today is as healthy as ever, with venues for reviews ranging from the Web to weekly alternative newspapers to daily newspapers. Longer art criticism can be found in a wide range of art magazines published throughout the world. Except for the staffers of art magazines, most art reviewers and critics are freelancers, often college art professors. The most lucrative art criticism markets are exhibition catalogs and art books (individual artists or schools)—work that is usually written by gallery or museum directors, though also by academics and freelancers.

Architecture—This is a very specialized field, and for good reason: there aren't that many new buildings being constructed at any given moment. Indeed, most architecture reviewing and criticism is done by art critics, who see it as part of their purview. It is also a job that requires considerable travel, as new architecture has not only become a global phenomenon, but many of the most interesting new architectural commissions are now taking place in the developing world. Books about architecture remain as popular as ever and can offer a good income to veteran criticswith an established name. The one individual to break this mold—and arguably the most influential architecture critic of all time—was Ada Louise Huxtable, whose column on architecture appeared first in the *New York Times* and then the *Wall Street Journal*.

Culture—Cultural criticism is often confused with political writing (across the political spectrum), which it can sometimes be, but in fact it covers everything from obituary writing to profiles of emblematic individuals to extrapolations from unusual news events to larger cultural shifts. Cultural criticism can also range in format from standard "thumbsuck" pieces to actual field reporting. Thus, the list of important cultural critics of the last century ranges from the Marxist book critic Edmund Wilson to gonzo journalist, Hunter Thompson, and novelist/social essayist Tom Wolfe to political observer Christopher Hitchens. Cultural criticism can also reach very high art, as in the Depression-era writings of novelist and movie critic James Agee and trenchant columnist Alfred Kazin, who often wrote about the immigrant experience, and Dwight MacDonald, critic of middlebrow culture. It is extremely difficult to become an influential cultural critic, but in the Internet Age it is quite easy to become one: you simply announce yourself as one, start a blog and get writing. The hard part is finding an audience that wants to follow you.

Products—Product reviewing is distinct from the other forms described above because its emphasis is not rhetorical but empirical. This type of work also has its own venues: product review publications and web sites such as *CNET, Popular Science/Electronics/Mechanics, Car & Driver, Motor Trend* and that most influential provider of consumer product reviews, *Consumer Reports*. Many major newspapers, such as the *Wall Street Journal*, also have in-house reviewers who produce weekly features. Getting into product reviewing often requires little more than a workmanlike prose style, but considerable expertise in the subject and the ability to conduct, and cogently organize the results from, systematic evaluation. This is particularly true when reviewing for dedicated product-review publications. At the highest levels, product reviewing does require superior writing skills—especially for automotive publications, which pride themselves on entertaining copy. Product testing and reviewing can be a well-paying full-time job with considerable job security, but often with a long apprenticeship.

Keys to good criticism

Deep knowledge—You need to know your subject well. Indeed, you need to know it better than your readers. If you don't—especially in the Internet era, with its emphasis on reader comments and interaction—you will hear it from every reader who knows more than you and who will be happy to point out every one of your mistakes. Deep knowledge will also provide your writing with content: if you can describe the performance of a product in-depth, compare it knowledgeably with competing products and even place it in a historic context (that is, precedents, past practitioners, earlier models), you will not only easily fill your allotted editorial space, but provide your readers with a valuable service. This kind of knowledge doesn't come easily; that's why many reviewers and critics are academics with advanced degrees, or individuals who have worked in the field for decades. If you don't have that education or experience, and especially if you are starting out in the field, *do your homework*. Don't guess and don't assume you know what you are talking about—it will quickly come back to bite you.

Strong opinions—Anyone can be ambivalent; we read reviews and criticism for strong opinions, incisive judgements and, when necessary, devastating takedowns. If you are of two minds about your review subject, *don't write the review*. You won't help either your readers or your own reputation. Ponder the topic a little longer, until you finally do come to a strong opinion one way or the other. Then write. Also, beware of the pathetic fallacy: if you feel unexcited or wishy-washy about the subject— say a dull play or a weak musical performance or a mediocre novel—don't let your review be equally dull or second rate. Find a way to write about your subject in a dynamic and interesting way.

Sense of duty to standards—Criticism is a craft with a noble history and an important role in society: that of identifying and celebrating works of superior quality, calling out weak, indifferent or corrupt works, and educating the audience both to appreciate good art and to understand its historic antecedents. To do this on a consistent basis demands that you never coast or produce anything less than your best work—the profession's phrase is "mail it in"—every time you write. You owe that to your subject and to your audience. A side benefit is that consistently working at your best will also make you into both a better critic and a better writer.

Intellectual courage—Being a reviewer or critic means making people angry. It's the nature of the business, and if you are afraid of causing offense then you shouldn't be in this profession. To be a good critic you must have the courage of your convictions. If a work of art is flawed, you must say so, even if it will anger powerful or famous people. By the same token, you cannot be afraid of being publicly embarrassed and humiliated: if you suspect that your judgment will go against popular opinion or taste, your attitude should be "damn the torpedoes" and you should publish, confident that you are in the right and that history will redeem you.

Strong, muscular prose—Just as critical writing should have a strong point of view, so too should it have a strong style. Wishy-washy prose undermines your argument—which is something a true critic should never allow to happen. You not only need the strength of your opinions, but also the strength of your logic if you are going to convince skeptical readers, not just entertain them. Live performance reviewing in particular requires strong, rich prose because you want the reader to actually feel as if he or she is actually there, sitting beside you, watching the performance with you. That's why reviewing should be much more than a mere accumulation of titles and plot points, but the description of an experience.

Consistency—Great reviewers and critics have a firmly established point of view, a yardstick of quality, that they develop early, hold to strongly, and apply consistently to all their subjects. A critic or reviewer who has a flexible value system that is applied inconsistently is not someone whose writing can be trusted, nor can it be used as a reference for readers. That's not to say that a critic or reviewer cannot evolve with time, experience and maturity—but that is a matter of decades, not weeks.

Self-discipline—Reviewing is a fast-moving profession, with tight deadlines and—especially with television and movies—a rapid pace, particularly during certain seasons. For that reason, successful reviewers have excellent time-management skills, can pound out copy quickly, and are dedicated to producing clear prose. When necessary, they can file a quick piece off their phone or laptop in the field without having to wait to get into a newsroom or home office. They are also obsessed with precision and accuracy: they get names and roles right every time, because editors often don't have that information at hand to check.

Healthy Lifestyle—This isn't discussed often enough. The best reviewers, and especially critics, are older as lengthy experience provides the best context and the most developed sense of quality. But you've got to get their first, and much of the lifestyle of reviewers—late nights, wolfing down fast food rushing to the theater, short deadlines, decompressing in a bar after filing your story—is hardly conducive to leading a long life. And there is no shortage of immensely talented critics who died too soon to achieve their full potential—Agee, Kenneth Tynan, Baudelaire, Oscar Wilde, Andre Bazin, Apollinaire, rock critic Lester Bangs. Dying young is only romantic to people who are young and healthy. If you want to live long enough to both create a sizable body of work and achieve the kind of quality criticism that comes from the wisdom of a long life, you should aspire to follow the example of the great French-American social critic, Jacques Barzun, who produced his masterwork, *From Dawn to Decadence*, at the age of 93. Few of us will reach that kind of milestone, but we can try—and that means staying healthy and living at a sane pace.

The ethics of criticism

1. Fully experience the work of art or product you are reviewing. Read the book carefully and take notes. See the movie, twice if you have time. Same with the television episode. Listen to the CD or MP3 files multiple times. Go back to the restaurant a second time and try something different. This will not only give you more time to ponder the experience,

but will assure that your initial opinion was not affected by your bad mood or an anomalous event (the chef, or the actors, had a bad night).

2. You owe it to the work you are reviewing or criticizing to take it seriously—even if you choose in the end to mercilessly mock it. Go into it with an open mind, or don't go in at all. You should always reread your copy for accuracy and grammar; but also for balance.

3. You are allowed to be opinionated—indeed, that's what criticism is—but you must disclose all biases other than those created by your aesthetic judgment. Transparency should be your rule. If you have a conflict of interest ("the reader should know the lead actress is my cousin") or a prejudice ("I bloody hate musicals"), announce it, clearly.

4. You owe it to the artist and your audience to experience the work in its entirety—or explain why you abandoned it early ("Half the audience was so bored it walked out at the intermission. For the same reason, I joined them.") Don't let your editor convince you to walk out early just to meet a deadline.

5. Beware hyperbole—Save extreme comments ("the best movie I've ever seen," "the worst play of all time") for a once-in-a-lifetime experience. Even then, you should modify the remark ("this may be the best movie I've ever had the honor to review").

6. Recuse yourself if you have a true conflict of interest—for example, you helped edit the screenplay, or you are a consultant to the product's manufacturer. Be honest about it, set a precedent for this kind of honesty early and, with time, it will be easier to do. Train your boss to respect your integrity.

7. Make your money off your publisher—not off free tickets, free books, or free review products—unless it is allowed by that publisher. Find out the rules from the start. Also, if you have been given expensive tickets to an event and decide not to attend, you should return those tickets immediately—don't deny the venue its revenues or keep seats from people who do want to attend. (more below on cut-outs and reader's copies).

8. Do not accept gifts from people or organizations you are writing about. The one exception is when you are dealing with a culture that typically gives gifts at important events. Even then, you must *always* refuse an expensive gift, and must give all inexpensive gifts to charity. During his saloon-reviewing days, the author (and his wife) once had dinner and drinks at a bar. The owner adamantly refused to let me pay the bill—so I left the entire amount as a tip to our waiter. A week later, a friend had a drink at the same bar and complimented the owner on the positive review in the paper. "It ought to be good," said the owner, "I comped the guy and his wife a full dinner."

9. Do not abuse review items or the people who provide them. During his
    days in corporate public relations, the author regularly sent expensive
    electronic devices to trade reporters for review. Many simply kept the
    items—their homes looked like electronics stores. One reporter couldn't
    find the power cord, so used the one from his electric razor, burned
    out the device and then sent it back, demanding a replacement.
    Another returned it in a too-small envelope that was duct taped to hold
    it together. The reporters did those things because they could: they
    knew that I couldn't complain and risk a bad review. This is despicable
    behavior, and if you do it, you can be sure your victims will remember
    and figure out a way to get even, including notifying your employer or
    suing you.

The work of criticism

As with every genre of professional writing, criticism is a craft, with specific
practices, tools and instruments. Here is a quick overview.

Reader's copies—In the publishing business it is common practice to
provide reviewers with "reader's copies" of new books a month or more
before the official publication date. These copies usually have plain paper
covers, an unfinished table of contents, and lack an index. They also
usually carry information about the publication date, PR contacts and
a warning that this version may still be edited before final publication.
The proper treatment for one of these reader's copies is to use it as
source material if you are, in fact, writing a review (and to check with the
publisher if you intend to quote from it, in case the copy has changed)
and, whether you use it or not, toss it away afterwards. If you want an
official copy, contact the publisher and request one.

Gallery and museum openings—Remember, you are a journalist, not a
guest. Don't overindulge in food or drink. If there is a separate media
event, go to that, not the public opening (unless you want to remain
anonymous). Keep your note-taking discrete or retire to a quiet area and
do your write-up there. Don't interview visitors inside; do it outside, and
approach them politely, give your job title and keep your questioning
brief. Try to get any press materials ahead of time, so that you are
prepared. In your review, include information about the show's location
and the dates and times of the exhibit.

Concerts and show opening nights/premieres—Dress appropriately (that
is, formal clothes for the symphony or opera; business clothes for plays

and musicals). Study the program beforehand—including researching the music or play, learning its history, web searching the major performers. If possible, get press materials beforehand. Learn to take notes in the dark—*do not* use a flashlight, light pen, cellphone, tablet, or anything else that may distract actual paying audience members and diminish their experience. Write your notes in the lobby or during intermission. If there is a final rehearsal or media performance, attend that and let the theater make money on the expensive opening-night seat you would have taken. As with art gallery reviews, include details on the show's run (dates and times).

Private screenings—Many major cities have small private theaters, run by Hollywood publicity firms, that enable movie reviewers to see films before they open and with minimal interference. Typically, local reviewers are notified which films will be shown at a given date and time, and when they show up are given a media kit and escorted to a theater with no more than a dozen seats to watch the film. No effort is made by the theater's operators to influence the reviewers—only to make them as comfortable as possible, and this is the best frame of mind. As a film critic you may or may not choose to participate in this process—many reviewers choose to watch new films—especially comedies, where they can gauge the audience's reaction—at public cinemas. If you choose the latter, be sure to be on the routing list of the major studios to get publicity materials in advance.

Review copies/items and cut-outs—Publishers, other media companies and publicists often send reviewers content material that they don't want returned—often because to mail twice is more expensive than the material itself. This includes CDs, DVDs, some books, and cheap consumer products and electronics devices. For TV reviewers, some of those DVDs will be recordings of upcoming television episodes. For audio, these items will have the print insert clipped in the corner—a "cut out," this is called. Increasingly, these items are being transmitted over the Web, but many remain in traditional formats. After you've written the review, or decided not to do so, the question then becomes: What do you do with all those items, which can represent a score or more per *week*? Rather than throw them away, the temptation is to sell them. This is an ethically gray area, and one you should address with your employer. You'll find, especially if you are a freelancer, that many publications and web sites consider this resale part of your compensation. Always check first.

Backstage access and sneak previews—One of the rewards of being a reviewer is *access*. With proper warning many artistic productions, from plays to rock concerts, will provide you with badges or backstage passes in order to see the actual workings of the production and, possibly, interview key participants. Needless to say, you will be there as a professional, not a starry-eyed fan, so you must be low-key and stay out of the way. Don't ask for autographs or free tchotchkes, and always ask permission to record conversations, conduct interviews or take photographs. Otherwise you may never again be given permission.

Sneak previews are more structured events also designed to give you special access. In this case you will be invited to see a production in advance of its formal opening. It may be a sneak viewing at a local theater of a new film—sometimes also attended by cast members, the director and studio representatives. For plays and performances, you may be invited to see the final rehearsal. And for gallery openings, you may get a private viewing. Implicit in these preview invitations is the agreement that you will quickly turn around your review and have it published *before* the official opening.

Deadlines—The hardest part of being a reviewer or critic is not the esthetic analysis of the event, nor even the writing of the review. It is meeting your deadlines. Criticism is work that largely takes place in a vacuum: you may have the plot of the play, or the biography of the artist, or the song list of the band—but there is nothing there to tell you how to render your opinion honestly, compellingly and of interest to your readers. For those things you are on your own. And it only gets worse the longer you wait to start writing. That's why many critics and reviewers start immediately— even to the point of writing the lede in their minds, while they are still at the event, and then finishing while they are still in a white heat from the experience. They do this even if it is 3 a.m. and the deadline is a week away. That said, there is rarely that much time; that's why reviewers must be able to write immediately and write fast, and be able to write their way through any creative wall.

Carving out a niche—Smart reviewers quickly learn to carve out an area of expertise for which they are the acknowledged expert (to keep away competitors), yet enjoy a large enough reader audience (to guarantee job security). Being known as an acknowledge expert has other advantages. For example, it presents the opportunity to write a book in your field, give speeches even become an adjunct professor or lecturer at your local university. Establishing such a niche can be as simple as writing a couple of hundred reviews on a single topic—say, your city's symphony—over the course of a decade, such that you can compare current performances to those of years before, or you personally know (and can get quotes from) key figures; or you can identify improvements or weaknesses. Needless to say, you can accelerate this process by doing a bit of research or field work.

Creating an audience—Successful critics are conscious of their audience and cultivate them at every opportunity. Loyal readers make for enduring careers—they buy subscriptions, read ads, write comments and positive letters to the editor. While it is natural to elevate your writing to impress your professional peers—or in the name of art for art's sake—you should never forget that your first duty is to your readers: educating them, developing their critical faculties, warning them against wasting their hard-earned money on bad experiences and alerting them to positive experiences. Take care of your audience, and they will take care of you. Review, say, a new movie, and write only about the cinematographer or the film's relationship to an obscure 1920s silent film and, while you may impress other reviewers, you will lose your following—and eventually your job.

Building a career—Like all writing jobs, the career of a reviewer or critic has a trajectory, one that you need to manage in a professional manner if you are going to enjoy long-term success. Typically, this means taking what is an established position and leveraging it into something larger that offers the prospect of ever-greater wealth and fame. Here are some ways to do that:

The right venue—It is difficult to make a comfortable living (that is, support a family, buy a house, retire comfortably) being a reviewer or critic for a small local, or even regional, publication, web site or television news show. You need to have the ambition, and willingness to do the hard work, to land a job at a big-city newspaper, a national magazine or a national web site or television program. You do this several ways: by taking on bigger projects (like subject profiles, extended features, investigations) than are part of your normal job description; by building your resume with more prestigious freelance work; and by constantly applying and interviewing for jobs at the next higher position in your profession. At some point, you are going to bump up against a ceiling on your career but, if you are good, that will come later than sooner, and you will have landed a well-paying gig.

Conferences and festivals—At a certain point in your career, your professional reputation will likely reach the point where you are invited to give speeches or serve as the master of ceremonies at industry events or university conferences. You may see these invitations as distractions (if they're not paying) or intimidating (if you are not comfortable as a public speaker), but nevertheless you should accept every one you can. They are a quick way to elevate yourself among your professional peers; they certify you as a leading expert in the field and they are a great way to network for career promotions. At some point, you will be able to command a sizable fee—often the equivalent of several month's salary for a weekend of work—and you will become one of the leading figures in your field. The pinnacle of this kind of work is when your name is attached to just such a conference or festival—thereby cementing your position at the top of your field. If you do have stage fright, or (like most people) are uncomfortable with public speaking, start small, join a toastmaster's group, and get used to it.

Compilations—An important career step for any reviewer or critic is making the jump to writing books. We'll explore this more in the next topic, but for now note that the easiest way to get into the book business is with a compilation of your writings, including reviews and essays. Needless to say, you have to have written a fair number of pieces and have an established reputation before any publisher is going to give you such a deal (unless you choose to self-publish). But once you reach that level, this should be an easy decision, and a crucial next point in your career development. Best of all, it turns what was short-lived, fugitive work into content that will sit on library shelves—and in the hands of your descendants—for generations. And isn't that, ultimately, why you write?

Books and biographies—Compilations aren't the only book-writing opportunities for veteran reviewers and (especially) critics. Having established an expertise in your field, you become the most likely candidate to write survey or history books on that field—biographies of key figures within it. Books like this often have the possibility of becoming best-sellers and thus command large advances or produce considerable royalties. A successful book of this kind will only further advance your reputation and lead to future book deals.

Career: The Good

Lifelong work—Reviewers and critics typically enjoy considerable job security (in part because editors don't really much care as long as deadlines are met and editorial holes filled). It is not unusual for, say, a music critic or movie reviewer to retire from a publication after decades of employment. Though the likelihood of hitting a salary ceiling is there (see "The Bad"), over the long haul, critics and reviewers may very well enjoy a higher lifetime income because they don't suffer the long periods of unemployment often suffered by their editorial peers.

Get better as you get older—A second reason why critics and reviewers have high job security is that their critical skills tend to improve with time.

Their insights grow sharper after they've written several hundred reviews, and their historical knowledge of the field only grows stronger. This makes it one of the rare careers, even in writing, where you can be better at what you do at 70 years old than you were at 25. That means you may well be spared the career obsolescence experienced by many of your professional counterparts.

Tremendous power and influence in your field—Unlike many other careers, where you can feel like just a cog in the big corporate wheel, being a critic can give you influence and get you respect from the very beginning of your career. And, while your corporate counterparts are still enjoying only limited influence even at the general-manager or vice-presidential level, by the middle of your career you can be enjoying a sizable amount of fame—and a profound influence on your field of interest. By the time your counterparts have hit career ceilings (other than the handful who make it to the CEO's office) you will have become the "dean" of critics in your field, your influence may be as great as any artist. That's not a bad career trajectory

Enduring work—Criticism is one of the most long-lived of all types of professional writing. We still read criticism of Greek life and culture *three thousand* years later. That may not seem important at the beginning of your career, but in its final years, when you are thinking about your legacy, it will be very important. In the Internet Age, you can pretty much assume that everything you write will be traceable somewhere, probably for generations. But if you want to improve the odds of that happening, you'll want to pursue the creation of books—from compilations of your writings to original works.

Independence—Critics were among the first journalists to mostly work away from the office. That's because they typically had to attend screenings, gallery openings, and so forth, away from the newsroom, and while some then would go back to the paper or magazine late at night and pound out copy, others would simply write from home and send in their copy. In the twenty-first century, it's rare for a critic or reviewer to visit the office at all—except perhaps to occasionally remind their editor who they are. Needless to say, for web sites and online magazines, there is no "there there" anyway, so the critic's office is his or her home office. Hit your deadlines, and the life of the modern critic is one of almost complete independence—even more so than home workers at corporations, who still must report to their superiors and attend virtual meetings.

Free stuff and collectibles—We've already noted the ethical challenges regarding "review" copies and gifts. And those rules at your employer must always be followed. That said, if you are a music critic you are inevitably going to be sent hundreds of CDs or free music downloads—with no expectation of returns. The same with book criticism or electronics reviewing. And, even if you are not receiving free items, your expertise will likely enable you to make smart purchases in your field—such as art and engravings—the average gallery patron might not make. The result is that, in the long run, you will likely develop a valuable collection of superior works in your area of specialty, and for many critics such collections have proven to be a nice added retirement—or a donation to a local library, university or museum.

Career: The bad

There aren't a lot of negatives about a career as a critic or reviewer. That said, if the work doesn't fit with your personality it will become increasingly difficult to maintain over time.

Pay—If you don't make the leap to authorship, national media or conferences (and sometimes even if you do), the income from criticism and reviewing is, at best, average. At a newspaper you will make the salary of a mid-level reporter or editor, and rarely more. It is possible to jump to national syndication—but few critics do. Few freelance reviewers ever earn enough to make a living from it; but rather, you'll likely do this kind of work as a supplement to a regular job.

Voyeurism—Ultimately, criticism is about looking at and judging the work of other people. This can get old after a while, especially (as noted) if you want to be doing that work yourself. But even if you aren't envious of artists and are content with your own career work, it can seem as if you are intruding on others' lives—and don't deserve to do so. This can be especially the case if, in the course of your work you learn something private, but salient, about an artist or performer's life and feel obliged to publish it.

Contempt and fear by people you admire—Also, as mentioned above, you can assume that you will never have a sincere relationship with anyone you write about. The power relationship is just too one-sided—in your favor. Your subjects, often unconsciously, will either suck up to you or keep their distance, simply because you have their fate in your hands. Worst of all are the subjects who will be friends to your face but attack you to others. If you get into the business to get to know the important figures you write about—famous artists, movie stars, authors and so forth—you have made the wrong choice. Most likely, they will look upon you the way the French novelist Andre Gide did critics in his era, quoting the old Arab proverb: "The dogs bark, but the caravan moves on." In their eyes, you will always be one of the dogs.

Bias—Developing biases is an inevitable part of the profession of criticism. There will be mediocre artists you like and great artists you truly hate. The challenge is to keep your criticism balanced and fair in the face of both emotions. But that can be a heavy burden: the only thing harder than honoring someone you hate is to give a bad review to a friend you like and admire. If you allow your biases to affect your work, then you are no different than the type of critics (described above) who abuse their power and authority by picking winners and losers for their own gain. And, like those power abusers, letting your biases color your work is a sign that you need to change careers.

Turning points

You become bigger than your subjects—Though it is comparatively rare, in most artistic fields, and about once per generation, a critic can be so esteemed and influential that he or she becomes more powerful than the subjects of their writing. This kind of reputation can actually distort the entire field, as the critic begins to attract all the attention, and the actual practitioners are reduced to operating in their shadow and compromising their work to appeal to that critic. When this happens, it is sometimes better for the critic to move on to other subjects where his or her influence is not so great

You abuse your power—This is the corollary of extreme fame. Critics who enjoy considerable power in their field, if they lack sufficient professional integrity, can take advantage of that power—picking winners and losers for their own advantage, allowing their judgment to become personal and even earning money under the table. It takes a strong character—and considerable pride—not to succumb to this kind of power. If you find yourself drifting toward this kind of behavior, *get out* while your reputation is still intact.

You grow tired of being an observer—It goes without saying that, given your job of making or breaking reputations—and with great fortunes sometimes hanging in the balance—being a critic or reviewer is a job that enjoys a lot of respect, but not a lot of love. The artists themselves often hold you in disrespect, if not downright contempt. They, after all, are doing the hard, risky work—only to have you come along and judge them. If you can't live with that treatment, you probably shouldn't be a critic. Almost as common are those critics who initially set out to be creative types themselves, and when it didn't pan out did the next best thing and became critics. But they never abandon their original dream, and it haunts them to watch others succeed while they can only write about them.

Intellectual cycles—Criticism is a dynamic field, with universities producing new schools of thought every decade or so: the "new"

criticism, critical analysis, postmodernism, and so forth. It is extremely difficult for someone who has made his or her reputation with one of these schools to maintain their reputation in the next. These shifts don't really affect reviewers at newspapers and magazines—mostly because their readership just wants thoughtful and decisive opinions—but, at intellectual journals, such shifts can signal the end of a critic's career.

Essayist

What is an essay?

An essay is a venerable form of nonfiction writing that endures because of its power to influence readers. Essays are typically short (500–5,000 words), tightly constructed, attack a single and comparatively narrow theme and drive the reader quickly and directly to a conclusion. Typically, essays have an obvious structure, reference larger outside forces and are topical and timely.

Essays can take a number of forms, including many found in the other professions described in this book, including art and literary essays, political tracts, one-off columns, extended blogs, opinion pieces and editorials.

Why write essays?

Because essays are so powerful. All the great minds of the last three thousand years have written in the essay form. Some essays (see below) have changed history. Part of their appeal is that they are the equivalent of a compressed argument transformed into print. Another reason is that they are comparatively brief: for writers, that means essays can be written quickly and can be sold to magazines and newspapers. For readers, a lot of the appeal is that the average essay typically can be read in a single sitting and doesn't require the commitment of, say, a nonfiction book. Finally, because they can be turned around so quickly, essays can be timely, and hooked to recent events, in a way impossible for longer formats.

For writers the biggest problem with the essay is that the form is inevitably bound up with bad memories of having to write "essays" in school. This is unfortunate, because the true essay has almost nothing to do with that debased form, which is little more than a form of punishment. The trick is to not let those bad memories deter you—there are few more enjoyable and rewarding forms of writing.

History

The essay—or at least a prototype form of the essay—can be traced to the Greeks, in particular to the post-Socratic philosophers. Plato's dialogs, such as *The Republic* are structured as conversations in which Socrates is prompted by interlocutors into extended monologues that are almost indistinguishable from short essays. This is particularly the case with his celebrated "Parable of the Cave." Aristotle, in turn, achieves the essay format with his *Nicomachean Ethics* and *Eudemian Ethics*. Other essay-like writings from the era include Epictetus's *Golden Sayings*, a founding document in Stoicism.

The Romans made many important contributions to the essay. Notable are the writings of emperor and Stoic Marcus Aurelias, Cicero's speeches, St. Paul's letters in the New Testament, and Augustine's *Confession*. With Aristotle's ethics, all had a profound effect on the story of expository writing because of their rediscovery during the Renaissance. In imitating these works, the leading writers of that later era adopted the essay form and perfected it.

A parallel development of the essay occurred in Japan, most notably Shonagon's *The Pillow Book* (written circa 1000) and *Tsurezuregusa* by the Buddhist monk Yoshida Kenko, written three centuries later.

The literary side of the Renaissance is synonymous with the essay, and its leading practitioners are among the greatest figures of that age. They include political essayists such as Machiavelli (*The Prince*) and the poet John Milton; personal essayists such as Montaigne (*Essays*); cultural essayists such as Castiglione (*The Book of the Courtier*); scientific and philosophical essayists, including Francis Bacon (*Essays, The Advancement of Learning*), Pascal (*Pensées*) and Descartes. Besides the historic precedent, another source of the appeal of essays during this era was the rise of printing. Essays could be written quickly and produced cheaply for mass distribution to an increasingly literate populace. As a result, essays enjoyed an enormous influence that would have political implications in subsequent centuries.

The eighteenth century constituted something of a Golden Age for the essay. During the Enlightenment, the essays of Coleridge, Addison, Burke and Samuel Johnson enjoyed considerable popular support; while Voltaire and Swift wrapped social commentary and criticism in satire. Romanticism was launched with Rousseau's attack on reason and rationality in his extended essays, many of them embedded in his novels.

The nineteenth century saw the creation of some of the most important essays ever written, including those by the Romantics, notably Hazlitt's and Goethe's essays on science, literature and aesthetics. The middle years of the century featured cultural critic Matthew Arnold (*Essays in Criticism*) and in the United States the rise of the transcendentalists, Emerson and Thoreau. The last years of the nineteenth saw important philosophical essays by Nietzsche on human will, power and morality. The century ended with one of the most powerful essays ever published: Zola's "J'Accuse," which called out French government corruption in the Dreyfus Affair.

The twentieth century saw an explosion in essays, propelled by both newspapers and a medium that proved a perfect home for a growing literary form: the magazine. The list of major essayists during this century is too long to enumerate in these pages, but here are some examples, many of them famous in other writing fields:

- C. P. Snow—Most famously identified the growing schism between science and the humanities. "Two Cultures."
- G. K. Chesterton—Literary essays and Christian apologist. "A Piece of Chalk."
- T. S. Eliot—Literary critic. "The Metaphysical Poets."
- Isaiah Berlin—Social science, culture, human liberty. "The Fox and the Hedgehog."
- Hillaire Belloc—Religion, travel and history. "On Them."
- Dwight MacDonald—Radical politics, cultural criticism. "The Book-of-the-Millennium Club."
- Rebecca West—Travel, politics. "The Strange Necessity."
- Stephen Jay Gould—Paleontology. "Ladders, Bushes and Human Evolution."
- Loren Eiseley—Anthropology, human culture. "The Star Thrower."
- Virginia Wolfe—Literature and arts. "The Death of the Moth."
- Martin Luther King Jr.—Race and America. "Measure of a Man."
- Tom Wolfe—Social criticism and culture. "Sorry, Your Soul Just Died."
- Jorge Luis Borges—Literature and history. "Borges and I."
- Ramdhari Singh Dinkar—Nationalism and anti-colonialism. "Memorial for Dr. Kashi Prasad Jaiswal."
- George Orwell—Politics and literature. "Down and Out in Paris and London."
- Frantz Fanon—Africa and anti-colonialism. "The Fact of Blackness."
- Felicien Marceau—Art and literature. "Balzac et son Monde."
- Thomas Mann—Literature and German culture. "Dostoevsky in Moderation."

The essay in the twenty-first century has evolved to reflect the dominant issues in the early years of this already-tumultuous century: international terrorism, globalism, the technology revolution (in particular, the Internet) and the biotechnology revolution.

- Marilynne Robinson—Religion and faith. "Open Thy Hand Wide."
- Christopher Hitchens—Politics and society. "From 9/11 to the Arab Spring."
- David Foster Wallace—American culture and sports. "Consider the Lobster."
- Alain de Botton—Philosophy and human relationships. "Why you will Marry the Wrong Person."
- Theodore Dalrymple—Medicine and the underclass. "The Heart of a Heartless World."
- Roger Scruton—Conservatism and English culture. "The Politics of Culture."
- Roger Angell—Sports. "Distance."
- Kate Jennings—Feminism and language. "Home Truths."
- Mark Steyn—Music, politics and culture. "Dependence Day."
- Camille Paglia—Feminism and literature. "Junk Bonds and Corporate Raiders."
- Gerardo Fernandez Fe—Cuban culture. "Cuerpo a diario."
- Sebastien Lapaque—French culture and politics. "Salauds de pauvres!" (Poor Bastards!)

Types of essays

Centuries of essay writing have shown that almost every topic can be the subject of a compelling essay, from personal confessions to the latest twists and turns of world affairs to the meaning of the universe itself. But whatever the form, the key to a great essay is a tight focus on the subject, a logical progression to a strong and compelling conclusion, and powerful prose. Here are some the subject areas essayists have found to be rich subjects.

Politics—Political essays cover the entire spectrum, but typically focus on larger ideological themes. News related political writing usually takes place in columns.

Culture—Perhaps the most popular topic for long-form essays. Topics range from art and literature to popular trends to classical themes. There is a venue for just about every one of these subjects.

News—These are comparatively rare, as the extended time to create an essay works against the timeliness of breaking news. This is more the subject of short columns. That said, major news events—such as war—that extend over time have been the subjects of some great essays.

Technology and business—Popular topics in the twenty-first century, given the electronics revolution and the emerging global marketplace. The best essays on this topic deal with the implications of these changes on civilization, work and leisure and what it means to be human.

Personal life—Essays of this type can range from the deeply moving to the riotously funny. They typically deal with real-life anecdotes, parenthood, marriage and ageing.

Nature and science—Some of the most celebrated essays of the last century have taken recent discoveries and inventions and extrapolated them to human culture and mankind's place in the universe.

History—Each new generation needs to revisit the past to reevaluate key events, discover new lessons and provide context for the present. Some of the best essays offer a reappraisal of important historical figures and events, elevating some reputations, lowering others, and discovering the long-forgotten.

Entertainment—An important role of the essay is to identify new trends and schools of thought. The essay also serves as a vehicle for surveys of new art, music, film, television and so forth.

Call to arms—One of the most important essays ever written was Thomas Paine's "The Crisis," with its famous opening: "These are the times that try men's souls [...]" As a ringing call to sustain the American Revolution it was unmatched (George Washington had it read to the Continental Army), and ultimately changed history. That said, the "call to arms" is a common essay form beloved by every fanatic and ideologue—and is usually a wasted effort.

J'Accuse—This type of essay has a very distinguished history. Zola's essay of this name was a legendary attack on the corruption and anti-Semitism of France's Second Republic. J'Accuse essays are very risky: some have gotten their authors murdered. And they must be very accurate—or the author (and publication) risks libel suits. But as instruments of justice they are all but unmatched.

Sports—Sports writing attracts top-flight reporters, but they rarely are given the chance to put that talent to work. When they do—in essays that celebrate great athletes, teams and sports moments, that follow the mixed fates of sports heroes and limn the contradictions between sport and real life—the results can be haunting, hilarious and unforgettable.

Profile—The difference between a profile-type feature story and profile-type essay is that the former typically restricts itself to telling the story of the subject, and usually features extensive quotes. The latter usually has fewer quotes and, instead, places the subject in the larger context of history, culture, antecedents and influence.

Satire—The satirical essay may be the most difficult form of all of these to pull off successfully. One reason is that while a mediocre straight essay can still be readable, a mediocre satirical essay is indistinguishable from a failed one. Great essayists can be created with a lot of work and effort, but great satirists seem only to be born. If you are one of those rare individuals, start with small venues and perfect your craft. With satire you usually don't get many chances to succeed in major venues.

Markets

Magazines—Some mainstream magazines regularly publish freelance essays; more publish essays from staffers. Arts, culture, political and academic journals are the largest and most consistent publishers of essays.

The web—The Internet has proven to be a major new opportunity for essayists. Though the blogosphere is increasingly defined by ever-shorter entries, there still remain numerous opportunities for long-form writing, especially essays. The bad news is that there is rarely much pay (if any); the good news is that a top-notch essay has a good chance of being linked to scores of other sites and result in millions of readers—the kind of audience that builds reputations.

Newspaper op-ed sections—The editorial pages of newspapers feature regular columns (by staffers, often without bylines), guest columns (bylined) and, less regularly, actual essays. The boundary line between the last two is not well-defined, nor does it need to be. That said, a short (500–900 words) opinion piece on a particular topic is usually considered a column. While an in-depth analysis by a guest expert, not hooked on an immediate news topic, and typically running twice as long, is usually considered an essay. This type of essay writing is typically given special treatment, appears most often in top-tier newspapers and commands a premium price.

Newspaper arts & review sections—These sections, which appear in major publications (*The* (London) *Times Book Review, The Wall Street Journal Arts & Review*, and so forth) are dedicated to book reviews, arts criticism and, typically, to one or two extended essays, usually of cultural criticism. These are very high-prestige venues, and usually only major national figures are solicited to write for them.

Opinion journals—The publications, which range from national magazines (*Commentary, The Nation*) to political journals (*Foreign Policy*) to cultural and academic journals (*Hudson Review, The New Criterion*), are home to most of the essays published each month. While these publications lean toward authors with either the right credentials or recognized expertise, they still offer an opportunity for new writers to build their reputations.

What makes for good essay writing?

We'll look at this more in-depth in the "Tips" section below. For now, we'll take a high-level look at what makes an essay "work" for the reader, who is, after all, the person—not your editor, not yourself, not your friends—to whom your writing should always be targeted.

Engaging opening—If you don't grab your reader from the first sentence, before they even realize they are reading your essay, you'll lose them. When that happens, no matter how good the rest of your writing, how strong the message or how compelling the conclusion, it won't matter. They'll be gone.

Strong organization—You need to drag your reader through the whole length of the essay. That's done with smooth transitions and a logic that pulls them through to find out what comes next.

Precision—The intelligent reader will be challenging you at every point, and nebulous, imprecise phrasing will not help your case. You must make your points clear.

Twists of thought, irony, powerful phrasing—Why read anything if it isn't fun, or at least compelling? The best essays are not only powerful in their logic, but also delightful in their style and their insights into the author's thinking.

References and appeals to higher authority—Back up your case with references to other, official, sources. That gives your work legitimacy. And support your argument with references to acknowledged experts in the field. That gives your work credibility.

Clear, elegant writing—Once again, it is important to be entertaining. Experts have a common weakness for lapsing into the jargon of their profession because it offers an even higher level of precision. But it can also make the prose unintelligible—even insulting—to the average reader. Be precise in your argument, but mainstream in your prose style, as well as simple.

Powerful close—In following your entire argument, your readers are taking a journey with you. So why, when you've taken them to the mountaintop, would you show them an empty vista? No, your job is to blow them away with a strong closing, one that vibrates in their brain for hours, even days, afterwards. Creating a powerful close to an essay is just as difficult as writing a great opening—and takes just as long.

The good news

- *It is the best writing you'll ever do.* Being an essayist puts you in the company of some of the best writers alive. It is the big leagues. You can build your reputation on it, and it is something you will look back on with pride.
- *You can influence events.* More than any other form of writing (other than speeches), essays mobilize the citizenry, impact legislation, turns opinion and sometimes changes history. Other than novels (and perhaps film), essays are a writer's best chance at fame and immortality.

The bad news

- *It's hard to make a career.* Essay writing tends to be a collection of one-offs. There are very few full-time essayists, so, as you might imagine, there is a lot of competition for very few positions.
- *It's usually a sideline to another job.* It follows that, since there are few full-time essayist jobs, if you want to pursue this line you'll need another job. One possibility is academia, but that, unfortunately, can also be a burden, as you are not considered a "real" expert. But careers in most other professions don't leave much time for writing.
- *Lots of competition.* It's not just at the top. Some people think they can write novels or epic poems or even movies. But *all* people think they can write an essay: "It's just like a school paper, isn't it?" As a professional writer you can usually rise above all that competition, but it's still noise, and your work can get lost among all those other submissions.

Careers

Academic—You may have lower odds getting an essay published in the mainstream media, but your odds skyrocket when writing for academic journals, literary magazines and so forth. And term breaks and summer give you large blocks of time to write. Moreover, getting an essay published doesn't just get you paid, and a readership, but it can also be a career builder.

Columnist—See the chapter on "Columns." For now, note that writing a column offers the independence and personal creativity of essay writing, with a lot more job opportunities (and a much faster pace).

Full-time essayist—As already noted, this is a very difficult job to get, but if you do, it is one of the best jobs a writer can have. As with columns, pacing is everything: don't burn yourself out. And if the frequency is too fast, try to negotiate a slower publication rate (but don't lose the job in the process). If you can maintain high quality at a reasonable pace, this is one of the most secure jobs any writer can find.

Editorial page editor—The opinion page(s) editor typically grants himself or herself regular authorship of the lead editorial. These pieces are often of flexible length according to the subject, thus, making them resemble essays. On the other hand, they also are almost always anonymous, take positions aligned with the owners and are linked tightly to daily news events (often local). If you can live with these compromises and willing to put in the time to climb the career ladder at a publication—usually a newspaper—this is a very influential position with considerable power in the community.

Tips for essay writing

Think before you write. This isn't school. You don't just start writing and continue until you run out of things to say. You need to organize your argument to be seamless, logical and powerful.

- What is your main point?
- How are you going to support that point?
- Can you logically carry your argument from suppositions to conclusions?

Spend 50 percent of your energy on the lede. If you don't pull your reader in before they even know they are reading, then you have failed before you've begun.

- Are the first two sentences as tight and as powerful as you can make them?
- Have you buried the lede? The key point of the essay had better be in the first two paragraphs, preferably in the first sentence of the first paragraph. If you need to "clear your throat" with sloppy words and phrasing to start writing, go ahead and do it, but edit them out later.

Use the human voice wherever you can. Use famous quotes, lines from poetry or literature, and so forth.

- It connects your writing with the reader.
- It is authoritative and legitimizes what you have to say.
- Always give recognition to your sources.

Summarize the question or problem to be addressed.

- Devote a paragraph early in the essay to stating the situation briefly and cogently to make sure all readers share the same basic knowledge.
- If you can, quote an authority in your summary to show you are being fair.

One paragraph per point—even if the point takes one sentence to make. This isn't an ironclad rule, but the more you can expose the "bones" of your essay the easier it will be for readers to navigate through it. Placing your key points in separate paragraphs is one way to do it; another is to simply enumerate them: that is, "first, [...] second, [...]"

Let the conclusion find itself.

- If you know at the beginning how you want the essay to end, write that ending down and work toward it.
- If you don't know the ending as you begin to write, follow the logic of your argument.
- Don't fit your text to your pre-determined ending; instead, abandon that ending and write a new one that follows the logic of the preceding argument.
- If the ending you ultimately reach disagrees with your lede, go back and change the lede.
- If all else fails, and you can't come up with a clever ending, just repeat the lede, but rewrite it to incorporate the points you've made in the essay.

Re-read the essay as if you are the audience. That can be difficult to do soon after you've written the piece. So, if you have time before your deadline, set the essay aside for a few days, and only then revisit it as a tough editor.

- Fix logical holes.
- Give the essay "air." That is, break up paragraphs that "look" too long on the page.
- Ask yourself:
  1. Does the essay answer the problem posed by the lede?
  2. Is it intellectually complete?
  3. Does it answer the assignment?
  4. Does the piece physically "look" appealing to read?
  5. Can you find more opportunities to include a human "voice"?
  6. Can you rewrite the conclusion to make it more accurate, more encompassing, and more clever?

Use the technology you've got. Always take advantage of your available tools.

- Use the Internet if you have access. Gather supporting documentation, quotes, data, and so forth. Keep track of your sources, especially if you need to footnote.
- Make full use of word processing: spell check, insert key points, footnote, tables and charts, even write in non-linear fashion and piece together the diverse paragraphs if that helps you compose.
- Unless it has been assigned, write the title last. Make it pithy and memorable.
- Look at how the copy lies out on the page. Try different fonts and type sizes, italicize and embolden. Change margins to get rid of widows, and so forth. That won't change the final published appearance of the essay, but it may help sell your submission.

Submit electronically with a brief cover note.

- Don't write a long message—let the essay sell itself.
- If you get an acceptance, invoice immediately.
- If you get a request for edits or changes, make them immediately and resubmit.

Promote yourself.

- Don't depend on the publication or web site to find all of your readers.
- Have a developed e-mail routing list of friends, family and influential people who follow your work or the subject matter of the essay.
- E-mail the essay (as a file or a link) to that list.

EXAMPLE: The opening to an op-ed piece published in the *Wall Street Journal*. Note how the structure of the argument is made explicit.

Two-tiered Careers

Why do some high performers—in business, politics, and life—maintain optimal performance throughout their lives, while others, some of whom possess even greater talent, quickly fade and fall behind? And why do some lesser performers suddenly take off in mid-career and accomplish astonishing things?

Interestingly, two very different high tech leaders—one a legendary Silicon Valley figure, the other a successful, but almost-unknown outside his industry, founder/CEO who makes his home in Massachusetts—offer the same answer to this question.

Anil Singhal is the latter figure. Born in India, he co-founded and runs a billion-dollar Internet infrastructure company, NetScout Systems. Singhal has developed a business philosophy he calls "Lean But Not Mean." And part of that philosophy is that he needs to help his employees—especially his best employees—to change their careers mid-stream.

In particular, Singhal believes that a person's *primary* skills—"those talents by which you earned your college degrees and first made your professional reputation"—can take you only so far [...] about ten or fifteen years. After that, *secondary* skills—those capabilities, often underrated, such as your ability to interact effectively with others—define one's career.

Book Author

What is book authorship?

The authoring, co-authoring or compiling and introducing of a full-length (40K to 300K word count) hardcover, softcover or electronic nonfiction book. Such a book typically takes 12–15 months to complete, of which the actual writing is about 9 months. Time to publication after completion of the writing can range from days (e-books) to more than a year (traditional hardcover publishers). For the purposes of this book, we distinguish "author," which we will use for nonfiction books only, and "novelist," a term used exclusively for fiction.

Why write nonfiction books?

Because some subjects are of sufficient importance and complexity that they can only be treated at book length. Also, putting one's work between covers confers on it a value and gravity impossible in any other publication format. Finally, more than any magazine or newspaper article, books are substantial physical objects that can endure for years, even generations.

Types of books

The range of subjects for nonfiction books is as wide as the range of human interests. In other words, it is almost infinite. Here is a partial list of broad topics. Under each topic you can probably create a list of subtopics just as long. The point is that, especially in the modern global marketplace, there are probably enough potential readers in each of thousands of subgenres of nonfiction to make it commercially viable for you to write a book on that subject. And if you are willing to write out of love (or for reputation building) instead of money, the potential topics are probably ten times that.

History	Biography
Natural Science	Political Science
Computers	Health
Politics	Travel
Religion	Culture
Business	Technology
How-to	Repair
Personal Finance	Tutorial
Philosophy	Government and Politics
Professional Development	Humor
Autobiography	Military
Memoir	Cookbooks
Lifestyle	Autobiography
Self-improvement	Celebrity
Health and Fitness	Diet
Architecture and Design	Photography
Compilation	TV, Cinema and Radio
Survey	Review
Textbook	Reference
Gardening	Sports

The book-writing process

Writing a book is a major effort, one that can take thousands of hours and months out of your life. Too many people become obsessed with an idea for a book, sit down and just start writing from page one, devoting many hours per day for the first couple of weeks. This is a recipe for disaster— which is why only a small fraction of books started are ever finished. Most often, these writers simply burn themselves out. Or other responsibilities call, and they abandon the effort. Or they discover they don't have enough material for a book-length work.

By comparison, professional authors treat book writing as a long-term, complex campaign that can consume a year or more and requires a long-term strategy, short-term tactics, logistics, considerable preparation and pacing of the work. They know that writing the book itself is typically less than half the process, with the rest taking place either before they type the first word, or after the finished manuscript is sent to the publisher.

We will now take a closer look at this entire process, segmenting it into phases.

Phase one: The idea

Writers come to book ideas in different ways. Some, academics or experts in their fields, often reach a point where their knowledge of a subject is superior to just about anyone else, or they have unique access to unmatched source material (such as the papers of a famous person). They may then decide it is time to put all of that knowledge together into a book.

Other authors find themselves obsessed with a topic and want to use the writing of a book to explore the matter more deeply—and perhaps even get paid for that research. Finally, some professional writers decide to write another book first—and then go in search of a compelling, marketable topic.

Whatever the approach, the subsequent steps are the same.

Subject—You need to take the time to determine two things:

1. Are there other books on the same topic? If so, do you have anything new to offer—original sources, recent discoveries, a different style (mass-market versus academic)? If there are comparable books, how long ago were they published? If more than a generation ago, you may still get a publishing deal.
2. If there are no other books on subject, why not? Is your idea so original that no one has ever thought of it before? If so, be very careful that you aren't deluding yourself. Consider the possibility that other writers have thought of doing the book and, for one reason or another—a paucity of source material, a litigious widow, and so forth—they have abandoned their efforts.

Rough research—You need to be able to tell the "story" of your proposed book, initially to yourself and then, as we'll see below, to your agent and potential publisher. Work in broad strokes. Don't worry about the fine details of your narrative—you'll get to those when you start writing the book. For now, be able to give an extended "elevator pitch" on your book idea: What is it about? What range of time or topics or ideas does it cover?

Theme—Just as important: what is the book's "theme"? That is, what is the point of the narrative? Don't confuse this with the "message" of the book, which is something you usually want to stay away from, as didacticism is usually the kiss of death for a nonfiction book. Rather, "theme" deals with what a book is *about* in terms of its storyline. Is it a look at the darker side of a famous figure? Does it look at the formative younger years of a celebrity? Is it a new approach to learning a particular skill? The theme is the action that works upon the subject of the book.

Content—This is something that new authors don't expect. You've found your subject, determined that there is an audience for it with little competition, and you have a good idea what the book will be like in terms of theme. You may think that you've got everything in place and the sale of your book is assured. But, in fact, your book may have been doomed from the start, and all of your efforts so far have been in vain, because the narrative of the book isn't what publishers are looking for *at that moment*. You may still get the book published with a smaller publisher (with no advance), and of course you can publish the book yourself as an e-book. But any chance of selling your book to a major publisher—and getting a large enough advance to cover your expenses while writing it—may *never have existed*.

Why? Because the book-publishing business has changed, and as this textbook is being written there seems little chance of it ever coming back to the status quo ante of its golden years before the end of the last century. The predations of technology and the distractions of other media have forced the big publishers to cut their annual publications lists and to focus more on blockbuster books. The era of these publishers (and there are fewer now, thanks to mergers) publishing well-reviewed but low-selling prestige books is almost over. And many will hesitate even to publish a potential bestseller if they don't see guaranteed mass sales even before the book is published sales (corporate purchases, book clubs, links to television series, and so forth).

Publishers don't like to talk about this change, especially to authors—and barely even to each other—because it represents the death of the old, elegant model of publishing. So instead, the truth is often wrapped in an alternative explanation. You'll know it when you hear it. The response from a publisher will be: "We think you've got a terrific idea there. However, it seems more like an extended magazine article than an actual book." That is the kiss of death, from which there is no appeal—no offer to expand the scope of the book to contain more content will work. You are done: find another publisher or come up with another book idea.

What can you do to protect your book idea from this fate? Not much. But you can at least look at your book idea and see if there is a way to expand its scope in such a way as to also increase its potential market size. Meanwhile, if you can find a source of volume sales for your book—or even a sponsor (considered unethical years ago, it is now not uncommon)—so much the better. All that still may not be enough to convince a publisher that is being very selective about its catalog; but if nothing else, it will help your sales with a smaller publisher.

Phase two: Preparing and pitching

Having a great idea for a book is not enough. No publisher is going to go looking for you; rather, you must find a publisher. And that is no easy task. Like all great institutions—indeed even more than most—publishers have constructed very sophisticated filters to keep outsiders from penetrating their walls.

Your task is to get past those filters. And really the only way to do so is through a combination of good representation and a strong proposal/pitch. In many ways, certainly at the start of your writing career, this phase may prove even more difficult than the actual writing of the subsequent book.

If you think the steps that follow are easy, you are kidding yourself. Probably more serious book ideas have crashed on the shoals of this phase than at any other point in the process. Give each of these steps the seriousness it deserves.

Write a proposal—A book proposal is the vehicle by which you will gain an agent who then will convince a publisher to buy your book. Successful book proposals have been as short as a cocktail napkin (literally) and 50 single-spaced pages in length (or as much as a quarter of the length of the finished book). You will not sell a book with the former—that is reserved for veteran and highly successful authors about which there is no doubt of their abilities or the market size. Nor will you likely need to prepare the latter—that's also for veteran writers, in this case who are going for a huge advance.

The proposal you will write for your first books will be between 6 and 20 pages, double-spaced. In it, you will introduce the themes of the book, its potential marketing, the book's length and delivery date and include an expanded table of contents. You are likely also be asked—after more than a score of books, this author is still asked—to write a sample chapter of the proposed book.

In other words, preparing a book proposal is hard work. It is not simply a matter of dashing off your idea and expecting to learn about the book's topic as you go. Rather, you need to think about your book in advance—enough to be able to describe the entire narrative of the book and its formatting, as well as how you are going to support its sales and marketing.

Here's the standard formatting of a book proposal:

1. *Cover letter*—This is appended to your proposal when you send it to your agent (your agent will send *all* copies to publishers; *never* circumvent your agent). Don't try to sell your editor in the letter about representing your book—the proposal will do that. Just be friendly, remind your

agent that he or she expressed interest in seeing your proposal, and say that you look forward to their thoughts. Done. Act like a pro: crisp and professional. Don't try to draw an agent's pity or convince them how ardently you want to be a writer—that's what amateurs do.

2. *Format*—The key here is readability—for your agent, and ultimately for your publisher. Don't send proposals that are single-spaced or with wide margins. Let some light into your layout: 1.5 or double-spaced, relatively wide margins, extra spacing between sections, page numbers, subheads, and so forth. Use a good, readable font.

3. *Title*—Start the first page with titles—the title of the book, plus subtitle. Don't worry, you can change both later. Format it as follows:

Book Proposal
THE WORLD OF VIDEO GAMES
A Survey of the Best Games Ever Created
By
Mary C. Jones

Put your name and contact information in the upper right corner. Don't assume that just because that information is on your cover letter that it will be enough—they often get separated.

4. *Summary or overview*—This is the main part of your proposal. It should consist of several hundred words that provide an overview of the proposed book. Again, be professional: no hyperbole, no exclamation points, a minimum of underlined or italicized copy, no personal appeals. Just a precise and well-written section that includes the following:

   a. The need for such a book
   b. The importance of such a book
   c. The key points of the book
   d. New material in the book
   e. Why you are uniquely suited to be the author

5. *Production and delivery*—This section, usually quite short, explains what the final manuscript will be like—in particular, if you will be including charts, graphs, illustrations and/or photographs. More important, this section needs to include when you expect to deliver the book. Nine months to a year is typical—though if you need more time, don't hesitate to say so.

   You also need to say how long the finished book will be. Again, it isn't crucial to be exact—but you need to give a likely range in order to help the prospective publisher prepare. The rule of thumb is that a book shorter than 50K words is hard to sell and earn a profit from (unless it is a paperback), the standard informational nonfiction book is 50–100K words), and anything longer is typically a book of history or biography. Usually only specialty and reference books are longer than 200K works.

6. *Audience*—In this section, you describe your likely readers and their numbers. Typically, this is done by describing different audiences (historians, classic automobile owners, citizens of Michigan, corporate C-level executives, and so forth) with a rough idea of their numbers.

7. *Marketing*—In this section you talk about how you can help the publisher promote your book to those audiences. List your connections to publications that reach those audiences, your prospects for print or television reviews or interviews, potential volume purchasers, potential for speeches, organizations to which you belong, and so forth.

8. *Author biography*—Here is where you talk about yourself. Obviously, list your key academic and career achievements. But also list any affiliations that may enhance your image as being knowledgeable about the subject of the book—including past writings, organization memberships, personal affiliations and anything else you can think of. This section can be as much as a page and doesn't have to be prose, but can resemble a resume or CV.

9. *Table of contents*—Besides the overview, this is probably the most important part of a book proposal. This is not what you think of when you read "table of contents"—rather, it is all that *plus* a paragraph or two with each chapter giving a deep insight into its intellectual content. These paragraphs should be written in prose, not telegraphed in shorthand. Be sure to touch on all the main points. This section may consume half or more of the proposal.

This is the book proposal your agent will submit to publishers (a first draft that needs no editing is rare). When this happens, it doesn't mean your proposal work is done. If you are a neophyte—but even if you are a veteran writer proposing a work that is outside your usual turf—a prospective publisher will want to cover his or her bet on you by asking for a *sample chapter* of the proposed book.

This sample chapter can be a tricky business. For one thing, you probably haven't done enough research yet to write such a chapter. You will need to do that. There's also a likelihood that the chapter you write will look nothing like its final version in the finished book.

There's no easy way to get around either problem, but you can minimize its wastefulness. In particular, don't choose a later chapter in the book, even if you know the most about its contents. Rather, write the introduction or the opening chapter because they are the least likely to be changed by later work and, thus, whatever research you do is less likely to be thrown out. It also is the chapter that usually explains the rest of the book which will help sell the book to the publisher.

Now, with your book proposal written, it is time to establish a relationship with the person who will be your representative to the publishing world: the literary agent.

Get an agent—Welcome to the "Catch-22" of book writing. As the phrase goes: "You can't get a book published unless you've got an agent; but you can't get an agent unless you've already published a book." This isn't entirely true. Every year a few unsolicited book proposals or finished manuscripts get picked up by the big publishers, but the numbers are so small that they almost seem like a publicity effort to convince first-time writers to keep trying.

Literary agents typically take two forms: those based in the world's publishing centers—notably New York and London—and those based everywhere else. They both do the same work, but how they go about that work is often different. For example, an agent based in New York City typically spends his or her day racing around Manhattan meeting with publishers. By comparison, the non-centralized agent will often gather together a batch of book proposals and carry them back to a publishing center once per quarter.

In practice, what this means is that not only is it hard to get a literary agent, but it is even harder to get a certain *class* of literary agent. There's no reason not to try contacting an agent to see if he or she will represent you (only send a letter, *never* send an unsolicited manuscript), you may get lucky, but chances are you will receive a reply that says some variant of "I'm sorry, but we currently are not taking new clients." That is half true: they are just not taking new clients like *you*. Should a former president of the United States contact them for representation on an autobiography likely to get a $10 million advance, or even an award-winning veteran writer wanting to switch agents, they will take that person on in a heartbeat.

So, how do you get an agent? Connections. Why do you think budding writers sign up for masters of fine arts programs? Or show up at book readings and industry conferences? Because the best way to get an agent is to get walked into an agency by a writer who is already a client. Even literary agents who publicly announce that their rolls are filled will still give a hearing to a writer with such a connection.

If it sounds cynical suggesting that you should get to know a veteran for that purpose, it is. But the simple fact is that you should be getting to know your fellow writers, anyway, especially those who can serve as your mentor. And, truth be told, it is also part of the profession: chances are that older writer got his or her agent the same way.

Targeting—Once you get an agent he or she will likely begin by having you polish your book proposal. What you initially prepared may have been enough to interest your agent, but chances are he or she has some very specific ideas how to revise the proposal to make it more saleable to publishers. This is not a time for pride: your book proposal is merely a tool, and no one is better at wielding that tool than your agent. Take his or her advice and edit the proposal according to their instructions—even if it means taking the book in a slightly different direction. Just remember, your agent understands what publishers want *at this moment* far better than you.

Pitching and selling—This can be the most frustrating part of being an author. During this period, your book idea is largely out of your control. Your agent has contacted editors at different publishing houses whom he or she thinks is likely to be interested in your project. If you are lucky, your agent has also set a general deadline for a reply. Either way, you are likely to spend several weeks waiting restlessly for that reply. At some time during this period you may be asked to take a phone call from one or more publishers to answer some of their concerns.

There are basically three scenarios for the final reply:

- The publisher wants to buy your book. Celebrate—you are about to become an author.
- The publisher wants your book, but wants you to make major changes. Find out in detail what those changes are—and decide if you are willing to make them. Keep in mind that publishers look at one hundred or more book proposals each year and likely have a much better idea of what will make a successful book than you do.
- The publisher turns down your book idea. Don't worry—your agent has likely sent out the proposal to a half-dozen other publishers. Wait until you hear from all of them. And even if they all say no, your agent still has more on a second list. If all of them turn down the proposal, then either go back to the drawing board and come up with another book, or look as an alternative to second-tier publishers, regional publishers and e-book publishers.

If you are exceptionally lucky—or more likely, you have a terrific book idea—you will land more than one interested publisher. In that case, your agent possibly will organize an "auction" of your book. Typically, this means a day set aside in which the publishers involved can place their opening bids, then outbid each other until one is left standing—or, at the deadline, the book contract is awarded to the highest bidder. Book auctions are rare, and most authors are lucky to experience one in an entire career. But if you are to ever see that fabled seven-figure book advance or sale, it will likely come as the result of a book auction.

Negotiating—Just because you have agreed on a deal doesn't mean the deal is done. There is a still the matter of agreeing on a contract. This is the other way that agents earn their fees. Publishers have their standard contracts, but most agents do, too, and where they differ is grounds for negotiation. The publisher's draft contract will contain the expected stuff: your advance, delivery date and manuscript length, and your royalties. Those royalties are pretty much standardized among major publishers but may vary with the smaller and regional publishing houses. Among the big houses, the deal will probably be a royalty of about 10 percent on the first few thousand books sold, then going up in increments of 2.5 percent to 5 percent with larger increments of book sales.

By comparison, there are other publishing operations, some of them run by the big houses themselves, others independent, that offer different deals to writers. For some of these, if the author will eschew any advance, will turn around the book in a fraction of the time required by traditional publishers (six months or more) and will split profits 50–50. E-book deals often require the writer to pay an upfront fee, but will also split profits.

Even the traditional book contract will contain a number of other points that few writers ever think of, including: television, film and radio rights; reprints; serializations; and, usually most important, international publishing rights. Regarding the last, as the global marketplace grows, so does the value of book rights sold outside the country of origin. These rights, though small by country, can add up in total. Who gets that money is often a matter of dispute between the agent, representing the author's interests, and the publisher, which wants to get as much of its advance money back as possible.

Typically, within days of signing and returning the contract, you will receive the first advance payment, if you are to get one. How those payments will be made is also the subject of negotiation and will be included in the contract. "Advance" is kind of a misnomer, as you will never get all of the money when you start the book. That may be in your best interest, but for the publisher it isn't. The publisher wants to pay as much of your advance as possible when you finish the book, but before it is published.

The final agreement will lie somewhere in-between. Likely the best deal you will get will be 50 percent upon signing, 25 percent upon delivery of the finished book and 25 percent upon publication. Note that means you may not receive that final payment for as long as a year after you finish your manuscript. That's a very long time to await being paid. Ask your agent to try for 50 percent on signing; 25 on completion; and 25 percent upon acceptance of the edited final manuscript by the publisher. But don't be surprised if you don't get it.

You now have a book contract and money in your pocket. It's now time to deliver on your side of the agreement and *write your book*.

Phase three: Writing and editing

It is now time to get to work. For the first three to six months you have two immediate tasks:

1. Research and gather source materials
2. Develop a thorough and complete outline that you will use to guide your writing of the draft manuscript.

It is best to do these two tasks simultaneously, because it is hard to know what to research before you know what you'll need for the book; and it is equally hard to write a detailed outline until you know what materials you have to work from. So, what this means is that you'll want to take the table of contents and use it to rough out the outline chapter-by-chapter. Then, as you do your research, use those results to flesh out your outline.

That said, don't be a slave to process and procedure when writing a book. As a teenager, as I began to transition from writing to impress girls to considering writing as a career, I happened upon a public television show about writing. The host was a very serious woman, a librarian who wrote freelance magazine articles, who spent the next half-hour explaining her system of putting all her research and notes on separate file cards, color-coded for every imaginable category. Then, she explained, when she had enough of these cards to write a story, she would lay out the cards in some sort of organizational matrix, from which she would write the first of several drafts.

As I watched in growing horror, I decided that I would never be a writer because I was utterly incapable of being *that* organized. On top of that, I realized professional writing, if it was anything like what she was describing, couldn't be very much fun at all.

Happily, I didn't listen to her. In fact, after two dozen books, a thousand newspaper stories and editorials, and several hundred magazine articles, I have *never* done anything like the process she described. Instead, my process was simple: get each piece done in the quickest, most efficient way possible *for me*. All that woman was showing me was the simplest process for her—and she was insane.

So, that's my recommendation for you: find what works and do *that*.

The secrets to writing a book—On my first book I did *everything* wrong. I spent too much time gathering information and conducting interviews, leaving myself almost no time to write the book. I then started writing without a real outline and quickly went off the rails, ultimately writing a manuscript twice as long as agreed upon. I then started on the last day of October and wrote day and night—sometimes as much as ten thousand words a day—sleeping on the floor of my office, not eating, not exercising, and finishing (300,000 words) in mid-January. I then sent off the book—and collapsed. Exhausted and sick, I slept right through my thirtieth birthday. Worse, because of the timing, I ended up going through the publisher's edits on the manuscript during my honeymoon.

Roll forward twenty years and more than a dozen books. I contracted in January to write an even bigger book than that first one for a much larger advance (more than ten times). I also knew I would be leaving on safari in Africa in mid-June. Luckily, I had all the notes I needed for the book, so I "merely" had to write 180,000 words in 180 days. I did just that, writing a thousand words a day every day, which gave me the time to enjoy the rest of my day, get outdoors, see friends and eat well.

In June, on the day before my wife and I and our two kids got on the plane for Africa, I e-mailed the finished manuscript to my publisher. I was healthier than when I started the book and was thrilled to get an e-mail from my editor a few weeks later that, incredibly, he had no big edits. That first book, which almost killed me, was an interesting book, but it also was a mess. The later book, which was almost effortless to write, was recently described by a business magazine as "the best business biography ever written." I'll leave it to the reader to determine which scenario he or she prefers.

Bravado—When talking with the publisher act like you know exactly what you are doing and what the book will be about—even if you don't.

Structure—Have a pretty complete outline in place so that you know where you are and don't lose your way. Going off on a tangent can be costly in time and effort, and it is painful to have to edit your way back.

Organize your work—Take the book one chapter at a time. Expand your outline to a high level of precision before you start each chapter.

Gather your materials—Put together everything you need to write the next chapter. Either mark or highlight the content you want to use in longer pieces (or you'll waste endless time trying to find it again). The author, when he has printed materials for a chapter, puts them in a semicircle on the floor around him, in the order of the narrative, and then picks up each item as he gets to it. When most of your content material is digital, put the articles in a separate file for the chapter, in order of use. If you are working on a desktop, use a big display and put the notes in a corner with the chapter you are writing in the center. Call down the content as needed.

Give credit—Never cut and paste content from another source unless you credit that source or quote in a footnote. Create the footnote on the spot—don't put it off to later. You will either forget or be unable to find the reference.

Discipline—Try to write each chapter continuously—that is, over a string of consecutive days. Try to write something every day until the book is completed. Aim for a daily pace you can maintain. If you need to take a break from writing, do it between chapters.

Continuity—Finish each session knowing what you are going to write next. If necessary, leave a quick note to yourself.

Stay in your game—Just as it is important to try to keep up a comfortable pace, it is equally important not to overextend yourself. If your pace is a thousand words a day, don't suddenly push yourself and write four thousand words one day. You will pay for it in the days that follow.

Don't look back—Don't worry about what you've already written. You can deal with that after the book is done. Just keep pushing forward to the finish line.

Stay healthy—You won't do yourself any favors if you break your health before you finish the book. Beware repetitive stress problems—get away from the keyboard and rest your fingers and wrists regularly. Eat well, get a good night's sleep every night, look out the window regularly, and exercise. You can party yourself sick after you've submitted the manuscript.

Writing technology—As a professional, you want the best tools for your work. On the other hand, you also don't want to waste your money on trendy junk that ultimately will reduce your productivity. Here's a list of basic items. Needless to say, with the pace of technological change, this list should be revised on a regular basis. Your goal should always be maximum comfort and efficiency—keep in mind, you are going to spend months using those tools every day.

A comfortable chair—Don't scrimp on your seating. Take it from the author, who managed to compress one spinal disk and herniate another spending a year writing slumped over in an old wing chair. Get a sturdy, ergonomic office chair with top-notch lumbar support and adjustable arms. Put it on a rug or pad so that it doesn't roll quickly and slip out from underneath you when you climb in or out.

Proper keyboard—Professional writers always have top-of-the-line keyboards, even at the expense of everything else. What this means is an ergonomic design (though you don't need those eccentric designs—just a standard design will do) with "positive tactile feedback." This last is important: it means keys that have a springiness and either a sensation or an audible click that lets you know that the letter, number or punctuation mark has registered. That is the fastest, more accurate way to type. Touch keys, like those found on smartphones and tablets, offer none of that and require you to constantly look to see if your finger tap has registered. That's fine for a phone number; it is exhausting for 100,000 words.

Good monitor positioning—In the best scenario you have a very large screen, or two screens, so that you can put up all your notes at the same time with your text. But even if you are using a laptop (as the author is writing this textbook), make sure it is in the best position for viewing, not reflecting ambient light (hello eyestrain), and is of sufficient brightness.

Wireless mouse—If you are using a laptop, don't use the touchpad or keyboard mouse for any length of time. You may start to develop thumb pain that will compromise your productivity. Get a nice, ergonomically designed, wireless mouse that minimizes hand strain. Even the nicest ones are pretty cheap.

Word-processing software—Most apps are so ubiquitous these days that we don't think about them. And, since you will be running your own writing business you'll likely be buying Microsoft Office or some other multi-use productivity software package, and it will contain the latest word-processing app. On the other hand, to save money at the start of your career you may choose instead to download some comparable freeware. That's fine too.

Just be careful. There are some features in these programs that don't really matter to a writer. For example, you likely never need more than a couple common fonts—all those other ones are for graphic artists. On the other hand, you want a powerful spell-checker and, if possible, a powerful grammar application (you may not need its advice, but it will help you identify problems). A good editing app, with "track changes," is also a necessity.

Internet—Writing isn't gaming; you don't need a huge amount of broadband Internet pumped into your computer while you're writing your book. On the other hand, during the promotional phase (see below) you may want to be able to generate a nice, clean on-line interview with the media, rather than having to travel to (and pay for) a college or corporate television studio. Same deal if you want to create and transmit any promotional videos for you book.

Memory—You don't need a huge amount of computer memory to write a book. These days your phone probably has more than you'd need. On the other hand, the one kind of memory you don't want to scrimp on is *back-up*. There is nothing more devastating than spending hours or days on copy for your next book—and then lose it. It happened to me once, and my wife found me at 3 a.m. banging my head against a wall.

Don't be me. Buy an external drive (they're free) or sign up with a Cloud back-up service. Set your computer on "autosave" so you don't have to remember to hit the save key. And if you fail to do that and you manage to lose a chunk of your writing—or your on-board disk crashes, or all of your files get encrypted by malware or ransomware—don't try to recover it. Take it to a professional and see what can be salvaged.

Copier/Printer/Scanner—Yeah, its Oldware. But there are occasions when you may want to take a newspaper or magazine clipping and make a copy of it on a full-sized sheet of paper for filing. Or you want to print out a chapter to do some careful editing by hand. Or you just want a hard-copy of your book. Here in the twenty-first century, a copier/printer/scanner isn't really necessary—you can always go the local copy shop. Having one of your own—and they are getting cheaper too—is just more convenient.

Wrap-up—Once you finish writing your book (Congratulations!) celebrate. Go out to dinner, sleep in for a couple days, read that book you've been putting off. Chances are that you'll be bumping up on your deadline, but if you do have a couple weeks, set the manuscript aside so you can see it with new eyes. What you've written may surprise you—after all, you wrote some of it months before and only saw it once.

But whether you have the time to be leisurely about it, or you only have day or two before the manuscript needs to be sent in, there are certain steps you need to take.

Assemble—If your chapters, appendices, graphics, photos, and so forth are in different files (not a bad idea, because if something crashes you won't lose everything), now is the time to assemble them. Take your time: this can be a difficult process, as you have to keep track of where you are at any point. Append page numbers and the title of the book on each page at a top corner. BTW: this may be the first time you've actually seen a precise word count—feel free to let it blow your mind: *you* wrote all of those thousands of words.

Check-through—Run a spell-check on the entire book. Make any corrections on the spot. Look for misspellings of names (you'll be amazed how they can change through the book). Check twice before you hit the "change all" button.

Read the manuscript—It will likely be difficult, even if you have the time, to read through the entire book at this point. So, don't fight it: just race through the text, making sure nothing clunks or leaps out at you. Use the grammar checker to locate awkward, fragmented or run-on sentences. Again, don't be a slave of your grammar checker—the choice is yours—but just use it to spot potential problems.

Titling—Now is the time to create a title page, a dedication page, acknowledgements, and to go through and establish both the final phrasing and font style/size for your chapter headings. If you have photos, digitize them as needed, and write captions for them (your publisher will determine where they will go in the text).

Now, send your finished manuscript off to your publisher. You've done it. Go celebrate again—and then be prepared to wait a month or two.

Phase four: Marketing and promotion

There is a lag time between when you complete a book and when you move on to this, the final phase of publishing a book. If you are publishing your own e-book, that lag time is as long as you want it to be to do your own editing, layout and packaging. If you are working with a quick-turnaround publisher you will have a few weeks while the editing, layout and publishing are done for you. If you are working with a big traditional publisher, you may wait as long as a month while your manuscript is being edited by a contracted editor (typically a graduate student).

For this section, we'll mostly be looking at the latter two publishers (that is, not you as a self-publisher). Here are the usual steps:

Deliver manuscript at deadline or earlier—(or beg for more time). If an e-book, publish. This is the necessary first step. The publishing process doesn't start until you deliver the complete book. Your editor may ask to see sections of the book after you write them, but that is solely for content editing before you get too far along. None of the rest of the machinery at the publishing house starts until your big file arrives.

Answer line editor and fact-checker questions—If your editor has any important changes to be made in your manuscript you will need to make those immediately. Then, once those are accepted, and after a few weeks, you will receive via the mail a printout of your book. It will look pretty beat up and will exhibit numerous edits per page in red or blue pencil—in total, depending on the size of your manuscript, it can total several thousand edits. Most of these edits, notably punctuation corrections, you will not have to deal with, merely initial in the margin. Other edits, especially when there is a question mark or an actual question, you *must* answer—every one or the book cannot be published. Write in the answer in a different colored pencil, then attach a sticky note on the side of the page to notify the line editor where it is. You may also get requests to create footnotes, add a definition to an obscure term, and so forth—do them all. Finally, you may also get a sheet or two, single-spaced, with more explicit questions. These need to be answered in the text—you should list on the separate sheets where those edits were made.

When you have finished with all the edits, package up the now well-worked-over hard copy of your manuscript and ship it back to the publisher. Now wait another few weeks.

Write, help with, or approve publicity and marketing materials— During this time, you will hear from your publisher's marketing department. Typically, you will receive a document to fill out with your personal data—in particular, groups and clubs you belong to (including alumni organizations); local newspapers, radio stations and television stations, and any publications you regularly write for. You will also likely be asked to provide a brief biography and photograph (for both the book jacket and the press release).

If you so choose, the publisher will write the press-release copy for your book. The good news is that they are pros, the bad news is that they need to write scores of these releases each year—and they know next to nothing about your book. As a professional yourself, you are usually better off writing your release for them and providing a list of targeted media that may be larger and more encompassing than the list they plan to use. That said, unless you have special access, let the publisher deal with the biggest media outlets and their book editors— they deal with them regularly.

*Receive the reader's copy—*A few weeks after you return the edited manuscript you will receive a box of "reader's copies" of your book. The pages inside will give you a glimpse of what the finished book will be like. But the cover will be paper, usually with a warning that this is not the final version of the book or its copy. This book has two audiences: book reviewers who want the lead time to prepare their reviews (hence the warning) and you. This will be your last chance to make any changes to your book. Don't take this opportunity for granted, give the book a close read and make sure that no errors were inserted in composing. Send your edited version back to the publisher. Meanwhile, the dozen or so other copies you receive are there for you to send out to other people of interest.

Collect quotes—Those people of interest are typically high-profile, influential people whom you would like to have provide you with a jacket quote, or in the case of one individual, your foreword. You may also want to send a copy to anyone who might be interested in a bulk purchase for his or her organization. Don't waste your copies on reviewers—have the publisher send those out at your request. For those to whom you do send copies, append a nice cover letter making the request. For the foreword writer, explain why you want him or her in particular to write it (how much you respect them, their expertise, and so forth) and how long it needs to be. Don't be afraid to politely suggest what you'd like their comments to say. Give everyone a deadline. Also, don't be afraid to follow up with a note reminding them of that deadline.

Promotion—A couple months later, just before the official publication date of your book, assist your publisher by distributing publicity materials to your personal list. Contact your print media sources with a letter offering the prospect of their serializing a piece of your book in single or multiple parts. Work with the publisher's PR people—or if you can afford it, contract a part-time publicist of your own, and work to set up bylined articles, interviews and book signings in your area.

Publication day—Celebrate. Enjoy that moment when a big box arrives on your doorstep and you tear it open to reveal your pristine books inside. Visit a book store to see your book on the shelf—or better yet, in a display. And, if you dare, read the reviews. If you get good reviews, don't entirely believe them. If you get bad reviews, don't entirely believe them either. All that really counts is that you got reviewed. Study where they appeared and where they did not—and develop a quick strategy to capture the latter.

Interview day—Some publishers, in lieu of a book tour, will set up for you a single intense day where you will do a score of interviews, one after another, with radio and television. This is a very efficient promotional strategy, but it will be hard on you. Get some rest beforehand (it can last up to 20 hours) and a headset (otherwise your ear will fall off). Put together a list of basic comments you want to make with each interviewer, then check them off with each interview so you don't repeat yourself.

Book signings and media tours—If you have a big book, you may be asked to go on a media tour, complete with book signings and interviews, in major cities around the country. Do it, but be prepared: these week-long events are exhausting. Lay off the booze, get to bed early and bring lots of changes of clothes. Room service, instead of going out every night, will let your get some extra rest. As for the rest: your handlers will take care of getting you to events on time. Enjoy the experience: it's great for the ego.

Sign with a speakers bureau—Smart professional writers know that the money you can make talking about your book can be many times greater than the money you made from writing it. I recently worked with an author who was willing to trade an advance for the chance to get published quickly. Thanks to a vast mailing list with his organization, he ended up with a big bestseller. But that was only part of his strategy. He quickly signed on to a speaking agency—at $20,000 per speech around the world. He made a couple hundred thousand dollars in royalties from the book; he's made a couple million from speeches on the book. You won't make that kind of money at the beginning of your career (or perhaps ever), but it should give you a good idea of how to make money from the secondary market for your book. In fact, some people write books just as a platform for their next run of speeches.

Start planning your next book—One mistake neophyte book authors make is to not think about their next book until the entire lifecycle of your previous book has ended. But that can mean as much as five years from when you first came up with the idea for that previous book. Pro-rate the money you've made and it can look pretty tiny per year after a half decade. Instead, when you first send off your manuscript to your publisher, start thinking about what you'd like to write next. Start doing some basic research and saving clips. And, since your contract likely says that your current publisher has the right of first refusal on your next book, you can use this time, when you are in regular contact, to bounce some of your ideas off them to see if you get a response.

Money—Did you skip to this section first? Here are the financials (in US dollars) typically associated with book authorship.

- Think in terms of advances, not revenues (there likely won't be any). Publishers plan it that way based on anticipated sales. It is often a self-fulfilling prophesy.
- First book advance—$0 to $10K. Note that several books per year—even from unknown writers—land gigantic seven figure advances. Dont count on getting one.
- Later advances (based on success of previous book) $10K to $300K (celebrities get *much* more).
- Royalties—10 percent, rising to 15 percent with sales.
- Foreign rights—Not much per individual country or language, but they can add up with multiple sales. Usually about $1,000 to $1,500 per language.

- Speeches—$1,000 to $50K.
- Movie rights—$10K to $500K, though films based on nonfiction works are much rarer than on novels.

Career: The good

There is a whole lot of good about being an author, which is why so many people want to become one.

1. You get to be a book author, with all of the fame, social cachet and satisfaction that accrues to that title. You also have a shot at having your name remembered long after you are gone, something even powerful businesspeople and government officials rarely enjoy. Your great-grandchildren will read your writings.
2. You have the potential to make big money. A bestselling book that goes through multiple printings and then is adopted by high schools and universities, can make the author a fortune. Short of that, with even modest success your advances will increase with each book you write.
3. You can leverage your authorship into other careers. Merely writing a book makes you, to some degree, an expert on the subject. That can mean speeches, consulting gigs, teaching positions, and board positions.
4. That expertise can also be converted into becoming a *thought leader* in the field, with the potential for follow-up books, later editions, spin-offs, workbooks and so forth. Some self-help and business book authors have built entire careers—even business empires—off one highly successful book.
5. You are the master of your own career and your own creation. It has your name on it and you get credit for your hard work.

Career: The bad

Frankly, if you follow the advice on book writing so that the project doesn't turn into an endless, unending nightmare, there's not a lot of bad about being an author. It certainly beats most office jobs.

1. Isolation. There's no way around it: you will spend thousands of hours, alone, hunched over a keyboard. You can minimize this by spending time with your family and friends when you aren't writing.
2. You are betting a year of work on a single roll of the dice. Spending all that time only to have the book not sell, or earn bad reviews,

can be dispiriting to say the least. But at least you have been in the arena, not just sitting in the bleachers. And take some consolation in the knowledge that your friends won't care, and no one else will remember anything other than that you wrote a book—and they will respect you for it.

3. Still, bad reviews are bad reviews. Speaking from experience it is not a wise response to go to bed with a bottle of whisky. Just get on with your life. No one else really cares. Promise yourself you'll do better next time. And keep in mind that you have no idea how the future will treat you: that book whose bad review put me to bed? It recently was described as "a classic." Meanwhile, a couple of my books that I'm particularly proud of went out of print long ago.

The author comes from Irish bricklayers, railroad laborers and body-and-fender car repairers. I learned long ago that words are just bricks, and my task is to mortar them together and stack them the best I can. When I've laid a couple hundred thousand bricks, I can step back and discover what I've built. It may be a cathedral, or it may be a very big lavatory. What really counts is that I've laid those bricks the best I can so that I can take pride in the process.

I recommend that philosophy. It'll get you through the bad times, and give you the right perspective on the good times.

Television and Radio News Reporter

What makes TV and radio news reporting different?

All writing is colored by the medium in which it appears, but with television and radio news, the writing is largely defined by the nature of those media. With television, almost all writing is subordinate to the visual imagery available, and the words almost always precede the image. As a result, television news reporting (as compared to print reporting) is typically more of a headline-and-caption production. In radio, the limitations are almost always due to time, as the spoken word is much slower than the read word. Also, in radio any nonverbal sounds (from real-life recordings to sound effects) are almost always subordinate to the spoken word—or used as a set-up to those words.

Why pursue a TV or radio news-writing career?

One reason is that television and radio news—especially the former—are just more glamorous than print. That's because an on-air face or voice is much more individualized than a simple print byline. Still, as the years pass, the three media are growing closer together as the Web enables television and radio reporters to write in a longer format; and print reporters to go on-air with Web videos.

Television and radio news also typically reaches a larger audience than print, especially in an era when newspapers are fading and dropping editions, and television and radio news is extending across the 24-hour cycle. Also, because of the delays created by press runs, TV and (even more) radio news is typically more timely, with updates and breaking news presented throughout the day.

But perhaps the most important reason for pursuing television or radio journalism over print is the personal connection you make with your audience. This is especially true with television, where viewers can come to believe they actually know you—and will sometimes come up and talk to you in public places as if you are an old friend. That can be irritating, but if you have the right, outgoing, personality becoming a local celebrity can be an added reward. That kind of attention almost never happens with print reporters, even popular columnists.

History

Radio—Radio had a nearly complete monopoly on non-print broadcast news for thirty years, beginning in the 1920s. As a result, it essentially defined the nature of modern mass-media and broadcast "stars"— including journalists such as gossip reporters Walter Winchell and Louella Parsons. Radio also created the first media news stars, many of whom went on to even greater influence and fame on television. The most famous of these journalists was Edward R. Murrow, who first made his name in radio covering the London Blitz in 1940, then went on to become the most important journalist in early television. Radio evolved over the course of eighty years from mostly music to dramatic and comedy programming (much of which—such as *The Lone Ranger*—migrated to early television) then back to music and, in a major transformation in the late 1980s, to 24-hour news and "talk" programming. In the process, radio brought news and culture-related conversational programming to the masses—notably through the likes, in the United States, of Studs Terkel, Rush Limbaugh, Teri Gross, and "shock jocks" Opie and Anthony and Howard Stern.

Radio remains the single most-influential (in politics and culture) and largest audience medium in most countries around the world—with top radio celebrities drawing tens of millions of listeners.

Television—The defining medium of the modern world. Though it made its first appearance in the 1930s, television didn't find widespread adoption (both because of cost and limited programming) until the late 1940s. Though popular throughout the developed world by the mid-1950s, when the first television celebrities appeared, television news really only found its footing at the end of that decade. Once again, Edward R. Murrow was a seminal figure: he all but invented most of the tropes of television news, including the investigative documentary, the incisive interview (he famously helped pull down the reputation of Senator Joseph McCarthy), and the celebrity profile. Murrow's last important appearance was hosting the news coverage of the Kennedy inauguration.

Television news became a dominant cultural force in the 1960s through the coverage of NASA spaceflights, US presidential assassinations and the Vietnam War. As television news coverage expanded, both nationally and locally so too did the celebrity of network news anchors—notably Walter Cronkite, in the United States. Television news only expanded its influence in the 1990s as television fragmented into hundreds of channels—especially with the arrival of 24-hour television news from CNN/ CNN International and Fox/Sky News. During crises, elections, national celebrations, major sporting events (the Super Bowl, World Cup and Olympics), and national celebrations, television remained the medium of choice for national populations to gather during a shared news event. That said, the Web increasingly has challenged this hegemony—especially when television couldn't keep up with unfolding events such as 9/11 and the death of Princess Diana.

What makes for good TV and radio writing?

It is important to remember that writing for television is essentially the equivalent of writing headlines for print publications; while writing for radio is mostly the equal of writing the two or three lede paragraphs for print. What that means is you need always to write economically and front-load your copy. That is true for all news writing, but for these two media it is absolutely essential. Radio and (especially) television are not places for nuance, extended description or repetition.

Television—Always let the visuals tell the story. What this usually means is that you will first tape your interviews, stand-ups and b-roll in the field, then go into the studio and record your copy. What writing you do should be not only economic and tight, but should also use strong verbs. Try not to repeat in your voice-over what you already are showing on the screen, but rather write to amplify those images or to explain what might be confusing to the viewer. The one time your words should be redundant with the image is when you are giving an interview subject's name, while showing that name in a title box on the screen.

If doing a report from the field—especially live—practice your copy beforehand to make sure you don't trip over any words or stumble over a name. Use your on-air time to quote sources for whom you have no visuals. Prewrite a nice, tight wrap-up. On your voice-over, don't try to explain complex terms unless you have to—try instead to find another word or phrase to make it intelligible to your audience.

Radio—Radio is the opposite of television in the sense that everything of content must be conveyed in words, while mood is best captured in the audio backdrop. Keep in mind that radio, because of the limitations of the human voice, cannot convey information as swiftly as either television or print. That means your writing must be very, very tight—and you must love the sound of words. Great writing for radio almost always exhibits a perfect sense of timing—pacing, pauses, the balance of sounds, and the mixture of long and short words. Some of this is the product of the reader, but that can go only so far if the writing doesn't have those attributes.

Writing for radio takes practice and a lot of editing. If you are reading your own copy, then find a mentor or other radio veteran who can show you how and when to breathe, edit your copy for enunciation and teach you timing. Very few people are naturals at this—and it is a valuable skill that will improve with time and experience.

Types of TV and radio writing

There are at least as many writing jobs in television and radio as there are in print. And, for the most part, the work itself is quite similar: it tends to be divided into beats, has deadlines and largely is targeted at the same audiences and markets.

That said, there are some fundamental differences. TV and radio newsrooms tend to be much smaller, so it is not unusual for reporters to cover other beats than their own or be sent out on breaking news. Moreover, while newspapers have radically cut back the number of editions they produce, TV and radio news seem to be still expanding, adding shows in the morning, lunchtime, evening and late night, some even jumping to 24-hour coverage. This can add stress to the job—at a minimum adding the requirements for ongoing updates on the original report or story. On top of that, as with print, most television and radio stations have added a online presence, and that can mean not just pouring over the prepared audio or into the web site, but also the creation of added copy.

Finally, tightening budgets at many stations means work that used to be done by a small team—for example, with television, a reporter, shooter, sound person, a producer and even a van driver—is now handled by just the camera person and the on-air reporter. The author was once interviewed by a television reporter in Montana who set up and ran the camera while asking me questions, then locked down the camera, ran around and shot her own reverses. Then, her competition, a reporter from another station, did the same—and then helped carry her gear out to her car.

Happily, the new camera and recording gear is much smaller and lighter than it used to be. Needless to say, you are increasingly on your own; it is no longer enough to be good on-air; you will also need to be expert at digital editing, graphics and voice-over recording/sweetening/editing.

Breaking News coverage—The bread-and-butter of television and news reporting. As the saying goes, "If it bleeds it ledes." Breaking news is exciting, dramatic, has very tight deadlines and is typically live. This work is for the young, and often for the neophyte—it is many a reporter's apprenticeship in reporting. The key is to develop your lede sentences on the spot, then look around for people (particularly officials) who can be interviewed to fill in any explanation. Don't draw conclusions, just present the facts. And if you can't get all the interviews you need, call and get a quote from an expert. Be prepared to present that story and any footage/audio live.

Trend stories—The nature of these stories is in the name. Your job is to combine multiple stories or events, using them as data points to extrapolate a "trend" to a larger story. For such stories, always try to get three examples and then support them with the analysis of an "expert"—anyone from a police detective to a college professor to a fellow at a local think tank or consulting firm. You are expected with these stories to draw some conclusions, even to make considered predictions, if you can properly support them.

Science and Technology News—Thanks to the technology revolution of the last sixty years, most stations have an in-house science and technology reporter. This can be a rewarding gig, as an endless number of science stories and technology product announcements come out every year, and medical researchers, hospitals and tech companies create an abundance of video news releases and b-roll footage. There is no shortage of visuals to accompany these stories. Often this beat also incorporates a business beat as well, as the hottest companies in our time are almost always related to tech. The downside of this work is that if you are not based in a tech region you may find yourself occasionally sent out covering the dumbest, cat-in-the-tree stories. This can be particularly appalling when a major tech or medical story is breaking that day and your managing editor just doesn't understand its purpose. Thus, a crucial part of your job is educating and pitching your superiors on the value of your stories.

Lifestyle news—Lifestyle features are a standard part of television news (because of the appealing videos) and, to a lesser degree, of radio news. "Lifestyle" covers everything from the opening of a new restaurant or public park to the growing popularity of a children's exploratorium or new kinds of plastic surgery to a fad diet. Typically, these stories place audience entertainment before actual news reporting, are heavily visual in television and defined by ambient sound in radio. These stories typically have multiple user interviews. And, for television, the reporter often inserts himself or herself into the story as a participant. Because they don't have the same tight deadlines as breaking news, lifestyle features are expected to have much higher production values.

Crime—The reporting of crimes is a subset of breaking news and usually done by the same reporters. These stories usually are much more stereotypical in their construction, combining (for television) an image of the crime scene, a precise description of events (usually provided by a police spokesperson), the naming of the victim (if approved by the police) and descriptions or mugshots of the perpetrators (if known). This can be exciting work but, like investigative reporting, it can be debilitating over time as you can develop "cop's disease"—a dark and depressing view of mankind after spending too much time living among its dark side.

Sports—The best part of sports reporting is that you never run out of stories. In modern life, there are always a half-dozen major sports in the thick of their seasons on any given day, and especially so on weekends. The other thing about sports reporting is that it requires an expertise that is both wide (from Formula One to NBA basketball to horse racing) and deep (you need to know the key players and have an in-depth knowledge of each sport). That keeps down your competition; while many people want to cover sports, few can successfully do so. The downside of this work is that it is something of a career ghetto: it's hard to jump from sports reporting to any other beat. Moreover, it is mostly a headline service: other than a few highlights, to which you can add commentary, most of the coverage is reading scores. That said, sports news on both radio and television is a guaranteed daily segment of a generally set length—which means you get your airtime and are unlikely to be sent on another beat.

Features—Feature stories are a superset of lifestyle pieces, but can cover many more topics, including negative stories. Television and radio features are like mini-documentaries and as such, the reporter may be given several days to prepare one. Features also usually enjoy longer time segments to tell their stories. The trade-off is that viewers expect more in-depth reporting than a typical news story. For that reason, features are usually reserved for the more veteran reporters who can be trusted to do a superior job.

Segments—Segments are expanded feature stories. They may be one-off stories, or they can be regular (weekly/monthly) or irregular components of news broadcasts. Segments are the usually the highest level of production at both the local and national news levels. They get their own logo and are generally assumed to be candidates for Emmys and other industry awards. Today, some large city stations have their own investigative units that can spend weeks preparing a dedicated segment. Other segments amplify a local news trend and can be the product of a smart pitch by a news or beat reporter. You should always be looking for a chance to bump up one of your stories to become one of these larger features. It's a career-builder and award bait.

Profiles—Profiles are yet another form of feature story, in this case focusing upon a single individual. Typically, these individuals are important local figures passing through a milestone in their lives: career promotion, election, award, retirement and so forth. Production normally involves interviews with the subject supplemented by historic footage (or, if radio, biographical material). Another form of profile is the story about an individual who is emblematic of a larger trend (an activist, a homeless person, and so forth). Profiles, because of the time devoted to them, as well as the importance of the subject, are usually given to experienced reporters—though that rule is regularly violated with younger reporters who have unusual access to a subject (typically because it is part of their beat).

Interviews—Needless to say, interviews are the heart of television and news reporting, and a typical reporter may conduct a half-dozen short interviews *per day*. But full-blown interviews, which may last three to five minutes on air, are a specialty form, a hybrid of the profile in which the conversation almost wholly replaces any feature components. In radio, interviews almost completely replace profiles. Thus, the in-depth interview is typically a back-and-forth between reporter and subject, face-to-face, recorded in real time in radio and with a minimum of reserve camera shots in television. Edits are kept to a minimum. For that reason, interviews have a shorter turnaround time than profiles and thus can be more timely. Interviews, including any raw footage left on the editing floor, can be valuable assets for stations as the years pass and, if the subject becomes sufficiently famous, may end up in museums and libraries.

Documentaries—Extended features or investigative stories, documentaries are the highest form of the television and radio reporting arts. They are rarely ever integrated into the usual news programming but instead placed into prime-time programming where they can be promoted and draw the largest possible audience. As this often means preempting popular existing programs, documentaries represent a sizable financial risk to the station and thus must be of the highest news value and production quality. Being given the opportunity to report, host or produce a documentary is the greatest honor in a television or radio journalist's career. And the result will almost always be put up for local, regional even national awards. Great documentaries, such as Fred Friendly/Edward R. Murrow's "Harvest of Shame" about migrant workers, can lead to new legislation and change the nature of daily life in a country. Any time a reporter gets the chance to be part of a documentary production, he or she should take it: not just because it demands the highest use of their skills, but also because, career-wise, it is the best ticket to a better job, either at the station or in a bigger market. Great local documentaries are the ticket to a position at national news.

News magazine shows—The growing importance and quality of television news, including documentaries, led to the creation of a new form of prime-time news programming: the television news magazines. These began as extensions of evening news shows, then evolved into their own distinct formats. These "newsmagazines," which typically are composed of several segments, each weeks or months in development, have proven to be among the most popular and enduring of any TV productions: *60 Minutes*, a one-hour prime-time series on the (American) CBS network, has been continuously on the air since 1968, winning numerous awards and consistently ranked among the most-watched shows on television. In the UK, the BBC's *Newsnight*, a public affairs program, began in 1980 and is shown every weeknight. Similar programming can be found in most large nations around the world on both the radio and television. Because of their audiences, newsmagazines typically have the highest production values and attract the top news talent on any network. Landing *any* writing position on one of these shows—including intern—is considered a major career coup. Such an offer should never be easily dismissed: you may not get a second chance for decades, if ever.

Opinion—Comparatively rare on television, but more common on radio, are opinion pieces. These are the equivalent of editorials in print and on the Web—that is, preset intervals of editorial time in which a representative of the station or network (news director, station manager, station owner) is free to read a commentary, usually on a news topic or subject of concern to the audience. Though these opinion pieces are usually presented as being from the speaker, they are often written by a professional on the staff—usually after consultation with the speaker. This type of work is usually not a full-time job, but rather one of many responsibilities of a veteran staffer. Opinion pieces can be an interesting distraction from the usual reporting work and a platform for expressing views that wouldn't be proper (or ethical) in a news setting.

Markets

Most populated regions have their own (few) television stations and (many) radio stations. Some stations are likely to be affiliated with national networks, while the majority—especially radio stations—are independently owned. The typical career trajectory of writers, reporters and producers in radio and television is to begin fresh out of college at a small market station to learn the profession and gain "seasoning." From the very beginning, and throughout one's career, it is considered acceptable to be constantly updating one's "demo reel" and applying for a new job—either a higher position at the current station, or a comparable (or slightly lesser) position at a bigger station in a larger market.

The other side of this career trajectory takes two forms: (a) Personal development, often done with the assistance of professional advisors and consultants, to improve one's on-air appearance, presentational skills, voice, use of technology (such as weather maps) and so forth. This is typically for reporters who wish to pursue on-air careers; (b) Career development, which involves the pursuit of high visibility, stylistically diverse, award-targeted stories in order to build the strongest resume and demo reel.

The following job markets for radio and television writers are listed below in a typical career trajectory, from entry level to a top position in the profession:

Local TV and radio stations—This is the bread-and-butter work of the profession. Local stations serving mid-sized cities and their surrounding regions feature brand-new reporters and writers just out of school and serving the equivalent of an apprenticeship. These youngers are usually mentored by older reporters who typically have chosen to freeze their careers in place in order to settle down in their hometown or to have families. This creates a unique dynamic not really found in the markets that follow.

Upmarket stations—These stations operate in the metropolitan areas of large cities and often reach audiences of a million or more viewers or listeners. Unlike smaller stations, upmarket stations can be career destinations for reporters and writers, as the pay is good and a certain amount of celebrity attaches to the job. It is not unusual for reporters and writers, once they reach this level, to stay for their entire careers. That said, upmarket stations can be excellent launchpads for jobs at the national level.

Regional stations—Regional stations take two forms. The first are stations that are attached to mid-sized cities but have the transmission power (or repeaters) to serve much larger, less-populated regions that might hold dozens of smaller towns and cover sizable geographic areas. These jobs resemble those at upmarket stations but require much more travel and are less likely to present the opportunity for high-profile, career-making, stories. The second form includes stations that serve very large cities and their environs and reach audiences of several millions. A legendary regional radio station, Mexico's XERF, was located on the U.S. border; its combination of 250,000 watts (five times the U.S. legal limit) and disk jockey Wolfman Jack gave it a loyal audience throughout North America, and, when the atmosphere was right, even in the Soviet Union.

Syndicated news shows—These programs are typically created by an independent production company and then syndicated either on a cable network or placed with individual stations. Content ranges from cultural programming (*The South Bank Show*), entertainment news (*Entertainment Tonight*) and regional features (*EveningMagazine*). These shows can have astonishing durability, with many still on the air after decades. This is stable, if not always respected, work for writers. That said, it can be a good platform early in one's career to launch to the national level. The key is to take on major assignments of the type that look good on the demo reel. The downside is that, other than cultural shows, these programs are rarely award winners.

Network news—The queen of television and radio reporting. These productions are given key time spots on network television and radio networks and are designed to reach a national audience. Network news regularly deals with major issues, interviews the most powerful people in the world and can have a major influence on public opinion and government policy. Among the writing positions available at network news are investigative reporting, news reporting, features and interviews— and the work can take you around the world (including long-term posting as a foreign correspondent). The pay is superb, and combined with the quality of the work, this is a job most people in the profession try to keep until retirement. Other than the occasional intern, work at this level is only for proven veterans. Network news productions usually take two forms: the nightly news and primetime network news "magazines," the most famous being *60 Minutes*. These program types capture most of the major television awards.

Documentary series—The production of television and radio documentaries normally comes from one of two sources: in-house productions by staff or independent productions by contract producers. Most documentaries are presented as one-offs, or as limited-run series. Sometimes, however, they are aggregated from multiple sources into quasi-series. At the network level, many news operations have in-house documentary teams; at regional and local levels the work is done by members of the news staff (who often take it on in hopes of capturing national recognition).

Cable news/specialty—The rise of 24-hour cable news (CNN/CNN International, Fox/Sky)—both breaking news and business/stock market coverage—presents a major career opportunity for news and feature writers and reporters at the national level. What was once a small number of positions at a handful of network news operations, has now blossomed into hundreds of jobs—in the process making the jump from local and regional to national easier than ever before. Moreover, as cable news ratings now challenge their network counterparts, the opportunity for premium salaries, reputation and awards has grown commensurately.

Web radio and video—The migration of viewers/listeners from network to cable to Web continues apace, and the trajectory seems clear: over the next few decades, most news- and feature-writing jobs will be found on productions targeted at a global audience on the Internet. Some of this programming will be on Web-only sites, while some will originate on other platforms, but will be reached by the majority of the audience via Web Radio or the Internet directly. Most of this work will be similar to the older forms—but given the unique nature of the Web, will likely also add additional multi-media work, including video production, links and the enlistment of listeners/viewers into crowdsourced story creation.

Jobs

On-air reporter—Traditional reporting, comparable to print, but with some twists. In both radio and television you will be regularly required to do live feeds. With prepared stories, you will need to record or tape your story in editing: with television you will need to add visual content (new footage, b-roll from the station archives). Improvisational skills required, as well as the ability to compose in real-time. A good clear voice in radio plus an appealing, unthreatening appearance on television. The ability to consistently conduct interviews that yield at least one good sound bite.

Off-air reporter/newsroom editor—Traditional reporting/editor work. Superior reporting and writing skills. Ability to work seamlessly with on-air staff.

Managing editor—Strong news sense and ability to spot news angles. Talent for picking the right reporter for the story. Organizational skills of a traffic policeman.

Producer—Superior story-telling and writing skills. Mastery of the editing suite. Ability to construct features quickly in a long or short formats.

Researcher—Web information drilling skills, strong empirical sense and comfort with data, charts and graphs, understanding of libel laws and searching through official records.

Correspondent—Domestic (such as the White House or Parliament): quick development of a network of contacts and sources, familiarity with official sources and spokespeople, ability to work independently. International: ability to immerse oneself into different cultures. Strong language aptitude. Ability to go extended periods without airtime—then sudden immersion into high-stress situations. Resourcefulness in both getting stories and getting them on the air.

Investigative reporter—Similar to print investigative reporter, but usually with tighter deadlines and shorter presentation of content (even with multi-part stories). Ability to identify the core story, develop strong ledes, and explain complicated concepts. Willingness to conduct confrontational interviews. Fearlessness. Precise understanding of libel laws. Comfort dealing with everyone from law enforcement to politicians to criminals.

Freelance producer—Similar to staff producer, but greater need to pitch stories. Ability to run a profitable business.

Documentary producer—Similar to producer, but with a greater need to organize all of the resources and content for long-format creations. Top-notch storytelling skills; understanding of multi-part narratives and story arcs.

Executive producer—Personnel skills. Resource management and routing. Critical path monitoring. Scheduling. Marketing and promotion.

Anchor/host—Appealing looks and manners. Teleprompter-reading skill. Ability to improvise on a moment's notice. Ability to deal with crisis—breaking news, extended airtime, orchestrating multiple incoming reports—with accuracy and cool.

Career: The good

- If you are on the air, you will likely become a star of some magnitude. You will be recognized when you are in public, be asked to give speech and host events, and regularly be listed as one of the most influential people in your community. You will also never worry about getting a table in a restaurant.
- You will be at the center of the action. No matter what major event occurs in your viewing/listening audience—be it your town or the entire nation—you will be involved in the reporting of it.
- If you are a daily beat reporter, everything is new each day. When you finish your shift, you can clear off your desk and not think again about it.
- You will have impact. With one of the largest media audiences (print and Web will usually be only a fraction of yours) you will largely establish the conversation with your audience for every news event. That is considerable power—one envied even by elected officials.
- The pay is excellent, as long as it lasts. And it will last a whole lot longer if you aren't in front of the camera.

Career: The bad

- There's not a lot of original reporting, and what there is, is brief. Radio is limited by the speed of the human voice, television is mostly voice-overs to images. As a result, both are largely headline services. Even long-form documentaries carry fewer words than a single newspaper or magazine news story.

- It's not real writing. Again, television and radio are essentially headline services, and what writing there is must often be dumbed down for the general audience. This kind of writing takes its own kind of talent to produce. But other than the rare documentary or feature, there just is no demand for the kind of prose styling and lyrical writing found in print or on the Web.

- It is a gypsy existence. Just about the only way to advance your career in television or radio is to move to a larger station or a larger market. And if you don't even do that every few years, your career is considered to have stalled. That can be fun at the beginning of your career, but at certain point you may want to settle down, get married, have children. Then those moves get a whole lot more painful. When this happens— usually at an age when your corporate peers are beginning to enter senior executive positions—your own career progress will end.

- There is zero job security. This is particularly true for on-air personalities, and especially in television. Because the entire industry is in constant flux, no individual job is secure for long. That said, beat reporters, and especially newsroom writers and editors, have much more security.

- If you are a television anchor, you are only as good as your looks. On-air reporters can become more "seasoned." But anchors, because they are the "face" of the news, must remain young and fresh in appearance. Would that this weren't so, but audiences are very picky and unforgiving.

Turning points

1. You get stuck in a dead-end market. Radio, and television even more, are pretty ruthless businesses. The pyramid of advancement narrows very quickly, and there isn't much room at the top. As a result, the odds are that you will at some point find yourself in a job and a market for which there is no way forward.

2. You get tired of dumbing down your writing and not being able to tell the whole story. As a writer, you get bored with working for a de facto headline service.

3. You get sick of moving around. You want to settle down, own a home, raise a family and be part of a community.

Screenwriter and Playwright

In this chapter we look at two types of writing that appear in very different ways, but structurally, are nearly identical. Both are dialog-driven and both involve actors and actresses who perform the author's words and instructions. Where they differ has less to do with the writing and more with venue, modes of transmission, timeliness (one is "live," the other not) and cost.

Screenwriting

What is screenwriting?

Screenwriting is designed to be viewed or heard, typically in a reading or performance that involves someone besides the author, and delivered by mechanical/electrical/digital means. Screenwriters produce *screenplays*, which are typically converted into working *scripts*, which are used to make motion pictures, Webcasts and television shows. Screenwriting can take the form of a monologue or dialog, and may or may not involve instructions to other creative personnel (instructions for camera shots, actor actions, etc. are usually reserved for the "shooting script."

Screenplays share long-established formats that need to be followed by the screenwriter if she or he is going to have a chance at making a sale. You need to learn that format and be fluent in it. The world will not bend its century-old system to you; you must adapt to it.

Types of screenwriting

Though term "screenwriting" is typically associated with television or film, it actually encompasses just about everything creative you write for the electronic or digital media—even if it is just a few lines to announce the next show on the schedule. Here's some examples:

News stories—If you are writing for television or radio, the line between screenplay and script blurs. You are essentially writing copy, often under a tight deadline, to be read on-air. In this setting, you are often writing words to be either memorized and spoken, or to be put into a teleprompter to be read on air. Formatting is straightforward—it is rarely more than the news copy with the name of the reader(s) appended in a narrow margin, large font layout.

Announcements and interstitials—This is copy designed to be read in a matter of seconds to serve as a segue between shows or productions: that is, "Next, on tonight's episode of "What's Up?" Mary encounters an old friend." Needless to say, succinctness and economy of words, combined with the speaker's ability to read clearly and quickly, are of prime importance.

Introductions and lectures—Educational films, corporate videos, online class lectures and so forth are rarely extemporaneous, though they may seem so. Rather, these productions should be seen as screenplays written for a single actor or monologist. And, in fact, they often are formatted as a kind of simplified script, with instructions for when the speaker should pause, point to a screen, set up an image, elicit a response from the audience and so forth.

Ad copywriting—Non-print advertisements for the Web, television, radio or even for movie theaters are always carefully scripted. This is especially the case if there are actors involved. In those case, the screenplay will be treated just like a television show or film, using the full formatting—even with an accompanying storyboard. This shouldn't be surprising when you consider that top-tier commercials are often more expensive to film per minute than major movie blockbusters.

Radio scriptwriting—This work is basically news reporting with some added wrinkles. For one thing, you must write to the time available and incorporate any available audio—including interviews, ambient sounds, and so forth. You must also write to the speaking skills of the news reader (even if it is you) by playing to their strengths and minimizing their weaknesses, keeping sentences short and limiting vocabulary.

Television narration—This type of writing is for voice-over work related to a larger production. This is almost identical to radio scriptwriting in terms of writing to the abilities of the narrator. What is added is that this writing must also be done to the images in the production. That is, your task is to amplify, not repeat, the imagery—as well as talk during lulls and transition and shut up when powerful imagery commands the viewers' attention. This means that the writing should not occur separate from the production but at the same time, with one eye to what is appearing on the screen.

This can become complicated, as the production may also be organized by the narration. So, which comes first? The answer is: both and neither. In practice, the narrative is writing with a sense of the imagery available. Then, in turn, the imagery modifies the narrative in a process that may take several iterations.

Television screenplay—The screenplay that will become the script for a one-hour television drama or a 30-minute situation comedy must conform to industry-standard formats. This is highly creative (and very lucrative) work that is equivalent to being a short-story writer or novelist. This type of writing requires considerable work and polish and is often done under a tight deadline (a typical modern sitcom may run 30 weekly episodes). For that reason, unlike most of the previous jobs on this list, television screenplays are usually team productions, with different writers taking on different scenes, subplots or characters under the discipline of a predetermined plot structure—the pieces then being glued together by a producer.

Film screenplay—Writing for film is the most esteemed form of screenwriting. As with novels, this work is high-risk/high reward. The odds against any movie screenplay being optioned, much less produced, are astronomical. That is all the more reason to learn your craft, follow the rules (that is, formatting), and polish your dialog until it shines. There also are a number of external factors that come into play with films (and, to a lesser degree, television) including registering your screenplay with the Screenwriters Guild, obtaining a copyright, hiring an agent and working your contact list (which, in the case of motion pictures, usually means moving to Los Angeles).

What makes screenwriting different?

It is time-disciplined—Almost every form of screenplay, from the television interstitial to the theatrical film script operates under a clock—from, say, ten seconds for the former to the standard 120-minute running time of the typical movie. And because the narration or performance is created out of language, screenplays must by necessity deal with word counts that are much smaller than other media such as nonfiction books and novels. This demands considerable discipline—which can be seen as either a strength of the form or a compromise.

It is performer-disciplined—The content must be delivered by someone: an anchor, announcer, performer, and so forth. And so, though the words may be powerful, they typically cannot overcome the limitations of these performers; conversely, a great speaker or actor can take even weak writing and invest it with a power it otherwise might not deserve. It is important then to understand the strengths or weaknesses of the performer or narrative involved with a project and modify your text to their best advantage.

Imagery (or sound) comes first—The highly successful screenwriter and novelist Niven Busch ("Duel in the Sun") once explained to the author that "writing for the movies isn't that tough. All you need to do is to write as if you can only stare through the camera lens—you see only what the camera sees." This was his way of saying that you write to the pictures, or the soundtrack. Otherwise, you will spend too much time explaining what isn't seen, and you will lose your audience's attention. Save your explaining for those things that can't be seen, but *must* be understood, by the audience.

It is format-disciplined—Radio is audio only. Television is mostly restricted by budget; movies by presentation time. In other words, you cannot ask a radio audience to look at pictures, produce a $250 million television miniseries, or ask filmgoers to sit through a 20-hour movie. If you want to sell your work, you will have to write to those limitations.

Dialog takes precedence over narrative—Over and over in this textbook it has been noted that we human beings prefer the human voice over prose. Nowhere is this more the case than in radio, television and film. That's why even documentaries will use interviews with participants—or experts— whenever possible, instead of the voice of a narrator.

It is cost disciplined—Television is expensive: even a documentary or news show will cost several hundred thousand dollars an hour to produce at the national level. Movies are immensely expensive, with even "low budget" independent films costing several million dollars to produce—and studio blockbusters hundreds of millions. Even radio, while comparatively cheap, still can require millions of dollars in capital expenditures for the construction and upkeep of production and transmission equipment. The calculus of revenues versus operational overhead and operating expenses determines just how much these different media can invest into new productions. The easiest way to get turned down by one of these platforms is to pitch a project that doesn't fit with its budget model.

Screenwriting tricks

Buy screenwriting software—Even if you know how to format a screenplay, having to do so manually, even on a computer, is a miserable experience with constant shifts in margins and justifications. That's why it is recommended that you use screenwriting software—either commercial versions (typically under $100) or popular freeware versions. Both can be downloaded from the Web. The best of these programs will not only automatically format the page as you type, but will also provide prompts and remember names.

Read your work—Screenplays are all about the spoken word. So why would you write a screenplay without reading it aloud to hear how it sounds? Listen for the music of your words. If you run out of breath in a sentence, cut it in two. If it sounds choppy, bolt sentences together. And if it doesn't sound authentic, be ruthless; rewrite it.

Radio: paint a mental picture—Radio, because it must rely on a single sense, must make an extra effort to play to that sense. It is not enough to simply report the news; the writing must convey a fully rounded experience of the event. This is done with background sound and evocative writing.

TV, film: show, don't tell—Again, screenplays for the visual media should be written to see through the camera's eye, with narrative enhancing that vision. You can add more content through other means, including titles and graphics. But beware of trying to stuff too much information onto the screen—you can overwhelm the viewer.

Careers

There are a lot of different jobs in screenwriting, but they fall under a limited number of categories, most of them mutually exclusive. That is, it is hard to move from a job as an advertising copywriter to writing screenplays for the film industry. That said, skills learned in one of these fields—economic and vivid writing, skill with dialog, working in the script format—can give you an excellent start in another. We've already described most of these careers, but here's some added information on each:

Ad scriptwriter—This kind of work is typically open to an advertising professional who is already writing copy, as a lateral move that typically begins with limited work and expands to take on longer formats. A degree in advertising is a good start, but it very much helps to have taken some screenwriting courses along the way.

Radio announcer—Radio announcing work is often given to reporters who show an interest in the work. Happily, the same skills that are valued in radio reporting are useful in writing announcements. As scriptwriters often are expected to do their own recording, a good voice—that is, even better than the normal radio voice—is valuable.

Reporter—Television and radio reporters typically learn their craft in two ways—in college broadcasting courses (including working for campus stations) and during the long apprenticeship climbing the ranks from small local stations to large regional and national stations.

Editor—Because of the nature of the work, a radio or television editor usually does more writing than their print counterparts. This is because most station reporters are sent out into the field to cover stories, leaving editors to prepare much of the copy derived from wire service stories and other sources.

Producer—The title of "producer" is shared by two groups in this world: (a) individuals who organize and manage the resources for the creation of a television series or motion picture, and (b) the editor/writer of a news documentary or feature segment. The latter producer is of interest here: this work not only requires a considerable amount of writing, but writing of a very high quality. Producers often combine training in broadcasting or communications with an education in literature or creative writing.

Screenwriter—As history has shown, anyone can write a movie screenplay. But just because the door is open doesn't mean many newcomers are invited in. You need a great plot, strong dialog and interesting characters—and an understanding of how to organize all that into the limitations of time and format. Most of all, you need patience; because with few exceptions, you are going to write a lot of screenplays before you sell, or option, your first screenplay. So, though it isn't necessary, a university-level education in writing can be very helpful.

Script doctor—This is a rare, but extremely lucrative, career reserved for writers who have already created successful screenplays and whose skills are in demand to "fix" other screenwriters' works. It is a long road to become this professional, and few (if any) writers start out their careers with this job as their goal. Still, it is not a bad destination if you can keep your ego at bay.

Turning points

Screenwriting, even more the fiction side than the news-reporting side, can be a very volatile career. You can be a nobody one day and a star the next and a nobody the day after that. And if the rewards can be great, the losses just as great—and averaged out over time can prove to be no more remunerative than a less-glamorous writing career. You can find turning points for news screenwriting careers in the chapters dedicated to reporting. Here we'll focus on fiction work:

Failure—The chances of selling a movie or television series screenplay are even worse than for a novel. That means that even if your work is good you are still likely to be rejected. Indeed, it sometimes can seem as if quality doesn't matter when dealing with Hollywood—or at least it takes a back seat to industry connections, experience and luck.

Age—Television and film, like pop music, is mostly for the young. Thus, even veteran screenwriters, after long and successful careers, can find themselves left behind by the twists and turns of cultural change. And there is little remedy for it.

The hit production and its consequences—Success is its own threat. There is so much fame (at least within the industry) and money that comes from the successful sale of a major film or television series screenplay that it can distort your life. Expectations for the next screenplay will be raised, fortunes will be offered for you to take on second-rate projects and the new wealth itself will be a challenge. This may seem like a welcome burden to bear; but hold your judgment until you actually experience it.

You run out of stories—Writing a novel can take years out of your life; a movie screenplay can be completed in weeks, even days. That difference can make you exceedingly productive—but it can also mean that you run through story ideas quickly. If you are not adept at converting news events from the outside world into new and original storylines your screenwriting career will end early.

Playwriting

You can think of playwriting as screenwriting in a box. You can't call forth thousands of extras or spend fortunes on computerized special effects or relocate to exotic locales. All you have is a stage, a simple set or two, and actors that you need to give words as they move across that stage.

This may sound deeply limiting—and in fact, it is. But as any veteran painter will tell you, the discipline of narrowing the number of colors in your palette actually can lead to the creation of better and more-vivid work. Also, for the writer, working on a play can be a much more hands-on and personally rewarding experience: the playwright is much more welcome in the theater than the screenwriter is on the film set.

What is playwriting?

The simplest explanation is the creation of a dramatic narrative to be performed by actors on stage. Plays can be dramatic, tragic, comedic or musical, and can take on almost any facet of human existence—past, present, or future—as its subject is limited only by the playwright's ability to evoke imagery in the audience's imagination.

Types of playwriting

Because they are innately abstract, plays take only a small number of forms—and most of those differences are peripheral. But also, because they depend upon the audience's imagination, the potential content of plays is all but infinite.

Amateur and equity—This is one of those peripheral factors: in this case, dealing with the nature of the performers. Amateur productions—plays performed in schools, by local theatrical groups—are distinguished by the fact the actors work without pay. By comparison, equity—registered—actors *must* be paid. It would be easy to assume that plays by professional performers will be "better" than those featuring amateurs. But experience shows that this isn't always the case. So, don't prejudge the venue in which your work will appear.

Tragedy, comedy and melodrama—As has been often noted, tragedy and comedy are two sides of the same coin—often the only difference is one of perspective—while melodrama (also called tragicomedy, the modern "dramedy", or simply "drama") is a hybrid of the two. That said, television has made these dramatic forms seem far more simple than they really are. The great teacher of this is, of course, Shakespeare, and any budding playwright would be well-advised to read his plays closely—not just for their style and plots, but also for the depth of the Bard's understanding of human nature. That said, you must go back to the Greeks for the original definitions of both tragedy and comedy, and those definitions are not only not simple, but are even paradoxical. Thus, tragedy is a tale of human suffering designed to produce a catharsis, or pleasure, in the audience. Thus, in a weird way, the sufferings of Lear or Hamlet or Willy Loman are designed to uplift us. And, it is not unusual, by this definition, for tragedy to make us laugh.

Conversely, comedy was defined as a conflict between two dissimilar (power, age, culture) groups that results in enlightenment and amusement for the audience. In other words, a traditional comedy can also make us, briefly, cry or grow angry. Consider Shakespeare's *The Winter's Tale* which, to modern audiences, is dark, intense and deeply disturbing for three acts, resolved only by an "amusing" final act. Yet, it is classified as one of Shakespeare's comedies.

This is not to suggest that, as a playwright, you should follow the old rules, but as a reminder that your play doesn't have to be purely tragic or a string of jokes (the title of one of the darkest American tragedies—O'Neil's *The Iceman Cometh*—is actually the punchline to a dirty joke). And that the greatest plays ever written often contain bits of both.

Musical—Musicals, usually comedies but occasionally tragedies and melodramas, are essentially plays with songs. But the reality, particularly the process of creation, is much more complex. In practice, the "book"—the story—of a musical is usually written by a professional playwright, while the music is composed by a professional composer. Making things even more complicated, the lyrics may be written by yet another writer, the lyricist. Usually, the book comes first, but there are musicals created around a collection of pre-existing songs.

What this means is that unless you have a rare talent in multiple creative disciplines—Meredith Wilson, for example, wrote all of "The Music Man" (with assistance on the original story)—at the very least you are going to have to find a composer to work with you. And if you are not experienced at songwriting, you are going to need to find a good lyricist, too.

That doesn't mean that if you have the bug you shouldn't try your hand at writing a musical—they are among the most-beloved artistic creations in modern life.

Live or filmed—This isn't a big deal, but you should know about it. A play is a live event seen from the front of the stage (or nearly so, from the balcony). But the film/video of a play is a recorded event that can be shot in shorter segments, and from the best camera angles, to produce the most impressive result. Make no mistake: a filmed play is still a play, with a play's physical limitations. It is not a movie. But filming does allow you to "blow out the walls" of the live play to include added footage, long shots, limited effects (if you have the budget) and so forth. In other words, you can go a little ways down the path to actually selling your play to the film industry for a full-blown movie production

It is almost always a mistake to write a play with one eye to it being filmed—this approach usually distorts the staging. But it can't hurt to keep this other potential opportunity in the back of your mind.

What makes playwriting different?

Think of playwriting as a more extreme form of screenwriting. It is almost completely dialog driven. Personality and character must be presented almost completely in the interaction of a character with other characters. Context and setting, beyond a few words in the program, must also be explained by dialog. Unlike film, where there is an army of performers, camera operators, editors, special-effects firms, hundreds of extras, and so forth to back you up, on stage it comes down to your words and the skills of a handful of actors. It is limiting, but also liberating.

One of the most surreal experiences in the life of the author of this textbook took place years ago when my play about railroad hobos received an equity production. With my young son, I drove down to the theater in San Jose, California, on a misty winter evening. As I drove up to the darkened theater—and its even darker parking lot—I was astonished to find the lot crowded with men in their late twenties, all scruffily dressed, and wandering about in the darkness. It got even stranger when I pulled into a parking slot—and heard a muttering sound. When I rolled down the window, the muttering turned into a score of voices: the men were all talking to themselves. It took several moments before I realized that the ghostly figures were reciting the lines I'd written months before.

They were there to audition for my play.

Stagecraft—The stage and the theater around it are not like the real world. Veteran playwrights know this and write their plays to recognize—even take advantage of—that fact. Neophytes often fail to understand this, and as a result their plays are more stilted, and less magical, than they need to be. The audience's experience in the theater should be one of stepping outside of everyday reality, where the suspension of disbelief never occurs: "Wait a second: this isn't really the battle of Agincourt, it's just a dozen actors on a plywood stage." This is accomplished by a deep understanding of the movement of actors in relation to each other and the set, careful management of the traffic of the actors on and off stage, pacing of the plot and, most of all, careful editing of dialog for the maximum impact in a live setting.

Limited visual support—To repeat: by its nature, the physical support of a play is necessarily limited. Even the most elaborate sets—like those found with opera (which are essentially "sung plays")—are still inferior to the outside, natural, world that can be captured in movies or on television. That said, a well-designed set—take the frame of the house in *Death of a Salesman*—can be profoundly evocative as it universalizes the audience's experience, rather than restricting it with details.

Blocking—The phrase *blocking* and *tackling* is from American football and describe the attention that must be paid to the basics of the sport before you can turn that attention to more advanced skills. But "blocking" is also a theatrical term for the task of the director working out how to move the actors around the stage for the best sightlines and greatest dramatic effect, key the lighting, determine the "traffic" patterns of entrances and exits by the actors so they don't have to run around behind the curtain or so they can have the time to change costumes or stop by the prop table. Blocking is the choreography of the stage.

As a playwright, you can help this process by thinking about it in advance. For example, you can't have an actor exit stage left, then reappear a few moments later at stage right in a different costume. Ultimately, being a traffic cop isn't your job—it is the director's—but if you want your play to be performed in a lot of places by a lot of acting companies, both equity and amateur, it can only help for it to have a reputation for being easy to stage.

Key success factors

If you are a writer, especially a fiction writer, you owe it to yourself to write at least one play—for the experience, for the practice in writing dialog, for the feel of a live audience and just for fun. Here are some things you can do to make the experience successful.

Practice, practice, practice—That's the punchline to the old joke about the tourist asking for directions: "How do you get to Carnegie Hall?" We assume that actors need to endlessly practice their lines and go through exhaustive rehearsals. But, by the same token, if you want to be a playwright chances are very slim that you will create a performable play on your first attempt. More likely, you will write several plays, none of which is performable in itself, but pieces from all of them may end up in a viable subsequent work. Playwriting is harder than it looks—and the only apprenticeship is actually writing plays, polishing them and, if you are lucky, getting them performed so you can see their flaws in performance. That means you will need a lot of patience.

Read-throughs—Even if you can't get your play performed, you can still get together a group of your friends (preferably actors) and do a reading. This is a great way to hear how your work sounds. Meanwhile, if your play does get produced, there will inevitably be read-throughs by the cast. If you can, you should sit in—with a copy of the play in hand—to make edits and rewrites on the fly.

Be able to adapt to cast, stage, audience—Like every novel, story or poem every play needs revisions and edits. But with plays, it goes beyond that: you should also be prepared to (slightly) modify your play for variations in the performance style of different actors and actresses cast in the same roles, and for the nature of the theater and stage (Are the wings narrow? Does the stage project into the audience? Will the performance be miked? And so forth). You may object that this compromises the purity of creation by pandering to the audience—and you are right. You can remind yourself of that purity when you put your unpublished play on the top shelf in your closet. Remember: a play has no value if no one ever sees it. So, improve your odds however you can.

EXAMPLE: A television screenplay. Note the minimum of instructions (directors will make those choices and include them in the "shooting script.") Also note the rigorous formatting: that's why you need to use screenwriting software.

6.

                    ANNIE
          You're going to remind me of the
          sacrifices it takes to be a
          successful entrepreneur. You're
          becoming *that* guy. And I can't
          handle that guy again.

                    LARRY
          Come on Annie, that's not fair.

Annie wipes her mouth with her napkin, then throws it on her plate and storms out of the room.

                    LARRY
          Annie, honey, please.

She storms back in. Not to see him, but to collect the bottle of wine and her glass. She heads back out.

IN THE LIVING ROOM

Larry, sunk down into a couch, legs up on an ottoman, laptop on his lap and work papers beside him on the coffee table, robotically flipping channels on the giant TV with the sound off.

ON TV

A crocodile launches out of some water and chomps down on a drinking wildebeest.

Channel changes.

An old Western with a white-hat and a black-hat duelling on Main Street.

ON LARRY

Barely lifting his arm with the remote, he flips to another channel. And then another.

Annie appears in the doorway, scintillating in her nighty and holding a bottle of champagne with two glasses.

She sits on the couch, takes the remote out of his hand, sets it aside and curls up against him.

                    ANNIE
          There may be 83 other drone
          companies...

                    LARRY
          ...In the LA Basin alone.

Fiction Writer and Novelist

What is fiction writing?

The creation of literary material, in one of many formats, based upon an imaginative construction of events, not directly from actual events.

Why do we need fiction?

Because real life, despite its extraordinary range, is often too messy, complex and undirected to present us with a coherent story that can amuse, challenge, ennoble, frighten and educate us the way carefully constructed imaginative fiction can.

Why does fiction seem so different?

No field of writing is more enveloped in myth than fiction: especially short stories, novellas, and most of all, novels. Even people who make their living writing nonfiction can find themselves intimidated by the prospect of creating fiction—to the point that they invest the process with a kind of magic. It is as if every other kind of writing is professional work, while fiction is an incantation: one apparently in which you wait for the Muse to appear and whisper great plots and dialog into your ear.

Part of the problem is that "literature" is considered an art form; while every other kind of writing is considered merely a professional activity, like journalism. Interestingly, we recognize that being a musician or a visual artist also requires creative inspiration, but also a whole lot of preparation and craftsmanship, proficiency with tools and materials, and a ton of work. Yet, somehow, fiction writing is seen only as genius and inspiration.

Here's the truth: *creating fiction is just writing*. It may have a strong creative component, but to one degree or another so does every other kind of writing, from creating a compelling press release to authoring a top-notch feature story. The fundamental difference is that fiction writing involves the creation of an alternative reality (setting or mis en scène) in which your subjects (characters) move through a storyline (plot). Creating those three characteristics is where talent comes in, but just about anyone with discipline and the right training can write a short story, even a novel. Of course, the quality of the result will vary.

Everything else is craft. Vocabulary, sentence construction, continuity, pacing, and all the other components of every type of writing. Take a sentence out of context from a speech, a corporate newsletter or a famous novel—and you probably can't tell which belongs where.

In fact, the sentence from the novel may be the worst written of the three. That's because many novelists aren't, in fact, very good writers craft-wise—and they overcome that weakness by being very good at the other parts of fiction. And there are some great novelists who are so good at just one part of the process—such as a plot that pulls you along, or an unforgettable lead character—that you overlook the fact they are lousy at almost everything else. But even that's not unique to fiction: think of how many nonfiction articles or essays you've read that held your interest despite awkward or turgid prose because of the story or the message.

The message of all of this is that if you are a writer you can be a novelist. The actual mechanics of the process of writing a novel already are within your skill set. As for the other factors, they are mostly a matter of practice: you need to write fiction—a lot of fiction—if you are going to be good at it. In fact (brace yourself) it is very likely that the first novel you write, the one you spent months on, composing tens of thousands of words, you will throw out. The key is not to think of it as a failure, that you are unworthy of being a fiction writer, but as your *apprenticeship.*

It's no different than pitching a bunch of feature stories and getting them rejected: you would rightly consider that learning your craft. So why consider your first novel to be any different? Just pay your dues and get on with it. If you're lucky you'll sell your first novel—something that is a lot easier to do in this age of regional presses and e-books. But even if you don't, don't give up. Keep writing.

Part of the problem facing new novelist might be described as *limited perception of the profession.* Most of the older fiction we read is the product of a winnowing process: we only read what survives—that is, the very best or most popular novels. The rest disappear down the memory hole. If you managed to dig out those forgotten novels you'd have a much better idea of the range of quality in newly published novels at any given time, and you wouldn't be intimidated. Instead, in school you only read the masterpieces, giving you a very skewed idea of the profession.

A second limitation is that few outsiders have any real idea of the actual process of writing a novel. Just as mathematicians often work backwards and forwards, and even follow hunches, in developing a proof—and then clean it up to erase all their missteps—so too do novelists like to treat their *finished* work as if it sprang fully formed from their imaginations. You see the polished author being interviewed on television, not the author in a pair of baggy and stained sweatpants shuffling down the hall to the home office and slurping cereal as they write. You also see the finished book, not the messy manuscript that several editors and friends tore apart several times because it was all but unreadable. If you could see all of that, you wouldn't be intimidated by other novelists.

One more note. Steve Jobs of Apple Inc. famously said: *Real artists ship*. He was talking about code writers, but his comment works equally well with word writers. The worst thing you can do as a novelist is to unilaterally decide that your novel isn't good enough. There are closets all over the world with nearly finished novels slowly yellowing on top shelves because their authors gave up. And those stacks of pages are still there because those authors still regret their failure.

There is no reason for you to join their ranks, especially not in the 21st century, when there are so many ways to publish. No, the biggest reason these days for not being published is *fear*. That their work isn't good enough. That the world will laugh at their creation. That they won't live up to the expectations created by years of telling people about the great novel they're writing. That the image they've carefully cultivated of being creative, and an artist, is *fake*.

That is the biggest difference between writing nonfiction and fiction: the latter takes real *bravery*. Write a nonfiction book and a bad review or two can be depressing; but after all, it's just your work. But write a novel to the same response, and it can feel like a judgment on your worth as a person; on your character; on what you thought was your life's purpose. Getting through that experience—and then starting your next novel—takes courage.

That, not talent or even discipline, is the real test of becoming a novelist. And if you have the guts to stick with it, you will succeed in becoming one. On the other hand, no matter how good that manuscript is in your closet— and it could be great—it won't matter. Because *real novelists publish*.

Types of fiction writing

There are more forms of fiction than we normally include in the genre. But if we throw a net out to include all kinds of imaginative writing, the list is very diverse.

Poetry—We discuss this genre elsewhere, but note here that it includes:

- Haiku
- Sonnet
- Ode
- Heroic verse
- Epic

And all the subgenres of form, style and meter therein.

Ficciones and flash fiction—This type of writing—short, highly imaginative, surreal, philosophical—is normally equated with the work of Jorge Luis Borges. Flash fiction (also called short stories) are works of fiction, usually less than 1,000 words that are nevertheless complete stories—often with shocking endings.

Yarns and Storytelling—This genre is among the oldest form of human communications and includes myths, tall-tales, amusing anecdotes, scary stories, heroic legends. Though they can be deeply serious and instructional, they are just as likely to be brief and humorous.

Jokes and Riddles—This type of fiction is also very old, though it is rare that a joke or riddle popular in one era will remain equally humorous or interesting in the next. Both forms are typically short, with a surprise punchline or solution designed to delight.

Short story—A form of fiction that derives from early storytelling that has a long and venerated history of its own. Short stories are rarely more than 5,000 words in length, differing from longer fiction forms by normally focusing upon a single plot line, limited characters and few scene changes. The greatest short stories are among the modern world's greatest intellectual creations.

Novella—The novella is a hybrid format, longer than a short story, but shorter than a novel (hence the name), and that is usually how it is created: beginning as one form and either growing too long or finishing too short. This is not to diminish the value of the novella; among the greatest literary creations in history—Tolstoi's "The Death of Ivan Illyich," Mann's "Death in Venice," Solzhenitsyn's "A Day in the Life of Ivan Denisovitch"—are in the form of novellas. Like the novel, the novella can allow for subplots and multiple characters, but works with a smaller palette (though no less complexity) than the novel.

Graphic novels—Graphic novels are essentially a hybrid between the novella and the comic book. Like the former, graphic novels are written for a sophisticated reading audience that is interested in experimental writing, mature plots and a powerful, even transgressive language and dialog. Like the latter, comic books, this writing is at the service of illustrations—again, many of them edgy and experimental. Though some graphic novelists do both the writing and illustration, some of the most famous graphic novels (*Watchmen, Dark Knight*) are collaborations between top-notch writers and illustrators.

Novel—The queen of fiction, the novel achieved its true form after several thousand years of development across multiple genres. It has remained in its supreme position in the human imagination because it is a supple format, able to deal not only with almost every possible plot, but also adaptive enough to evolve with human culture and technology. The novel emerged in the preindustrial, pastoral world and survives today in the world of the Internet, artificial intelligence and the global economy. We will look at the novel and its creation in a special section at the end of this chapter.

A brief history of fiction writing

The creation of fiction is older than written language—indeed, it may be older than *spoken* language. It is very possible that Neanderthal man, unable to enunciate words, may have acted out for family or tribe members the memory of a past hunt. Early modern man developed an extensive oral tradition of stories, myths and legends, much of it performed by shamans in mystical ceremonies. With the arrival of language, many of these stories made the transition into actual written forms. These written stories from the birth of writing are mankind's cultural patrimony from which all modern fiction is the descendant.

Here is a brief history of the modern novel and its antecedents, with some of the best-known examples.

Roots in the Epic Tradition—The form and style of modern fiction was born in extended oral epic poems and narratives, among them the "world's oldest story," the 6,000-year-old Sumerian epic poem, *Gilgamesh*, which contains many fiction elements still used by writers today. This epic tradition continued for Millennia and is still attempted today—often adopted by different civilizations as their national origin stories.

The Iliad and The Odyssey	The Aeneid	Beowulf
Sir Gawain and the Green Knight	The Faerie Queen	The Song of Roland
Arabian Nights	Bhagavad Gita	Shakespeare's Plays
Pan Tadeusz	The Sienkiewicz	Trilogy

Roots in religious tradition—Religious texts are not only an important source of stories, but those stories also become freighted with the power and duty of faith. We distinguish here between epic verse and religious text by whether they place esthetics before or after religious and moral lessons. Thus, most of the works described in the epic tradition are more about the plot; those in this section give precedence to religion.

Old Testament	New Testament	*Pilgrim's Progress*
Paradise Lost	Medieval Passion Plays	Augustine's Confessions

The Birth of the Novel—The earliest fictional narratives that can be described as "proto-novels" appear in the late Renaissance and early Enlightenment. Structurally, they retain some of the features of epic poems (no distinct story arc, tangential plots, inconclusive endings, and so forth), but their sensibility (a figure undergoing a profound change against a distinct landscape, consistent point of view, complex protagonist and antagonist) is distinctly modern. Unlike the often superhuman or divine characters in previous works, the reader can identify with the characters in these works—which makes them as readable today as then.

Don Quixote	Pamela (Richardson)	Candide
Gulliver's Travels	Robinson Crusoe	Tristram Shandy
Tom Jones	Moll Flanders	The Tale of Genji

Modern Novels/Nineteenth Century—This is the era in which the novel truly comes into its own, in a form that is still in its use today. A strong argument can be made that the nineteenth century represented the greatest era for novels—combining worldly (as opposed to academic) authors, complex social structures (including an aristocracy) and a readership not distracted by other media. Some of these novels will likely endure as long as there are human beings. [For the remaining sections, we will list by author name.]

Jane Austen	George Eliot	William Makepeace Thackeray
Anthony Trollope	Charles Dickens	Walter Scott
Robert Louis Stevenson	Oscar Wilde	Rudyard Kipling
Honore de Balzac	Alexander Dumas, father and son	Stendhal (Marie-Henri Beyle)
Gustave Flaubert	Emile Zola	Benito Galdos
Friedrich Nietzsche	Johann Goethe	Anton Chekov

James Fenimore Cooper	Nathaniel Hawthorne	Herman Melville
Mark Twain	Stephen Crane	Henry James
Fyodor Dostoyevsky	Ivan Turgenev	Leo Tolstoi

Rise and fall/Twentieth century—The twentieth century, thanks to improvements in printing technology, mass marketing and distribution, saw an explosion in novel writing. In the United States alone, perhaps 100,000 novels were being written each year by century's end, with perhaps 10 percent of that number being released by publishers large and small. That was the good news; the bad was that the novel, a static medium, was increasingly challenged by more dynamic media, including radio, television and the Internet. While at mid-century novelists were major figures in the cultural life of a nation, their latest works discussed by the entire intellectual world, by the turn of the twenty-first century, novels and novelists had been largely eclipsed by other forms of creative content. And while novels still sold in vast numbers, many talented writers had moved on to those other platforms. Here is quick list of some of the most important twentieth century novelists.

Rudyard Kipling	Thomas Mann	Andre Gide	Thomas Hardy
Jack London	Theodore Dreiser	Ernest Hemingway	William Faulkner
F. Scott	D. H. Lawrence	Virginia Woolf	E.M. Forster
James Joyce	Marcel Proust	Andre Malraux	Jean-Paul Sartre
Albert Camus	Aleksandr Solzenitsyn	Giuseppe di Lampedusa	Mikhail Bulgakov
Saul Bellow	Gunter Grass	Naguib Mafouz	Graham Greene
Gabriel Garcia Marquez	Toni Morrison Thomas Pynchon J.D. Salinger	Philip Roth	John Updike
Yasunari Kawabata	Abe Kobo	Vladimir Nabokov	Franz Kafka
J.R.R Tolkien	Philip K. Dick		

Types of modern novel

In part because of a desire by novelists to escape the heavy shadow of their famous predecessors, and in part because of the opportunity presented by a diverse and universally literate audience, the world of novels in the twentieth century fractured into scores of genres and subgenres. And, as each found its audience, those genres fractured again. With low-cost publishing, Web-based distribution and a growing number of MFA and

Creative Writing programs, that process is likely to continue throughout the twenty-first century as well. Here is a brief list of some of the dominant genres in modern fiction.

Literary
Mystery–Detective
Postmodern
Science Fiction
Fantasy
Historical
Horror
Multimedia
Graphic
Romance
Political
Experimental

Fiction writing careers

Writing fiction isn't just novels and short stories. Any kind of imaginative writing that isn't a precise reflection of real events is, to some degree, fiction. Here's a list of careers that can be characterized as "fiction writing." We address most of them elsewhere in the book; for our purposes here just recognize the breadth of this type of work—some of which pay very, very well.

Joke Writer
Screenwriter
Humorist
Stand-up comic
Romance Novelist
Science Fiction Writer
Novelist
Poet
Monologist
Dramatist-Playwright

Career: The good

- Being a fiction writer is the greatest career imaginable—with the potential for money, fame, respect and admiration, and a chance at near-immortality.
- You get to live your own life, use your imagination to its fullest on a daily basis, and do not have to answer to a boss.

- When someone asks what you do for a living, even if you are broke and currently living in your car, you get to say, "I'm a novelist."

Career: The bad

- Making a career as a fiction writer requires considerable talent (though not as much as you may imagine) and a lot of work (a lot more than you imagine).
- The various fields are all highly competitive, and your counterparts can be pretty ruthless. Everybody, it seems, wants to be a famous novelist—and there's probably only a dozen slots available for every million dreamers.
- It's very hard to make a living as a fiction writer. If you make it to the top as a novelist or playwright there are a lot of riches available in the form of royalties, speaking fees, grants, and so forth. For everybody else, it is a desperate struggle.
- In the face of those odds, you will likely give up and return to the real world of real jobs, disappointed and having lost valuable time.

Turning points

- When you are starving and decide you cannot fight the good fight anymore and give up.
- When you publish that first novel that gets blistering reviews and you are forced to take stock of your future.
- When you are successful, and the world moves on, with a younger generation stealing the attention that used to be yours.

The craft of fiction writing

Getting set up—There is a tendency, when a plot or character captures your imagination, to just start writing in a creative fever. Sometimes that can be successful with a short story—but rarely even then. And it is a terrible strategy when writing a novel. A novel is not a sprint, but a marathon. You need to plan ahead and pace yourself. Rush into a novel and you are likely to have to retrace your steps because you run into problems of logic and continuity that must be fixed—and can stop you dead. And even if you do manage to fix those problems on the fly, you are still going to burn out at some point.

Instead, think before you start. You don't need to outline every step in your plot and every nuance of character and setting, but at least have a good idea of all those things so there aren't any big holes anywhere. And you don't have to have the perfect ending yet, but at least have an idea of an ending to your novel.

1. *Find your story*—Get in the habit of making up plots. Do it all the time in your head. You are a storyteller, this is what you do; so, strengthen that muscle.

   a. *Start with the germ of an idea*—Something you've read or seen or heard. It might be a news story, an incident from your family's history, an anecdote someone has told you, and so forth.

   b. *Extrapolate that idea into a larger story*—There is no rule that says you must adhere to the original story. In fact, it is usually better if you don't. Real life isn't neat, and events don't fit into a distinct plot but are embedded into the rest of life. Fiction has a beginning, middle and end; it has a structure; and it has meaning. This is as true for the literary anecdote as it is for the novel. If you don't have those things, the story you are devising isn't complete.

   c. *Look for logical holes*—Go through your story line, think about your characters, examine the world you are creating. Are they real? Are they internally consistent—even fantasy must have an internal logic. Characters are allowed to have contradictions—that's real life—but their dominant traits must be aligned to the plot. As for the setting: can you imagine yourself living in that world?

   d. *Find alternatives and move on*—If you do find logical holes, develop some work-arounds. Sometimes these inconsistencies will resolve themselves as you write, but don't trust that to luck—plan ahead. Try to solve all your big problems in advance.

   e. *Don't sweat the little stuff*—If you've solved the big problems with plot, character and setting, move on. The little things—the color of the protagonist's hair, the details of the village in which the story takes place—you can resolve when you get to them. Don't let the little stuff stop you from getting to work—or worse, don't let it become an excuse for not getting to work.

   f. *Be critical of yourself*—Try not to fall in love with every story you come up with, but if you do fall in love that may be a good sign to write that one. Even if you have developed the complete narrative of a novel, challenge yourself before you begin. Ask yourself: Is this the story I want to spend hundreds of hours on over the next six months? If not, trust that you will come up with other, maybe better, ideas.

2. *Write down a brief plot summary*—This summary does not need to be long, just a couple of pages. But set down key turning points before you forget them—remember: you may not get to them for months. If you want to describe key characters or the setting, write that down,

too. See if the story you've just written still looks good on paper. Add to the summary as new ideas come to you. Finally, only use this summary as a reminder; if the demands of the story change as you write it, go with that new trajectory.

3. *Keep notes*—Keep a notebook and pen nearby at all times—in your car, on your desk, on your nightstand. When you are inspired, write down any scenes or bits of dialog or story that come to you. Don't assume that you will remember them—you won't, and you'll have to replace them with other writing that never seems as good. And don't put off writing those notes—even if they pop into your brain at 3 a.m., or at a stoplight or during dinner—they'll disappear with the next distraction. As you write the novel, keep those notes nearby, organized in the order of the plot, and don't forget to regularly refer to them so you don't overlook them.

The writing process

As has been repeated throughout this textbook, writing is writing; a sentence written for a press release is the same as that written for a book. That said, there *are* some differences with fiction writing that have less to do with the words than with the actual writing process itself. In particular, fiction writing tends to be more intense and focused. That's not to say that nonfiction writing isn't that way, but it is usually a lot easier to stop writing, do something else, and then get back to writing. You also tend to go "deeper" creatively with fiction—and once you're on a roll you don't want to stop for fear of leaving that imaginative space.

Keeping that in mind, here are some suggestions for making the fiction writing experience easier and healthier. Some of these will be a repeat from the nonfiction book writing chapter. (Needless to say, you can use them for other types of writing as well).

A comfortable seat with back support. Get a good ergonomic chair that provides lumbar support and reinforces proper posture. Don't scrimp on price: you are going to be in that chair much of the new few years.

Proper keyboard and monitor position. Carpal tunnel syndrome is a writer's worst nightmare. When your wrist is screaming in pain it's hard to concentrate on your writing. Also, most writers purchase special keyboards (or buy laptops with quality keyboards) that are "positive tactile feedback'—they click when pressed—rather than touch keys. The former will improve your speed and accuracy. Writers, almost uniquely, wear out the tops of the keys before they wear out the rest of their computers.

Get up and walk around once per hour. This is for the same reason you get up and walk around on an airplane: circulation, the danger of blood clots, for long-term circulatory health. A novel will take you thousands of hours to write—so get up and move around.

Don't write too much in any give session (unless it's going easily). This one is tricky. The rule of thumb is to not write more than an hour or two on any given day. If you try to push yourself too much you will burn out or break down—and in the end write fewer total hours. That said, if the words are coming fast and you are afraid to stop, then push on. But the moment you lose that momentum, back away from the computer.

Try not to miss a single day, even if you only work a few minutes. Momentum is everything. If you are writing a work of fiction, don't stop daily sessions until you are done. If it is a short short story, then try to write it in one sitting. If a short story, in a matter of days. A novel: seven days per week for as long as it takes. There are several reasons for this. First, it enables you to stay on top of the plot; a few days off and you may forget entire twists and subplots. Continuity also helps you stay in close touch with your characters and their motivations. Finally, in the setting of your piece, you can remember how to navigate around.

Set a baseline standard for a typical day's session (say, 1,000 words). Writing a novella or novel is like writing a nonfiction book: it is a marathon, not a sprint. Find your pace and, whatever it is—500 words per day, 1,000 words per day—stick with it day after day. The goal is to finish the book in the same shape as you began. If you can't hit your daily mark, don't sweat it—and don't try to make up the lost ground the next day. If you push too hard you will pay for it later. On the other hand, if you set your pace and then make it a habit over the weeks and months, the act of completing your book will be surprisingly painless.

Get a sheet of paper, or whiteboard, or bulletin board and record or stick up all your notes. Most of the details of plot, character and setting can be kept in your head with shorter works; but with a novella or novel there is just too much to keep track of. So just as with a nonfiction book you organize your notes in an accessible way, with fiction you'll want to keep track of your story elements in a manner that's clear and ready at hand.

As new ideas come to you, write them down and put them up there, too. You'll never be able to come up with every detail of a book ahead of time. And even if you could, it's pretty rare for the book you finish to be precisely the book you planned when you started. New, and sometimes better, story directions will come to you as you progress along. These epiphanies can come to you at any time, and if you try to remember them you will be disappointed. So, write them down. Immediately; even if it's on tissue paper or the money in your wallet. Never assume you will remember later.

If you hit a wall, inch your way through. If you give stuck, or hit a logical conundrum while you are writing, don't quit—rather, slow down your writing and work it through the best you can. Then mark it and revisit it later. By then, your unconscious will probably have come up with a better solution.

Back up everything you write. Get an app for your computer that will automatically save everything your write, as you write, and in every draft. Your memory storage can be on the computer (worst choice), on a peripheral hard drive (better choice) or on the Cloud (best choice).

Don't let the writing get stalled by a word or term you are stuck on. Your goal should be to reach your daily quota of words. And sometimes that means powering through any obstacles the writing puts up before you. For example, you may get stuck on a word or fact or name—it's on the tip of your tongue—and you could probably find it if you put in enough time searching the Web. But doing so will also break your train of thought and cost you precious minutes or even that day's work. When that happens, just type in a "TK"—the editing term for "to come'—in place of the missing word and move on. Come back to it later and don't interrupt your work.

Narrative

Inhabit the world you are creating. If the place where your story or novel takes place isn't real in your mind, it won't be so to your readers either. Before you start writing, imagine it in detail; walk its streets, picture the buildings, landscape and inhabitants.

Visualize the major characters. Picture them in your mind. What is their appearance? How do they speak? How do they behave in everyday life? How will they act under stress? How do they interact with each other?

Understand the cultural and physical setting. What are the customs of the people in your story? How do they behave toward each other and toward outsiders? What is the climate like—temperate, torrid or frozen? What is the dominant religion? What is the history of the region? The ethnicity of the people?

Remember that the plot must be logical. The laws of physics, of causality and logic are universal in this corner of the universe. So, don't violate them—unless you specifically explain why those violations are taking place. Don't take causal leaps that are so great that your readers can't fill in the gaps. If you violate logic you will confuse your readers and risk losing them.

Editing

1. Don't let editing get in the way of writing. If you have to, write all the way through, then go back.

2. That said, try to edit as you create. Reread each sentence or paragraph quickly after you write it. Does it make sense? Read aloud in your head for continuity, for transitions and to check for run-on sentences. But keep writing.

3. When you've completed the piece, put it aside for a week or two, then return to it fresh, and with new eyes.

4. On your first pass at editing, read the work all the way through, concentrating on continuity, pacing and flow. Keep an eye for unexpected changes in the characters and their behavior, for plot holes and for contradictions in the surrounding "world.'

5. For later rounds of editing, set out a block of time to edit. Try to get a sizable chunk of the work done in each session to maintain continuity.

6. Priorities (in order of importance):

   Macro

   1. Overall theme—Is it coherent and consistent with the real world?
   2. Overall structure—Is it consistent?
   3. Does the text have a continuous, logical arc?
   4. Is the text complete in resolving all plot elements?
   5. Are the chapters internally logical?
   6. Do the chapters contribute to the overall arc of the narrative?
   7. Are the characters well-defined and consistent all the way through?
   8. Do they speak distinctly and in the same manner all the way through?
   9. Do your descriptions of settings and actions contradict themselves?

   Micro

   1. Use a red pen or pencil for visibility.
   2. Put check marks on the margin for location of edits.
   3. Circle your edits when possible.
   4. Look for noun–verb disagreements.
   5. Check capital nouns.
   6. Break up long paragraphs and long sentences.
   7. Write down separately the spellings of key character and place names—make sure they are consistent throughout the text.
   8. Kill exclamation points and clichés.
   9. Incorporate your edits and quickly read the entire text.
   10. Edit as you create. Reread each sentence or paragraph quickly after you write it. Does it make sense? If you do not know a fact—leave a "TK" designation to remind you to search for the

answer later. Read aloud in your head for continuity, transitions and to check for run-on sentences.

11. When completed, put it aside if you can. If under a tight deadline, then focus upon the lede, logic, quotes and spellings of names. If under a long deadline, put the work aside for a week or two, then return to it fresh and with new eyes.
12. If editing someone else, read the work all the way through.
13. Set out a block of time to edit, try to get a sizable chunk of the work done in each session to maintain continuity.

Other tricks

1. Develop some simple rituals to get you in the writing mood and shift the side of your brain in use to creative over empirical:
   a. Say aloud "fiction"—cognitive scientists have found that it works.
   b. Have a cup of tea or coffee while you think about the day's writing content.
   c. Shift location: designate a fiction writing place for yourself.
2. Launch a day's work by reading what you wrote the day before.
3. Force yourself to begin, even if you aren't happy with what you first write. Tell yourself that you can fix it later.
4. Leave each day's writing with a clue or a start to what you will write the next day.
5. If for some reason—and it better be a good reason—you miss a few days, or even weeks, read a longer section of what you've written to get your momentum back.
6. Don't sweat dialog—polish it later. Just get it down quickly, as if you are overhearing it.
7. If you finish a chapter and haven't done your word quota for the day, start the next chapter. Or, stop, but put down notes about how to start the new chapter. Never stretch out a chapter ending just to achieve your daily quota.
8. Don't spend too much time on description. That's what amateurs do; and it slows the narrative. Move on with the plot. You can fix descriptions later (and you probably won't want to.)
9. Keep reading other stuff while you are writing—even if it influences your writing, it'll probably be for the good.
10. Don't write drunk or high. You'll think you are a genius—but you won't be. Even famously alcoholic writers only wrote well when they were sober.
11. Stay healthy—eat well, get enough sleep. The months you spend on a book can be debilitating.

12. Don't tell other people you are writing a book. You may abandon it—and your embarrassment will make it harder to write the next one. Worse, your friends may press you to finish a book that you don't want to. Only tell everyone (other than your agent and editor) when you are done.
13. Celebrate the completion of your book. Have a party, buy yourself a gift, go out for a nice dinner. These moments only come along a few times in a life—enjoy them.
14. Real writers publish. You don't get to act like a writer until you are one.

Writing a novel

Finding the plot

The Plot is the Story—and a story has a beginning, middle and end—though not always in that order. A great plot forgives almost every other weakness in storytelling.

Do you need the plot before you start? Almost always. You need to know where you are going—even if you never get there. Here's what you need to do every time you write fiction:

1. Write out your plot, including the key turning points.
2. Keep it with you as you write.
3. Revise as needed.

The plot defines your narrative pace. Don't get in its way or get too far ahead.

In practice, the plot is both the spine and the orientation of the work. All fiction must have a direction: it must start somewhere and end somewhere, even if nothing happens. Joseph Heller's *Something Happened* is a book in which essentially nothing happens—nevertheless it has a shape and form and it exhibits momentum. Even the most experimental work has a plot of some kind, even if it is not immediately apparent.

Why do we have plots?

1. It is the nature of fiction to organize and simplify reality; so, in creating fiction we need an organizing principle to do this.
2. We are chordates and vertebrates, we're bipeds and we are bilaterally symmetrical—so we see the universe as balanced and meaningful, and as a series of paths to be taken. As intelligent creatures we also see life as a series of decisions based upon limited information. And as conscious animals, we try to approach reality by seeing in a detached,

omniscient way. We search for conclusions. And we try to organize and simplify reality in order to learn from it.

3. Time is linear, and it has direction. The world we experience is finite: it has a start, duration and end.

What constitutes a plot? It is a *record of change over time.*

Change requires *conflict*: physical, emotional, existential. A complete work of fiction requires the resolution of its defining conflict—that is, "Okay, so what finally happened?"

Traditional construction of a work of fiction:

Rising action

- Introduction/setting
- Introduce characters
- Establish status quo
- Introduce defining challenge
- Spin out conflict

Climax

- Resolution of that conflict
- Impact

Closure

- Aftermath/anticlimax

Conclusion/continuation

- Coda
- Postscript

Type of plots

Aristotle says in his *Poetics* there are two different "change types" and three different "character types." Of the change types, there is the *tragic plot*, which features a movement or change between good and bad fortune. That is: change that begins in good fortune and ends in bad fortune. His description of the second type, the *comedy plot*—change that begins in bad fortune and ends in good fortune, has been lost to history.

The three possible "character types" are the characters of "decent" people—people "outstanding in excellence and justice"; "evil people"; and the "in-between man."

Of the six logically possible outcomes, Aristotle lists only four. Aristotle contends in *Poetics 13* that the most desirable plot involves "An in-between person who changes from good to bad fortune, due to hamartia, or "tragic flaw." Ranked from worst to best by Aristotle, these are the four logical possibilities of pathos, or appeal to the emotions of the audience:

1. Pathos is about to be elicited from the audience, with its knowledge, but does not occur.
2. Pathos is about to be elicited, with the audience's knowledge.
3. Pathos is about to be elicited from the audience, which is ignorant.
4. Pathos is about to be elicited from the audience, which is ignorant, but does not occur.

Okay, so that's the classical view. A more modern view is that there is a finite number of story types that are spun out in an almost infinite number of ways. Here are some of the best known:

1. Boy meets girl, boy loses girl, boy regains girl.
2. The low raised up—late: justice served, early: hubris punished.
3. The high brought low—restored ever-wiser, or replaced by the more worthy.
4. A misunderstanding creates conflict.
5. A new arrival threatens the established order: marriage, family, community, group
6. A person leaves for an adventure, returns forever changed.
7. A miscommunication or accidental comment tears apart a relationship.
8. A successful person isn't who he or she seems.
9. A person tries to survive great events.
10. A tiny action or decision destroys everything.
11. An obsession ruins a character's life or achieves justice.
12. A bad person is redeemed by a good act.

When do you abandon a plot? When you realize that characters wouldn't do what you've planned for them. That's not an excuse to improvise, but a demand that you rewrite the rest of your plot.

Point of view

What is a point of view (POV)?

1. The position of the **narrator** in relation to the story, as indicated by the **narrator's** outlook from which the events are depicted and by the attitude toward the characters.

2. The lens through which the author allows the reader to see and hear what's going on in a created world.
3. The manner in which a story is narrated or depicted.

Point of view is not the piece's "style," nor is it the author's "voice"—though it may inform the nature of both.

Every work of art has a point of view—writing no less than others.

There are essentially four points of view: internal, inside out, outside in and external. We call these meditative, first person, third person and the Eye of God. To this we add two states of knowledge: limited and omniscient. Then, we can add two perspectives: objective and subjective. Finally, we can include two modifiers: trustworthy or untrustworthy.

If you know your combinatorics, that gives you 32 different points of view—though God is always omniscient and truthful, so that reduces the number to 30.

So, the question becomes: Which point of view should you select? The answer to that is: Whichever one works best—and by that I mean, which point of view best serves the style, the subject and, most of all, the purpose of your story. Which POV will yield the best aesthetic result?

There is a second, subordinate, but no less important question: Which point of view do you think you can pull off? That's not an idle question. As an author, can you maintain 250 pages of putting yourself inside the head of a nineteenth-century, planter class, white 14-year-old-girl? How about telling the story of a Roman legionnaire from the perspective of his charming, but sociopathic fellow soldier?

So, in the end you need to conduct a mental calculation—an equation that combines the best POV for the story with your ability to maintain that POV. And sometimes, you just have to make some compromises.

A simple test: when you devise your story, what POV do you take? That's probably the best one for you. That said, you should at least look at alternative POVs to see if they might be more effective or provide you with a more compelling challenge.

The natural POV most writers take is limited omniscience. Why? It enables you to move the whole story ahead while still maintaining a comparatively narrow perspective. It also keeps the eye steady—you pretty much stay with one person and do not jump around into other people's heads. You also, like the character, are unable to see far into the future—and thus the resolution can come as a surprise.

Advantages

First person—really flesh out the character, add mystery
Limited omniscience—natural human story-telling style

Omniscience—can have fun with different narratives, perspectives, and so forth

Limited palette—taking away things to force a discipline on the author that can be advantageous

Second person—very rare; disguised first person, makes the author and reader partners in the story.

Disadvantages

First person—limited view of what's going on; hard to describe anything

Limited omniscience—common, everybody does it, author needs to take command

Omniscience—too much distancing from the characters, loss of the randomness of real life

Limited palette—can make the work too insular and bland

Second person—odd, forced quality, reader may object to being told what he or she is doing or feeling.

Great first person—*Moby Dick*, *Huckleberry Finn*, Raymond Carver novels, most detective and crime novels, *Catcher in the Rye*.

Great limited omniscience—*Don Quixote*, every movie you've ever seen, most science fiction, most comic novels (*Confederacy of Dunces*).

Omniscience—giant novels: Dickens, *War and Peace*, *Gravity's Rainbow*.

Limited palette—*Pride and Prejudice*, Trollope's *Barchester* novels.

Second Person—best known is *Bright Lights, Big City*

Setting and mise-en-scène

Definition of mise-en-scène

1. *a*: the arrangement of actors and scenery on a stage for a theatrical production
   b: stage setting
2. *a*: the physical setting of an action (as of a narrative or a motion picture): context
   b: environment, milieu

What is a "setting" in fiction? The setting is where the story takes place. The setting can either serve as a backdrop or be an active agent in the story.

Setting can take many forms (and these can be mixed and matched):

1. A natural space—woods, ocean, outer space
2. A constructed space—city, town, classroom
3. A cultural or social space—church, shtetl, refugee camp, family home

4. A historical space—*Killer Angels* (Gettysburg), *Romeo and Juliet* (Verona)
5. A confined space—prison cell, hospital room (*One Flew Over the Cuckoo's Nest*)
6. A psychological space—mental illness, hallucinations (*Johnny Got His Gun, The Diving Bell and the Butterfly, I Never Promised you a Rose Garden*).

Setting changes with the narrative. It does so in two ways:

1. Externally—the setting can move to a new location.
2. Internally—the setting can be changed by events in a single location.

Advantages of a confined setting: More like drama. Minimal need for description, throws characters into a tight close-up, narrative focus, lends itself to allegory.

Disadvantages of a confined setting: Starkness, loss of the richness of existence, hard to move the action along because it is all self-generated by characters.

Advantages of an expansive setting: Places the narrative in a real world, can draw upon larger themes. Narrative can be helped along by larger external/cultural/historical events. Telescope versus microscope. Readers feel like observers, not scientists.

Disadvantages of expansive settings: Characters can get lost in the landscape. Requires the distraction of a whole lot more description. Big events can seem more important than the characters or the story.

Creating a setting

The key is in creating verisimilitude—that is, authenticity that enables the reader to suspend disbelief. How it's done:

1. Presence—This is the backdrop. The world in a place and time in which the narrative is occurring. Crucial features:
   a. Know your readers—What do they already know that you can leave out? What are they likely not to know that you need to provide?
   b. Economy—Pulling back to the long view takes the reader away from the characters and story. So, keep these descriptions as brief as possible.
   c. Metaphor—Here's the place to use them. Go for something unexpected but illuminating.
2. Foreground—What are the precise physical details the reader knows to both get a feel for the setting?
   a. Location details
   b. Salient details for the narrative

3. Action—What is going on at this location at this moment in time? A busy street in 1890? A party in Rome in 1311? A group of surfers at Mavericks waiting for waves in 2015?
   a. From the character's physical location in a story, what can he or she see going on?
   b. Where in this action are the actual events that will unfold in the narrative?
4. Expertise—How is the action actually occurring? Can you name the precise acts, in sequence? The right tools or instruments? The larger expertise? Can you name the items within this action? Brands? "Big Two-Hearted River" (Hemingway), "The Things They Carried" (O'Brien)
5. The critical detail—Can you find that single image/object/action in the setting that puts it all together—that captures the heart of the narrative, or where it is going? Can you find that metaphor that captures the underlying mood of the narrative? Is there one bit of background dialog or piece of insider knowledge that makes the story's setting real in place and time and sets the stage for the story to unfold?

Finding the balance

This is the hardest part of scene setting. How much should you describe to get the narrative going? How much should you add along the way?

There is no easy answer to this. But there are rules of thumb:

1. Provide enough setting so that the reader sees a 3D world and can suspend his or her natural disbelief.
2. Imagine your targeted reader and determine how much they already know and need to know about the setting.
3. Provide enough detail so that the reader understands the physical space in which the action is taking place.
4. Use the right words to set the mood and the reader's expectations. Search for the perfect image.
5. Edit, edit, edit. Don't provide more description and setting than is absolutely necessary.
6. Use the setting as a stage to introduce your characters.
7. Every time your narrative changes location, provide new stage setting descriptions—but try to provide less with each change.
8. Use extraneous dialog and action to help provide a feeling for the reality of the setting.
9. Detail is your friend, always use a precise term or wording or brand name to ground your description in the real world.

Examples of rich scene setting

Raymond Chandler was legendary for the tightness and richness of his story openings:

> There was a desert wind blowing that night. It was one of those hot dry Santa Anas that come down through the mountain passes and curl your hair and make your nerves jump and your skin itch. On nights like that every booze party ends in a fight. Meek little wives feel the edge of the carving knife and study their husbands' necks. Anything can happen. You can even get a full glass of beer at a cocktail lounge.
>
> *Red Wind* (1945)

> Bunker Hill is old town, lost town, shabby town, crook town. Once, very long ago, it was the choice residential district of the city, and there are still standing a few of the jigsaw Gothic mansions with wide porches and walls covered with round-end shingles and full corner bay windows with spindle turrets. They are all rooming houses now, their parquetry floors are scratched and worn through the once glossy finish and the wide sweeping staircases are dark with time and with cheap varnish laid on over generations of dirt. In the tall rooms haggard landladies bicker with shifty tenants. On the wide cool front porches, reaching their cracked shoes into the sun, and staring at nothing, sit the old men with faces like lost battles.
>
> In and around the old houses there are flyblown restaurants and Italian fruit stands and cheap apartment houses and little candy stores where you can buy even nastier things than their candy. And there are ratty hotels where nobody except people named Smith and Jones sign the register and where the night clerk is half watchdog and half pander.
>
> Out of the apartment houses come women who should be young but have faces like stale beer; men with pulled-down hats and quick eyes that look the street over behind the cupped hand that shields the match flame; worn intellectuals with cigarette coughs and no money in the bank; fly cops with granite faces and unwavering eyes; cokies and coke peddlers; people who look like nothing in particular and know it, and once in a while even men that actually go to work. But they come out early, when the wide cracked sidewalks are empty and still have dew on them.
>
> *The High Window* (1942)

Ernest Hemingway, of course, is legendary for his precise and spare style, the product of an enormous amount of ruthless self-editing:

> In the late summer of that year we lived in a house in a village that looked across the river and the plain to the mountains. In the bed of the river there were pebbles and boulders, dry and white in the sun, and the water was clear and swiftly moving and blue in the channels. Troops went by the house and down the road and the dust they raised powdered the leaves of the trees. The trunks of the trees too were dusty and the leaves fell early that year and we saw the troops marching along the road and the dust rising and leaves, stirred by the breeze, falling and the soldiers marching and afterward the road bare and white except for the leaves.
>
> The plain was rich with crops; there were many orchards of fruit trees and beyond the plain the mountains were brown and bare. There was fighting in the mountains and at night we could see the flashes from the artillery. In the dark it was like summer lightning, but the nights were cool and there was not the feeling of a storm coming.
>
> *A Farewell to Arms* (1929)

Characterization

A *character* is a living figure whose existence or actions in some way affects the plot of a work of fiction. A character can make a contribution to the development of a narrative merely by existing—or by advancing the story in almost every scene.

Hierarchy of character types

Protagonist—the leading character, hero, or heroine of a story. Typically, the individual with whom we identify, who is changed the most in a positive way by the events of the plot, and who emerges as the victor of the story's climactic events.

Antagonist—the leading character, villain, enemy who stands in opposition or contention against the protagonist. Typically, the character we identify as the "bad guy," the negative force, or—positively—the individual who challenges the protagonist to become better, wiser, smarter or more experienced. The antagonist is typically the figure who forces the narrative to its climax, and is in some way defeated, overcome or exceeded by the protagonist.

Subsidiary Protagonists—characters who operate in the orbit—as allies, confederates, advisors—of the protagonist. These subsidiary characters typically take several forms:

Inner Circle—Family, close friends or disciples of the protagonist with whom the protagonist can share emotions, fears and so forth, and can give deep trust.

Outer Circle—Characters who are generally in support of the protagonist; who can provide aid and comfort. But they do little to advance the plot. Outer circle characters are generally less trustworthy than Inner Circle members.

Mentors—Older, wiser or at least more-experienced characters who can provide guidance and advice to the protagonist. These characters are typically used sparingly as they can make the plot mechanical. In some stories, the protagonist must break with the Mentor and his or her advice in order to succeed.

Subsidiary antagonists—characters who operate in the orbit of the antagonist. They typically take three forms:

Confederates—Those who work as lieutenants, partners, superiors, and so forth to the antagonist.

Henchmen—Those who execute the antagonist's desires.

Spies, gossips and sources—Those who, knowingly or unknowingly, provide useful information to the antagonist.

Secondary characters—figures in the story who are neither for or against the protagonist but who somehow advance the plot. These are often authority figures: attorneys, judges, doctors, police, bureaucrats, teachers. These individuals may also serve as a synecdoche for larger institutions.

Tertiary characters—figures who advance the plot as

- eyewitnesses to events,
- commentators,
- aids to plot transitions,
- crowds and
- vox populi.

Rule of thumb—Higher-level characters (protagonist, antagonist, inner circle, confederates) require the most complex and precise descriptions. Lower-level characters can be captured in a line or two. Tertiary characters can sometimes not be described at all, or with a simple adjective or two.

How to characterize

Go for the greatest amount of descriptive information in the
fewest words.
Doesn't slow down the text.
Present a compact message to create a coherent whole.
Come up with that unforgettable mental image.

Describe early, typically at the character's first appearance—otherwise you
create confusion in the reader's mind, an unresolved question.

Sources of characterization

Visual—hair color, length and style, shape of face, shape of features, eye
color, identifying marks, figure, hand shape, foot size, asymmetries,
height, weight, healthfulness (skin pallor), race, ethnicity, hair style,
glasses, clothing style, jewelry and so forth).

Auditory—voice range, pitch and color, vocal mannerisms, regional
accent, sound of movement.

Verbalization—vocabulary, grammar, long or short sentences, languid
or excited style.

Tactile—skin color, hand grip, hair softness, callouses, skin softness,
texture of usual clothing.

Odor—Sweat, perfume, natural skin smell, hair smell, clothing smell,
hand smell (denoting type of work), breath.

Skeletal—stance, asymmetries, body morphology, paralyses.

Muscular—overall health and strength, muscle size.

Locomotion—stride and gait, foot landing, quick-motioned or lethargic
and slow, limps and hitches. Nervous tics and repetitive motions
(hand-wringing, teeth grinding, and so forth).

Nerves—anxiousness, cool, jumpiness, rapid involuntary movement,
irrationality, paranoia, shyness, boldness.

Decoration—Simple or elaborate, rings, bracelets, piercings, necklaces,
and so forth.

Clothing—tasteful or garish, trendy or traditional, fabric types to
denote class, modest or designed to draw attention; coordinated or
confused; branding, slogans; shoe type, coat type, hat type.

Personality—alpha aggressive, beta easy-going or omega fearful and
reticent; talkative or taciturn; well-read or ignorant, opinionated or
passive, political or apolitical, strident or accommodating

History—veteran, leader, victim, successful, failure, contented or
frustrated, traumatized or triumphant, chronically ill

Rules for characterization

1. Try to capture the person in as few words as possible.
2. Use all your senses.
3. Try not to judge, but let the details convey the truth.
4. Take extra time on the protagonist; make sure he or she is truly 3D in the mind of the reader, such that the reader can readily predict what the character will do next.
5. Learn to like your characters, good and bad, and give them their due; remember Flannery O'Connor's remark that the terrible thing about this world is that everyone has their reasons.

His herringbone suit had a slight benzine odor which showed it was just fresh from the cleaners. He had worn it very little though it was four years old and now it was tight in the waist and shoulders, but not too tight. It was not a bad-looking suit at all and in fact it made him look rather like one of those suburban husbands you often saw in advertising illustrations, a whimsically comical man who peeked naively out of the corners of his eyes at his jolly and amazed little wife who was making a new kind of beaten biscuits.

Point of No Return (1949)

Dialog and the fictional voice

What is Dialog?

For our purposes, there are two definitions:

1. *The conversation between characters in a novel, drama, etc.*—These conversations are embedded within a larger narrative and help to move it along.
2. *A work of fiction composed entirely of conversation*—The conversations are the narrative as encountered in the *Plato's Republic*. Variant: Epistletory stories and novels (*Pamela*) in which letters replace spoken words.

Crucial point—Dialog in fiction is *synthetic*. It is designed to mimic real conversation, yet should not copy it. Fictional dialog should more resemble poetry—that is, all of the superfluous content needs to be cut out. The lesson they teach screenwriters: *Dialog should have the swing of everyday talk, but content well above normal.*

What makes great dialog?

1. *Distinction*—Everyone is different, and so everyone should speak differently. Even men and women of very similar backgrounds speak differently in terms of emphasis, verb forms, references, and so forth.

2. *Expertise*—The use of certain technical terms establishes a character in a certain profession or with a particular skill set.

3. *Location*—Every word a character says should locate them in place and time—accent, colloquialisms, jargon, fad phrases, regionalisms, personality and so forth.

4. *Brevity*—In real life, some people talk forever. We call them boors. Don't let your characters be boorish—unless it is intentional and, even then, you need to maintain control.

5. *Amplification*—Every word your character speaks, especially in a play or short story, should either drive the narrative forward or tell the reader something more about that character.

6. *History*—Dialog should provide insight into the history of the speakers, their experiences especially with each other.

7. *Absence*—What is left unsaid. If you have already presented a matter or conflict between two people, not mentioning that conflict in a subsequent dialog can increase tension.

8. *Misapprehension*—Showing two people in a dialog not understanding each other can be a good launchpad for future conflict.

9. *Encoding*—Not addressing a conflict, but replacing it with an alternative lesser conflict, can enhance the plot.

10. *Explanation and summation*—A quick way to make sure your reader is not getting lost or confused is to have a character summarize the events to that point or explain to another character what is going on.

11. *Confession and Expiation (Atonement)*—Dialog is the best way to bring an unresolved conflict to the surface: "I've always loved you"; "I've never forgiven you"; "I despise myself for what I did"; "I confess to the murder", and so forth. Often used as the climax of a story.

Tricks to good dialog

1. Put yourself in each character's shoes as they speak. Think like them. Know them.

2. After you write it, read it out loud. Does it sound right?

3. Plot it out: Where are the stresses, is there a rhythm, a regional music?

4. Stay away from awkward, colloquial spellings.

5. Tighten, tighten, tighten. Brevity is your friend.

6. Cut out superfluities: Again, if it doesn't define a character or advance the plot, cut it out.
7. Devote twice as much time to editing dialog as you do the rest of the narrative.
8. Occasionally use your characters' dialog to help readers keep up.
9. Never write it if you can get your characters to say it.
10. "Dialog only has to be true to the world of your narrative" (Calvin & Hobbes)
11. Lay off exclamations as much as possible.

Examples

Raymond Chandler

She laughed suddenly and sharply and went halfway through the door, then turned her head to say coolly: "You're as cold-blooded a beast as I ever met, Marlowe. Or can I call you Phil?"

"Sure."

"You can call me Vivian."

"Thanks, Mrs. Regan."

"Oh go to hell, Marlowe." She went on out and didn't look back.

J. D. Salinger

"Hey, Selena..."

"What?" asked Selena, who was busy feeling the floor of the cab with her hand. "I can't find the cover to my racket!" she moaned.

Despite the warm May weather, both girls were wearing topcoats over their shorts.

"You put it in your pocket," Ginnie said. "Hey, listen—"

"Oh, God! You saved my life!"

"Listen," said Ginnie, who wanted no part of Selena's gratitude. "What?

Ginnie decided to come right out with it. The cab was nearly at Selena's street. "I don't feel like getting stuck with the whole cab fare again today," she said. "I'm no millionaire, ya know."

William Shakespeare

Hamlet

How came he mad?

First Clown

Very strangely, they say.

Hamlet

How strangely?

First Clown

Faith, e'en with losing his wits.

Hamlet

Upon what ground?

First Clown

Why, here in Denmark: I have been sexton here, man and boy, thirty years.

Hamlet

How long will a man lie i' the earth ere he rot?

First Clown

I' faith, if he be not rotten before he die—as we have many pocky corses now-a-days, that will scarce hold the laying in—he will last you some eight year or nine year: a tanner will last you nine year.

Hamlet

Why he more than another?

First Clown

Why, sir, his hide is so tanned with his trade, that he will keep out water a great while; and your water is a sore decayer of your whoreson dead body. Here's a skull now; this skull has lain in the earth three and twenty years.

Hamlet

Whose was it?

First Clown

A whoreson mad fellow's it was: whose do you think it was?

Hamlet

Nay, I know not.

First Clown

A pestilence on him for a mad rogue! a' poured a flagon of Rhenish on my head once. This same skull, sir, was Yorick's skull, the king's jester.

Hamlet

This?

First Clown

E'en that.

Hamlet

Let me see.

[Takes the skull]

Alas, poor Yorick! I knew him, Horatio: a fellow of infinite jest, of most excellent fancy: he hath borne me on his back a thousand times; and now, how abhorred in my imagination it is! my gorge rims at it.

Here hung those lips that I have kissed I know not how oft.

Where be your gibes now? your gambols? your songs? your flashes of merriment, that were wont to set the table on a roar? Not one now, to mock your own grinning? quite chap-fallen?Now get you to my lady's chamber, and tell her, let her paint an inch thick, to this favour she must come; make her laugh at that.Prithee, Horatio, tell me one thing.

Horatio

What's that, my lord?

Hamlet

Dost thou think Alexander looked o' this fashion i' the earth?

Horatio

E'en so.

Hamlet

And smelt so? pah!
Puts down the skull

Horatio

E'en so, my lord.

Hamlet

To what base uses we may return, Horatio! Why may not imagination trace the noble dust of Alexander, till he find it stopping a bung-hole?

Execution: Finding the balance

1. How long should a work of fiction be? Two answers:
    a. As long as it needs to be to get its story across
    b. As long as it maintains the reader's attention and interest

Let's look at each in turn:
As long as it needs to be: In other words, how long does it take to tell the complete story. Defined by:

1. The complexity of the story
    a. Number of twists and turns to the main story
    b. Duration of the story
    c. Larger context—*Les Miserables, The Hunchback of Notre Dame, Life and Fate* (Grossman)
    d. Number of sub-narratives
2. The level of detail required—*Gravity's Rainbow, JR* (Gaddis), *Moby Dick*.
3. Amount of dialog—*Pamela*

As long as it maintains the reader's attention: How long can you keep the reader delighted or focused or in rapt anticipation?

1. Interesting characters
2. Complex plot

   3. Gathering threat or comic relief

How should you balance the plots of a work of fiction?
1. 50 percent or more should be the main story
2. 20 percent or less should be each of the secondary stories (Telamachus, Dumbledore and Snape, Starbuck and Ahab)
3. Usually no more than two secondary plots, and never overlapping with each other.

Balance of scene, description, action and dialog:
1. What drives the story—large events? Then mis en scène plays a major part.
   a. Main character's behavior? Then action
   b. Main character's personality or character? Then dialog
   c. The story? Then plot
   d. The mood? Then description

The easiest way to do this is to exert discipline on all the non-dominant parts—for example, edit heavily on plot and description, but lighter on dialog or action.

A story is like a song, a novel is like a symphony. The story has a single melody, two verses, bridge and big close (that is, rising action, counterpoint or change in viewpoint or style, then climax). A novel has an overall theme and direction, but can also have multiple movements, counterpoint, multiple tones and different instrumentation, varied tempo, overtures, intermezzos and a closing. A good novelist takes advantage of many of these, a great novelist uses all of them.

    Again, human beings are wired to respond to another person's voice, so if you see three or pages of narrative description or action, find an excuse to insert some dialog, or even internal monologue.

— Control the reader by controlling the pace: use dialog and rapid cut action to speed up the narrative; use description and detailed action to slow it down. If possible, alternate at ever greater frequency as you move through the plot.
— Give characters complexity, even contradiction, at the beginning of the narrative, but simplicity and purity of action at the end.
— Presage the end at the beginning through simple symbols or bits of dialog. But don't be heavy-handed or give the conclusion away.

Chapter breaks

Good—by length
Better—by plot turns
Best—by the demands of narrative velocity

Chapter titles

Not necessary. But if you use them, be elliptical or witty. Don't give away the chapter ahead of time—this isn't the 18th century.

Story title

Use it to make the sale to the reader.

Novel title

Use it to name either the overall theme or the main character. It's okay to have one when you start, but assume it will have changed by the time you finish. Trust others to help you with the final title.

Character name

Feel free to change character names, but search and replace all variants—then go through the text to make sure there are no orphans with the old name.

Academic Track

Until now we have been largely discussing writing careers in the commercial world. In this chapter, we'll take a break from that thread and look at an alternative writing career—one that may not carry the same potential for fame, but can actually be more financially rewarding, stable and fulfilling than what we think of as "professional writing": *academic writing.*

Like many writers, the author (without really knowing it) reached a decision point in his writing career in the months before his undergraduate college graduation. In one direction stretched the commercial world, in the other, graduate school and a life in academia.

I barely gave it a thought: I wanted to be a writer, not a professor. And, so, I went to work in corporate public relations and after four years became a newspaperman. I never looked back until decades later, when I finally did become an adjunct professor. And it was only then, as I looked at the life of a college professor up close—and even more when I finally identified the sophisticated parallel universe of academic publishing—that I began to wonder if I had made a terrible mistake all those years before.

The author will try to present this other world as objectively as possible, though you may notice a bit of bias—a combination of envy and amusement—creeping in.

Definition of the academic track

The academic track is the pathway by which writers establish a career by positioning themselves within academia and build a reputation—and earn awards—by writing for audiences and publishers largely within the academic world. The biggest difference between commercial writing and academic writing is that the former is typically the career itself, while the latter is a valuable sidelight to the primary work of teaching.

The academic pathway

If a commercial writing career can best be described as the zig-zagging pursuit of ever-greater opportunity, an academic writing career is much more of a straight, predetermined path where the only thing in doubt is when (and if) the next promotion will occur. The standard path, pretty much set in stone two centuries ago, goes like this. (Note for the senior positions we also show alternative, nonteaching, career paths in academia.)

Undergraduate degree—A bachelor of arts in English, creative writing or communications; or another major with a minor (or extracurricular work, such as working for the school paper) in writing.

Graduate degree—A master's in fine arts in creative writing or another major (or entry career) in writing. This two- or three-year degree is actually more popular for budding writers who want to become novelists and short-story writers; but some future academics will choose the MFA path initially with hopes of a commercial career, then change their minds and make the lateral move toward teaching.

PhD—In English, literature, creative writing, journalism, communications—today, a doctorate is almost the only prerequisite for most academic careers. To non-academics, the earning of a doctorate— after as much as a half-dozen years of graduate school—seems like the final step before a lucrative and highly respected teaching career. The reality is very different: in fact, in many cases it is just the beginning of a long apprenticeship. (Note that earning a PhD basically locks you into the academic track, as that degree holds little value in the commercial writing world—and those years would be better spent learning your craft.)

Adjunct Lecturer or Instructor—The author jokingly tells his students that "adjunct" is Greek for "slave." Unfortunately, it is not entirely a joke. Becoming an adjunct is typically one's first foot into an academic career. It is considered a training period, a high-level paid internship in which one learns how to teach, network, build a resume and live the life of an academic.

The modern reality is much different: as universities cut back on labor costs (usually to hire more administrators) more and more of the actual work of teaching is performed by adjuncts, even as attrition thins the rolls of tenured professors. In most US universities today, adjuncts teach a majority of the classes—and nearly all of the lower-division ones. Yet few are allowed to teach more than a handful of classes at any one university— and are paid per class only a fraction of that paid to their tenured counterparts.

As a result, adjuncts are often reduced to a transient existence: racing back and forth between two or more universities, cobbling together classes, struggling to cover their living expenses, and all but living in their cars—all with the hope of eventually getting hired as a full-time instructor or, better yet, a tenure-tracked associate professor. Meanwhile, their old classmates who earned MBAs or became lawyers, are already making big salaries and buying homes. It is the worst time in an academic's life, and it can last well past his or her thirtieth birthday. But at least their students call them "Professor."

Lecturer/Senior Lecturer—This position may seem to the outsider as just a glorified adjunct, but it is in fact a worthy career goal. Lecturers are faculty members who, for various reasons, have chosen not to follow the tenure path. What makes lecturers better off than adjuncts is that it is a real full-time job with a single institution. You are also free to move on to other instructor jobs at other colleges and universities if you so please, even dip into industry. Stick around long enough as a lecturer and you may get promoted to senior lecturer, a job that has even more job security and a higher salary. And, as a lecturer, you are not likely to be stuck taking on management jobs, such as department head, or sit on endless governance committees.

Assistant Professor (Lecturer in the UK)—This is the entry level position on the tenure track. As such, you have title and a good salary, but you still have to prove yourself—and that means publishing many papers, perhaps even publishing your first book. *Alternatives:* Section editor at a literary magazine.

Associate Professor (Senior lecturer or principal lecturer in the UK)—The middle position on the tenure track. The life of an associate professor is essentially one of a full professor who is still waiting for tenure. Associate professors are the workhorses of campus life, as they sit on most of the boards, committees and task forces. Because they are still proving their value, associate professors often still carry heavy class loads as well as produce endless papers, monographs—and populate academic conferences and associations. Job security is very high, though not a guaranteed tenure track. *Alternatives:* Editor at a literary magazine or academic publishing house.

Professor (Reader)—This job is the dream of most academics. It means more money and a reduced teaching load, in theory replaced by a greater emphasis on research, writing, editing, global conferences and all the other trappings of a life of the mind. Better yet, this work can be pursued without fear of being fired or laid off. Tenure, which is at the heart of professorship, guarantees employment for the rest of your working career. No more censuring your opinions or swallowing your pride in order to get along with the administration. Who wouldn't want such a career? Well, as we'll see below, there are some good reasons why some academics don't want this life. And, if you do manage to achieve tenure, enjoy it while it lasts: there is a growing backlash against tenure, especially by state governments, about funding public universities that carry unproductive, controversial and expensive faculty members. *Alternatives:* Senior editor or editor-in-chief at a literary magazine or publishing house.

Department head or dean—In the business world, promotion to a title like this is a major achievement. In the academic world, it can sometimes seem like punishment, as you have to deal with endless meetings, reports and unmanageable professors. Most people go into academia because they aren't interested in such skills as management, HR, budgeting and marketing. Being a department head—and even more, a dean of a college—means assuming all of those tasks and more. Luckily, most universities have a minority of faculty members who do have an interest in—or at least an aptitude for—those activities. Smaller departments (and unfortunately for writers, this includes many English departments) often don't have such individuals, so they typically rotate the assignment, convincing one of their professors to take on the job for a couple years. The results are usually mixed. The trade-off is a lighter class load and sometimes more pay—though many of these temporary department heads would happily get back to teaching instead. *Alternatives*: CEO of publishing house or international conference organizer/host.

Jobs

Teaching courses to college students in a classroom isn't the only work available to academics with writing skills. In fact, as the list of alternative careers above hints at, there are a lot of other ways to put those talents to use—in most cases as a source of additional income, but in others as a full-time career. Here are some examples:

Tutor—Writing is at the heart of higher education, and thanks to modern elementary and secondary schooling, a lot of college students are terrible writers. Many of them (or, more accurately, their parents) are willing to pay to get help.

Editor (academic papers)—A lot of professors are lousy writers, too. This is especially the case with faculty members not in the humanities—such as engineering, the natural sciences and even business. They need editing help and can afford to pay for it. Note, however, that much of the writing in academic papers isn't *real* writing (just try reading some), so a talented writer may find this kind of work hard sledding.

Editor (literary journals)—Literary magazines (both independent and university-based) often hire academics to edit particular contributions (poems, stories, creative nonfiction) at piece rate—or to actually serve as the nominal editor-in-chief of the entire publication on a salary. This can be interesting, though not particularly lucrative work—though the job can sometimes reduce course load.

Editor (books)—Academics have considerable involvement with the book industry. New graduates with advanced English degrees get hired as line editors, while professors are sometimes hired to be content editors in their area of expertise (though this usually involves professors in business and science, not writing). Veteran academics are often hired by publishing houses to assemble collections of papers, essays or tributes (for memorial editions) and provide their own introduction, and sometimes a contribution to the text. This work not only pays well, but also is a superb platform for enhancing the editor/professor's reputation.

Book reviewer—Many academics, at all levels, make added income and help their reputations by reviewing new books for newspapers, magazines and web sites. Typically, they write about their areas of expertise. For English and creative writing professors, this usually means novels. As noted in the chapter on criticism, this kind of work usually doesn't pay very well, but can do a lot for reputations—not least because it establishes the reviewer as both an expert and an arbiter of the field. It is also a way to get a lot of free books.

Arts critic—Art criticism is its own world, with the opportunity to write reviews, essays, monographs and books—and even to curate shows. A fine arts professor who can write, or conversely, a writing professor who knows art, can develop a very rewarding second career in this genre.

Opinion–Editorial writer—Universities regularly hold seminars and send out e-mails trying to convince faculty members to write editorials for local and national newspapers to help get the school more publicity. Some even subsidize this activity. Writing op-eds is nice work for professors—you get a soapbox for your views, you position yourself as an expert and you make a little money on the side. That said, editorial writing requires finding a news hook, really thinking about the topic, developing a strong argument and then presenting it with sufficient economy to fit the 500- to 1,000-word standard length requirement. Skill comes with practice, and learning from the brutal editing your early attempts will experience. It may look easy when you read an editorial, but it is quite difficult in practice. You also need a thick hide—because you will likely draw letters to the editor excoriating you for not knowing what you are talking about. That said, a great editorial can actually change government policy—one of the last remaining ways an academic can do that.

Columnist—Columns are a superset of editorials. They have the same structure but don't have quite the requirement of being immediately topical to the latest news. That said, column opportunities are rare—as most columns are written by full-time columnists. Still, many publications welcome one-off guest columns on a particular topic. Many like to have those columns written by credentialed experts. As a second kind of column—one that can sometimes turn into a regular part-time job—is the cultural column. These can cover art, literature, movies, television and so forth, and are a perfect opportunity for academics with expertise in one or more of those fields.

Feature writer—Feature writing is one of the few writing fields open to everybody, including amateurs. While most established publications have staff feature writers, most also supplement those staffers with freelance work. The bad news is that being a professor doesn't give you an intrinsic advantage over other freelancers in the eyes of editors. That said, editors also respect expertise—of which academics, by definition, have in spades. Pitch a story on something you teach, or are an acknowledged expert, and your odds of getting the assignment are high.

Poet, short-story writer, essayist (for literary magazines)—We describe this more in-depth in the next section, but academia operates in its own literary world of magazines and book publishers. In this world, professors who write fiction or essays have a distinct advantage. These publications usually don't pay, but they have considerable reputation value in the academic world. Given that there are scores of academic literary magazines out there, professors who write (and even more, professors of writing) have a greater chance of being published than their non-academic counterparts. And while some of this writing is world class, much of it is inferior—which further increases the odds of your writing finding a home.

Author (fiction and non-fiction)—For years, the author had noticed catalogs for books by academic publishers—including such famous houses as Oxford University Press and Yale University Press—but I had never given them much attention. The titles were obscure, and I almost never noticed those books on the bestseller charts. Only after I became a professor myself did I take a closer look. And I was amazed: what I discovered was an alternative publishing universe, one that had its own bestsellers, popular authors and awards. Many university presses have catalogs just as long as the big-name commercial publishers.

The difference is the business model. For example, only a few of these publishers give advances to authors—and those that do give comparatively small ones. The criteria for publishing books is also different: whereas commercial publishers look for books that offer either the potential for profits or prestige (for example, top-notch writing), academic publishers look for contribution to knowledge (often niche), particularly original research. The two camps even have their distinct awards, with only a little overlap (the Pulitzer Prize, Booker Prize). And, whereas commercial publishers give priority to professional writers, university presses give the same priority to academics.

Thus, my second thoughts on my career choice. What you need to know is that if you want to be a writer, if you want to be a published poet, short-story writer, essayist, nonfiction book author or novelist, pursuing an academic career not only doesn't preclude that, but in some important ways makes it *easier.* Yes, you may never write that big bestseller that gets turned into a hit movie, but you'll also never have to live on ramen noodles while struggling to sell your book. Plan your academic career right and you can have a nice paying job with (eventually) permanent job security *and* a shelf full of your books. Not a bad deal.

Advisor—The simple truth is that people trust academics to come up with good ideas, not make good decisions. This is not the place to argue that point, only to acknowledge its reality. But what this means is that there is always an opportunity for an ambitious academic to attach himself or herself to a powerful business executive or politician as an expert personal advisor or task force committee member. Indeed, this is almost the only way an academic can wield real influence and power outside academe. And it certainly makes for an interesting life.

Event/Conference organizer/host—What do academics do during the summer? Go to conferences, often in the nicest and most exotic places in the world—and just as often on the university's money or your taxes. It's a nice deal. But even nicer, if you have the right personality, is to organize and/or host one of these annual events. Then you can make a lot of money too, as well as burnish your reputation. Another version of this, especially for writing and art-history professors, is to set up in Florence, Rome, the Berkshires, or some other pleasant place, and hold seminars on writing or history for intellectual tourists with deep pockets. It's nice work if you can get it—and as a professor, you can.

Expert (law, patents)—Attorneys regularly have need of "experts" to give testimony in their cases. Though this opportunity doesn't happen often for English, communications and creative writing professors— it's usually for engineering professors—there are still occasional cases involving plagiarism, art valuation, or the use of language in contracts where a one-time job is available. Not only does this work pay well per diem, but if you can get known as a reliable expert, it can be a lucrative side activity.

Career: The good

As long as you recognize that your primary career is teaching, then the life of a writing professor can be very rewarding in every way Here, for a writer, are some of the best things about taking the academic track:

Even unintelligible, pretentious crap gets published—As a professional writer, you should never compromise the quality of your work. But because university and academic publishers have editorial policies that give primacy to original research and experimental writing, and because they are often short on content editors and line editors, an awful lot of all but unreadable books get published (some great books, too). That makes the odds of getting published—and added promotion—much more likely when you show up with a well-written manuscript. The danger, of course, is that you can get complacent. But that can be overcome simply by sending your best work to commercial publishers and competing in a much more challenging arena.

Once you get tenure, you're set for life—In our modern gig-based economy, having one job for your entire career may seem limiting to a young writer. But ask a middle-aged writer what they think of having a guaranteed paycheck every month for the rest of their working lives. And better yet, to be able to write what you please without fear (well, maybe a little) of getting fired or becoming a pariah.

All the money you make writing is on top of a good-paying steady gig— Don't feel like writing this week? No problem: you are still going to get a paycheck. Want to take a couple of years to research and write a book that will be read by only a couple of hundred people who share your interests? No problem; you are still going to be paid. That's the kind of freedom commercial writers dream of, and that only the most successful mainstream writers ever experience (if even they do).

Travel the world and go to conferences on other people's money—As already noted, it can be a very pleasant life. Like business conferences, there is no shortage of tours, cocktail parties and extracurricular fun; unlike business conferences, you aren't expected to be particularly productive even when you are "working."

Enough awards and recognitions to go around for everybody—Whereas the commercial publishing world is pretty tight when it comes to honoring writers, the academic world gives out honors and awards like jelly beans. To test that, just look up the biography of a mid-range commercial author and then compare it to a comparable academic author. The former will be lucky to have one or two awards from second-tier competitions, while the latter can fill a page with honors. So, if you want to fill your book covers and office walls with "best book" awards, compete in the academic world.

*You get to be called "doctor" or "professor" the rest of your life—*It sounds immodest, but there's a lot to be said for being called by an impressive title. It is an instant advantage in a social setting; it saves the time of having to prove or justify yourself and, frankly, it can keep you going on a bad day. Just don't take it seriously yourself.

Free summers, and even the work is pretty easy. Professors will tell you that teaching is hard work. And it is. But lecturing a roomful of sleepy 20-year-olds is whole lot easier than running a combat platoon in a war zone, or working a 12-hour shift as an emergency-room doctor, or managing a product division in a Fortune 500 corporation. Besides, you only have to work nine months out of the year—and get paid extra for teaching summer school.

Career: The bad

So, if the academic track is so good, why do people regularly quit and jump to the commercial world? Why do some academics choose not to accept tenure when it appears offer the dream career? Here's why:

A nasty apprenticeship (PhD) and journeyman (Adjunct) process— While your peers in the business world are working their way up the organization, enjoying the perquisites of corporate life, making good money and living in the real world, you get to spend your twenties broke, all but living like a hobo, and teaching an exhausting course load. During this decade of your life, you will ask yourself many times, "Is this worth it?"—especially when you realize that with your talent and intelligence you could be doing very, very well in business or government. And one day, the answer to your question may be: "No, it's not." Some of this may change with the growing efforts to unionize adjuncts; but probably not much.

*No one outside of academia really takes you seriously—*Look at old newsreels and you'll see in what respect professors were once held, and what authority they wielded in society. Times have changed—in large part due to professors themselves. As a result, despite your title and years of acquired knowledge, other than the occasional reporter, no one really cares what you know, or what you have to say.

*Only your students really respect you, and they don't really either—*Your students are far more engaged in the world than you are, and they know how the outside world sees you. So, even though you may develop a terrific mentor relationship with one or two students each year, the rest will only treat you respectfully because you have control over their grades—and they want to ask for a recommendation letter to graduate school.

Faculty politics can be crazy—It was Henry Kissinger, America's chief diplomat in his role as secretary of state, who said, "Academic politics are so vicious precisely because the stakes are so small." As a former Harvard professor, he would know. One of the refreshing things about careers in business or government is that you move around a lot, change jobs, and deal with different fellow workers. There, the secret to career success is devising win–win solutions. *None* of those things characterize a university department.

You'll be well off, but you'll never get really rich—Professors' salaries vary with the location of the school and its rankings; but, whatever the location of the university, you will enjoy a very nice standard of living. But, unless you manage to sell that one textbook that goes into eight editions, or that novel turns into a movie, you are never going to be rich. Not business-executive rich; and definitely not successful tech entrepreneur rich. If that matters to you, you are going to be disappointed.

It all may come crashing down, soon—If you follow the news, you know that universities, especially in the United States, are under considerable stress. Tuition inflation (thanks largely to investments in fancy new facilities, not adjuncts' salaries) is pricing students out of the better universities or forcing them to take out vast amounts of student loans. Meanwhile, online college courseware is nipping away at classes that used to only take place on campus. And, many states, weary of the cost of maintaining colleges that produce graduates with unemployable degrees, are looking at getting rid of tenure altogether. How much of all of this will ultimately challenge the future of the academic track? Only time will tell.

Turning points

For most of the careers described in this book, the turning points come near the end of one's career. In academia, the biggest one comes at the beginning: whether to follow the academic track at all. Still, there are others:

Can't get a job, no hope of tenure—There are two important jumps on the academic track. The first is making the leap from adjunct to a real position as an assistant professor. This can be surprisingly difficult—and, as noted, you may get weary of the struggle and leave the chase. The second takes place a decade or two later, when you have put in your time, paid your dues, and are up for tenure. Failing to make this jump can be emotionally devastating: these are your peers, your friends, people you've worked with for years, and now they've concluded that you are unworthy. You may choose to swallow your pride, or start over on the long path to tenure, or you may just decide that this is the moment to change your career.

You want to get taken seriously—As noted, professors no longer enjoy the prestige they used to—and less than you think you may deserve. That wouldn't be the case outside the campus walls in a career in business, nonprofits or government. And that difference may be enough to send your career along a different path.

You want to be actually heard—This is corollary to the one above. Academics mostly talk to students (who don't really care) and their fellow academics (who also don't really care). Even if you are writer, if your work is only reaching other academics, you are still in the same box, ignored by the general public and people with real power. You may decide that academia is not enough to leave the mark you want to make on the world.

You want to get rich and famous—You realize that, as an academic, you are only going to go so far in either category. And you want—and think you have earned—much more.

You get tired of the campus hothouse environment—As rewarding as academic life can be, it also means—especially with tenure—spending your entire career on the same campus, in the same office, dealing with the same people—many of whom you've learned to despise. From that perspective, the beautiful oasis of campus life can look a whole lot like a minimum-security prison. You cannot predict how you will react to this scenario beforehand. You can only live it and see what happens.

EXAMPLE: Sample opening to a feature story. Note the scene-setting and the establishment of a mystery to be solved.

Of Light and Leading

The archivist pulled out the white steel drawer. "I think you'll enjoy this," she said cheerfully.

I looked down and froze. At the sight of the old map, fifty years drained away—and I was again in the presence of one of the most unforgettable figures of my youth. . .

It was during a holiday break that I found myself walking into Santa Clara University's new library. A lifelong friend was in town. He had briefly attended Santa Clara and was curious about the many recent changes to the campus he had read about.

I had a second motive as well. The university had approached me about donating my 'papers' to Santa Clara – reporter's notes, book drafts, television episodes and all the detritus accumulated from 35 years covering Silicon Valley . . . and, to close the deal, invited me to visit the university's museum-quality archives to see where those items would reside in perpetuity. I found the whole idea both humbling and hilarious—but decided, if nothing else, to get a free tour.

And so we found ourselves in the library's basement, two gray-haired men being given a tour by the archive's gracious staff. Like most modern museums and archives, it was a disorienting combination of old artifacts and new technology: 19th century paintings of early university presidents, church vestments, panoramic photographs of students in letter sweaters and long-gone classroom buildings, athletic and scholastic medals and ribbons—framed by the great pale monoliths of automated storage bays. And all of it encapsulated in the thrum and slightly ozone smell of massive air filtration, temperature and humidity-management systems.

My friend and I entertained ourselves looking at the various artifacts for longer than etiquette demanded of our patient hostess. It was time to justify our visit. If I were to donate my papers, I asked, how exactly would they be preserved? I suppressed a smile at the absurdity of donating yellow old interviews with local grey market criminals to sit next to the dignified old Jesuits in their official portraits.

That's when the archivist walked us over to one of the bays, pulled open a drawer . . . and flung me back a half-century.

"Here, for example," she said, "Is an old map of one of the early Santa Clara Missions."

"I know this map," I told her. "I owned it for a while when I was a kid."

Both she and my friend gave me puzzled looks. "But how . . .?" the archivist asked.

"It's a long story," I told her.

Miscellaneous Writing

This chapter looks at the many kinds of occasional writing that you, as a professional writer, may be asked to do. It is a varied list, but the writing remains the same. Economical writing, strong phrasing, action verbs, factual accuracy, careful editing; good writing is still good writing, even if it is for a neighborhood brochure.

Some of this writing will be for nonprofits, others for profit-making clients, and still others for small businesses with very limited budgets. Again, as a professional, you should never write for free—the exception being for a nonprofit organization. But with very small businesses you may want to modify your fee to match their budget—balanced by whatever goodwill you may obtain (for example, if you are asked by your favorite coffee joint to help it write a neighborhood flyer, you may want to take your payment out in free drinks).

It is also not recommended that you charge an hourly rate. People can look at a work of art—and because they can't draw themselves, it seems valuable. But everybody can write—though most can't do it very well—and so when they see your completed work they have a tendency to believe they could have done it by themselves, that it wasn't that difficult and as such they undervalue your work. Also, different writers work at different speeds, and many bad writers work much more slowly than good writers. So why charge by the hour? And why try to negotiate a fee after delivery?

Instead, charge by the project and agree upon the price up-front. If possible, also get paid half up front as well. Then, if your client decides that his teenaged daughter could have written that copy as well as you and refuses to pay for the finished writing, you at least have the equivalent of a kill fee in your pocket.

As for working with nonprofits, good for you for being a good neighbor and citizen. That said, nonprofits are in the business of getting good people with special skills to donate as much of their time as possible—and one of the skills they need most is writing. So, while there's many good reasons to donate your writing skills it is also a good policy not to leave that commitment open-ended. Rather, you need to set a limit to the scope of your work at the beginning, and the magnitude of that commitment should be balanced against your need to earn a living. Don't worry about the folks at the nonprofit being disappointed—they will be grateful for the work you do and soon will be back asking you to do more.

Types of miscellaneous writing

Cover letters—These are letters that are typically written as an introduction to a report, packet of materials, gift, and so forth. The key is to write short (you should try to never exceed a single page), clearly and in the voice of the sender. Most of all, you must know enough about the attached content to be able to make a good case for the reader to look at it. If you don't have those materials on hand for reference, then you need to interview your client and then confirm with them your understanding. The good news is that, as a professional, cover letters are usually quick work. The bad news is that your client will see it as "only a letter" and will want to pay you accordingly—no matter how effective it is. You won't win that argument. Think of the job as extra money—and as opening the door for some future speechwriting work.

Recommendation letters—You will do this work for free, because it will either be for friends or the children of friends. And, you will soon discover that the requests for these letters pile up twice per year: when young people are applying for college, or trying to land their first internship or first job. That's the nature of the work, so get used to it because you will be unable to say no. That said, being able to help a young person, sometimes someone you've known since they were a baby, get launched on the next phase of his or her life can be immensely satisfying, especially if they get that job or college acceptance letter. And rather than think of it as a burden, look upon it as a compliment: that person (or his or her parents) look upon you as having sufficient reputation or influence to impress an acceptance committee or potential employer.

The trick to a good recommendation letter is to be short, but knowledgeable. You don't need to write more than a page. Focus on details of the subject's life, particularly those in which you participated and can speak authoritatively about the subject's personality and skills: "I helped with Billy's Eagle Scout service project and was deeply impressed by his organizational skills, leadership and commitment to service to his community." Always include that you think the subject will be an asset to the target of the letter. And don't stint on noting your own credentials and qualifications to judge the subject—either in the body of the letter or in the job title line below your signature. If you are an alumnus or former employee of the targeted institution, note that fact as well.

Try to write the recommendation letter immediately after you receive the request, or you'll keep putting it off. Find out the deadline, just in case. Once you've finished the letter, unless otherwise stipulated, send it to the subject for a fact check. Don't mail the letter to the targeted institution if there is a format for e-mailing it—otherwise, again, you'll put it off.

If your subject gets the job or the acceptance letter, congratulate him or her and say that they did it all on their own.

Brochures and booklets—Beware: these kinds of publications may look simple, but they can be endless, thankless jobs. In terms of word count, they don't take a lot of writing and can be drafted quickly. However, gathering the information and understanding what you need to do that writing can take a lot of time. But even that can seem minor to the approval process, which can go on forever and require numerous edits—even full rewrites—before every stakeholder in the organization is heard from.

On the other hand, if this is a corporate job you can usually charge a lot for this kind of work, as it has already been budgeted (find out the amount if you can) as part of a larger product or service roll-out. So, the trick is not to find yourself being punished, not for doing a poor job, but for the bureaucratic dysfunctionality of your client. One way to do that is to narrow the scope of the clearance process: stipulate that you will deal with only one representative of your client—let them work out the edits amongst themselves and have that person present the final decisions to you. You can also set deadlines on the project—both for your delivery of the draft, and for the delivery of their edits to you. With luck, the latter will force them to make a decision. Finally, if possible, see the layout—including photos and graphs—*before* you write, so you don't have to make major cuts to your draft.

If you are donating this work to a nonprofit, set a precise end point, otherwise the process really will go on forever. Better yet, agree to write the first draft only: they'll be grateful to get that (and will likely print that draft verbatim, so you probably are doing them a favor).

Ad copy—Freelance ad copywriting is very good work, if you can get it. It pays well and doesn't require a lot of writing. Still, that doesn't mean it doesn't take a lot of time and effort. You will likely be required to take several meetings, including brainstorming sessions (though you will probably be spared client meetings), and while your copy will be necessarily short, it will need to be well-polished (often going through multiple rewrites) and pass muster with the client.

The key to contract ad copywriting is flexibility. Remember, you are not writing for yourself but for your client—the ad agency or department—and through them, *their* client, and through them, their current and potential customers. That's a lot of different constituencies, so the chance of your ideas or words making it through all these filters intact the first time is essentially zero. So never fall in love with your words; instead, take satisfaction in getting to the final sign-off.

One good thing about ad copy work is that it tends to be cumulative. Ad agencies and departments are in a perpetual state of frenzy, which means they don't have time to recruit new contractor talent but will stick to people on their contact list. If you are on that list, you will get job after job unless you screw up, and then there may not be a second chance. So, never "dial-in" your work with these folks.

As for billing, your fee will probably be set in advance for the job, though if the job looks like it will require a lot of rework, try to bill by the hour. Invoice immediately on approval of the job—agencies can sometimes string out payables to 30, 60 or 90 days.

Press releases—PR work often requires the creation of more content than most miscellaneous writing jobs. But, because most contractors have no real understanding of how PR works or what a good press release looks like, you are likely to be spared amateur writers messing with your copy.

The key to writing a successful press release for a client is not to be creative. Gather the necessary quotes, product specifications, boilerplate information, and so forth. Make sure you get the names and titles right or the rest of your work will be suspect—and then write it in the standard release template. Don't show the client a rough draft; even if he or she wants to see one; it will only worry them. Only show them a polished version.

In the worst case, you may find your job is as much education as it is writing: teaching your client how PR works; not allowing them to hurt their odds of being successful by making overblown claims in the copy; not letting them disparage competitors in the release and so forth. That said, if they still insist on making one or more of those mistakes, there's nothing you can do, except decide whether you want to work with them again.

Poster copy—This is simple, fun work. It's usually just a few words, and there's no money (or very little) involved, but the takeaway—a poster you can save or even frame—often makes it all worthwhile. The key, of course, is whittling the copy down to the fewest number of words with the maximum impact, while keeping a laser-like focus on the poster's message.

Newsletters—This one is tricky, because writing the copy for a newsletter is not only a major job, but it can be an ongoing one. It's hard to argue with that kind of gig. But here's the downside: unless you are an employee and making an employee's salary, this could be a bad deal. Why? Because writing multiple articles on a deadline, especially with all of the reporting required, can be as time consuming as a full-time job for a lot less money. It's not very interesting content either, and no amount of good writing will make much difference.

So, seen as miscellaneous writing work rather than as a full-time job, newsletter writing is not particularly appealing *unless* you are just starting out, need the work and experience, and don't stick around too long. As for newsletter writing for a nonprofit: as a professional writer, don't do it. It is too much time that you otherwise need to make a living; it is too open-ended; and the writing itself is second rate. Leave it to the amateurs.

Public-service announcements—This work is exclusively for nonprofits and consists of either audio tracks or videos (typically 30 seconds or less) designed to promote the organization on local media. The fact is that, in terms of making a charitable contribution of his or her talents, this is one of the best things a professional writer can do. The work required is tiny—and the impact can be immense. The trick is to write tight—very, very tight—copy, stuffing the maximum amount of information into no more than a few sentences.

If you are doing a public-service video, this is the ultimate case of letting the imagery do most of the work. Make key points (such as contact information) as captions. If radio, choose no more than three key points, take out adjectives and adverbs, and hit the message hard.

Family histories—This is writing you will probably want to do, because you are likely the best writer in your family. Genealogy usually isn't of much interest to young people. But by age 40 many of those same individuals become almost obsessed with the subject. On-line family history research sites also have made the experience much more productive than in the past, when searchers often had to look through old church records. Now family histories are crowd-sourced by its members, sharing a vast cache of photos, stories and records. If you find this material interesting, you probably owe it to your relatives, to your ancestors, and most of all to your descendants, to turn those records into readable, entertaining stories.

Having done just that with a book, the author can tell you two things. First, it is easy to get obsessed. This is your family after all, and you may find your ancestors successes and failures deeply interesting—and often very moving. Second, prepare yourself, because many of your family's stories are wrong, having changed with the telling over the years. Meanwhile, you may well uncover events in the past that will shock you. In my case, it was a murder of one of my ancestors in which another ancestor was involved.

Skits and plays—Everybody knows you are a writer, so you no doubt would love to write a skit for the camp talent show or the corporate offsite meeting. And, wouldn't you write a historic play for your town's centennial, or one of your kid's schools? Nonprofessionals are often of the opinion that if you write for a living that you are both able to write successfully in any genre (sort of true), and that you can whip these things out in a day (almost never true).

Whether you want to donate your services to do this work is up to you. But you should be honest with the people asking for your help. If you don't know how to write comedy, tell them, and have them find someone who does to help you. Or just buy a book of skits and modify one to fit the occasion—no one will care where you got it as long as it works. And if you have no experience writing a play, just beg off: it is hard to write a good play on your first shot. That said, consider the audience: a group of nine-year-olds is hardly a discerning audience. They just want to have fun. If you are up for it, give it to them—don't worry about quality, just entertain them.

Forewords and jacket quotes—If you are successful in your career, particularly as a book writer or novelist, you may be asked to write content for another writer's book. It is quite an honor, so think twice before you refuse. That said, as a writer and not a businessperson or celebrity, you are expected to actually read the book. If you hate it, politely beg off because you are too busy, or some other excuse. If you like the book, agree to do it.

Jacket quotes are easy. Just come up with a couple sentences lauding the contents of the book and/or the way it's written and say good things about the author. If you don't know the style or tone of a jacket quote, pull out some books and study the wording of other jacket "quote–sters" and imitate it.

Forewords are much more demanding, but they are also a much greater honor—even more so if your name is mentioned on the cover ("With a foreword by ___"). You've no doubt read many forewords, so the style should be familiar to you. It is essentially an introduction to the book, a glimpse to the reader of the experience to come. Talk about what makes the book a good read, the new information it contains, how it answers a current need. You can also talk about how you experienced the book and what the reader will take away from it. Finally, you can talk about the author and how he or she is the perfect person to write this book. Also, if you have any particular expertise in the book's subject, use it to point out important facts or ideas in the book that non-expert readers might not notice otherwise.

Signage—Writing copy for signage might sound simple, but it is in fact quite complicated. Here, we're not talking about regular signage that gives directions or identifies a place. Rather, we're talking about historic markers, museum display information signs, lists of rules, and so forth. This kind of writing is the ultimate in fine editing. Your task is to be complete in terms of information while being limited by the physical size of the sign and the font. For example, if you are writing a sign for a museum exhibit of stuffed grizzly bears, you need to figure out how to include the names and classifications of the bears, their habitat, size, diet and behavior—all in a few dozen words on a small sign.

The trick is to gather the information you need for your sign, then write a first draft that contains all salient information. Next, start editing down the copy, throwing out any superfluous word or fact. This will get you most of the way there; then go through what's left and try to figure out how to say the most with the least number of words. If you are still too long, start cutting out bone: prioritize the facts by their importance, then start chopping off those facts in reverse order.

Part Four

The Work of Professional Writing

Being a professional writer means not just being a writer, but behaving as a professional. In other words, the writing is necessary, but it isn't sufficient. You must also be a businessperson as well—and if you intend to freelance, you must go still further and become an entrepreneur.

But even if you have a stable job as a writer at a large media corporation, such as a television network, you still need to keep records of your expenses, pay your taxes, stay updated on your tools and market yourself to potential future employers. If you choose to be self-employed you need to understand that you are running a business, with all that entails, including licensing, bookkeeping, employee tax withholding—and most of all, billing. Fail at this work and it won't matter how good a writer you are.

In this final section we look at the details of the work of a professional writer, from the "finishing" work of editing, to the business work of pitching ideas and invoicing and, finally, to the life's work of creating a happy and successful career.

Pitching

If there is one message that you should remember from this book, it is that professional writing is a *business*. It is a craft, a career. Your job is to get the work done in a professional manner—and, with talent and luck, the art will follow.

As with any business, the actual content is only a fraction of the work. You also must deal with bookkeeping, taxes, marketing, promotion, and sales. It is the last—the writing version of sales called *pitching*—that is the subject of this chapter. And just as with sales in other industries, the process includes qualification, contact, selling, negotiating, and closing.

Small business understand this. If they don't they go out of business quickly. But freelance writers, like other professionals in the arts, often seem to have the attitude that they because they pursued creative careers to escape the rules of business, that the rules of business won't pursue them.

No such luck. If you don't treat your writing career—especially freelancing—as a business, you will soon discover that there is a personal version of corporate Chapter 11 bankruptcy. And, suitably humbled, you'll have to go in search of a real job, one that, ironically, will also require you to perform some other version of pitching, negotiating and billing.

The good news is that being a good writer *and* being a good businessperson can be easy. It just takes practice, until the basic business work of writing becomes second nature. Until then, console yourself with the knowledge that you really have no alternative—at least not if you want this career.

It's important to understand that pitching a story to a publication, web site, or television series (we'll look at book pitching later) is not just a matter of sending an email or letter suggesting they buy your idea. It is, in fact, a multistage process—one akin to military planning or preparation for an athletic competition. Let's look at each in turn.

Preparation

This step is about improving your odds of acceptance by giving editors at your target publication exactly what they desire. You accomplish that by learning as much as possible about the publication, its editorial style and congruence (but not overlap) between recent stories and the one you propose. It is also useful, if possible, to identify the particular editor who is likely to read your proposal and assign you the story.

1. Study the publication, site or program. Learn its editorial style, attitude and philosophy, its interests and its readership profile.
2. Read or watch the most recent issues, entries or episodes. Never, ever, pitch a subject story it just ran. That proves that you haven't done your research—and that will insult the editors. Never put yourself in that position.
3. Do a web search to see if any of their reporters or editors have written in the past on topics similar to your idea. If it is an editor, pitch your story idea to that person—and reference their past story in a complementary way. If it is a staff reporter, note that person in your pitch to an editor and show how your approach will be different. This is important to let the editor know that *you* know—and make it harder for him or her to just give your idea to that reporter. It will also make it easier for that editor to explain why you, and not the reporter, should do the story.
4. Study the masthead and bios for the editor who appears to have both the right interest and the power to accept your pitch. If there is a story or assignments editor, pitch to that person. The next best target is the managing editor. The editor-in-chief is a long shot; pitch to that person only as a last resort.
5. Determine if you know anyone else who has written for this venue. If you are not a threat, contact that person and see if he or she can give you any tips: about how to pitch, who to pitch even how to invoice and get paid on time. Once you are established, do the same for other writers.

Contact

This is where the rubber hits the road. You've studied the publication and its editors. You've narrowed your story idea to the best fit for the publication or web site. Now comes the moment when you put all that knowledge to work. Pitching isn't difficult if you don't let it become so. Amateurs and neophytes tend to overthink a pitch—rewriting it multiple times, hesitating to send it out, second-guessing their story idea and so forth. Their hesitation shows through in the pitch letter. Veterans know that a pitch is all in the big themes, not in the small details, and they get the pitch out fast in order to get a quick response—that way they can either get to work or send the pitch to someone else. Their confidence shows through in the pitch letter. Try to be that cool and confident veteran from the start.

1. Unless you hear otherwise, use an email.
2. Keep your pitch short, but be sure to include the following:
   - *Set-up*—"I'm a regular reader" (you should be after your web search).
   - *Opening*—"I have a story that I think will be of great interest to your readers."
   - *Pitch*—Your story idea (two or three paragraphs—if you can't summarize your pitch that succinctly, then don't pitch it all).
   - *Biography*—Why you think you're uniquely suited to write this story (your knowledge of the subject; contacts in the field of the story subject; access either to experts or the story's main subject; your past writing related to the subject or the style of the piece: Q&A, profile, and so forth).
   - *Offer*—What you think would be appropriate for this story, but that you can write to whatever length the editor needs and can deliver it whenever they need it.
   - *Payment*—*Do not* discuss this in a pitch letter.

Delivery

It may seem obvious that you must meet your agreed-upon delivery, but you'd be amazed to learn how many writers regularly miss their deadlines. Neophytes often do so because they either underestimate the amount of time a story will take to report and write, or because they are afraid to submit a finished piece because they aren't sure it is good enough. They will keep writing ad infinitum until whatever gains were made by the rewrites is lost to the growing anger of the editor. Veteran writers miss deadlines because they either take on too much work and they can't finish it all in time, or they get jaded and assume their reputation and the quality of their work will get their tardiness forgiven. Not always. The answer for the former is to take pride in your work; be decisive; and trust your writing to get a fair treatment from the publisher. For the latter, it is to stay professional and respect the employer/contractor, not get complacent, and honor the craft.

1. *Meet your deadline.* If you can't, warn the client as early as possible, give an honest explanation (editors are genius BS detectors; but they also understand the foibles of reporters) and keep that client constantly updated on your current status and on your new estimated delivery date.

2. *Meet the length requested.* Always. You can be off by no more than about 10 percent to allow for editing. If you find yourself writing a longer story, discuss it with your editor as you go—never deliver it the wrong length. Even worse: don't deliver a piece that is too short unless you have an excellent reason, have prepared your editor beforehand and have helped come up with a solution (sidebar, graphics, chart, and so forth). Copy that is too short puts an extra burden on your client because he or she has to come up with something to fill the empty slot—which may mean another story assignment or ad, both of which can wreck layouts and print dates.

3. *Know ahead of time how the client wants the copy delivered.* If by email, make sure they have received it (ask for a confirmation email in return). If hard copy, send it registered and leave enough time for your deadline. If you use a specialty site, such as DropBox, make sure your software is compatible—and check to make sure your file has been picked up.

Follow-up

There is a tendency, even among veteran writers, to treat all freelance work as completed after submission and acceptance. But, again, writing is a profession—a business. And follow-up is part of any successful business. Why? Because it is what you are. And, even though you don't plan to, you may well work with that client again—and you want to have left a good impression. But most of all, you want to get paid.

1. *Drop a note to the client.* Make it crisp and short. Thank the editor for the chance to write for them, compliment them on being a good outfit to work for (even if not entirely true) and pass along any compliments on the piece you've gotten from readers. Leave the door open to work with them again.

2. *Invoice immediately.* It is best is to invoice with the copy when you deliver it. Short of that—especially if you've made an agreement with the client to be paid upon acceptance—invoice then. If the payment is to be made on publication, don't wait until then to invoice. Do it on acceptance as well.

3. *Find out who writes the checks.* It is usually a bookkeeper (with the publisher signing the check). Get to know that person. Use the excuse for calling them to confirm that your invoice has all the necessary information. Write a quick note to inform that person you got the check—and thank him or her for being so helpful. All of this may seem unnecessary, but someday, when your mortgage payment is due or the debt collectors are calling, getting that bookkeeper to write your check now, instead at the end of the month may be the only thing that saves you. Just think of your note as a "thank you" in advance for that day.

4. *Dialing for Dollars/Driving for Dollars.* If the day comes when you need that check immediately (or if the check never comes)—and you've developed that relationship with the bookkeeper, don't hesitate to call and see if a check can be cut immediately. And don't trust the old "the check is in the mail" dodge. Offer to pay for a delivery service (or at least ask for the routing number). If nearby, tell that person you'll be right over. Then get in your car and go. You may anger some people—even kill your chance of ever writing for that client again—so you must decide beforehand just how much you need that check.

EXAMPLE: Here's a basic invoice format. Note that it supplies your name and vital information (if you have regular relationship with the client you may want to add bank wire information. The due date can vary from "Immediate" to "30 days" or more, based upon what you've already agreed upon with the client. You may also list more than one project, then list the sum under "total."

Invoice

Michael S. Malone
May 21, 2018
No. 2018-04
Weather story (research, write, edit)..............................$xxxxx

Total: $xxxxx

Due date: 30 days
Please remit: Michael S. Malone

1234 XXXXX Ave.
XXXX, California
USA 9XXXXX

S.S.#XX-XX-XXXX

EXAMPLE: Feature story pitch letter. This is targeted for a small regional magazine. Note the summary of the story's hooks, all done in a few paragraphs, some quotes to establish the subject's character, and the mention of local connections. Note also that the letter ends with a wide-open pitch on the actual production and delivery of the story.

Dear Editor:

I have a story idea that would of great interest to your readers—and recognizes an influential member of our community.

Dr. J--------- D------- turned 80 this year, and this August he will celebrate his 50th anniversary as the dean of ophthalmologists in our area. Indeed, Dr. D------- is likely the oldest and longest practicing practitioner in his field in the region.

But this anniversary is perhaps the least interesting aspect of Dr. D------'s career. As a specialist in cataract surgery—indeed, he brought the modern version of that surgery to our region more than 45 years ago—he has saved the vision of thousands of our neighbors. And that is just the beginning, because for years he has travelled to Africa (Ghana and Nigeria) and South America (Colombia) to perform more than a thousand more such surgeries for free on people who would otherwise go blind. He has performed those surgeries in the most primitive conditions—from tiny cinder block buildings to even aboard dugout canoes. In the process, he has encountered a number of dangerous conditions (including having his canoe split and sink in a flooded Amazonian river).

One of a family of physicians—nine doctors, including his two sons—Dr. D------ is as busy as ever. One of his hobbies is hiking the world—thirty to fifty miles at a time in the wilder places of the world, from Sikkim to Kyrgyzstan. And, despite his age, he recently, completed such a trip to Uzbekistan. And with his wife he is raising two girls they adopted in China nearly two decades ago.

Dr. D------ has no intention of retiring. As he says, "If you like helping people, that's what you should do. And there's no reason to ever stop." These days his clients include seniors who have been his patients for forty years, and younger people whose parents came to him for surgery decades ago. "I still look forward to coming to the office every day," he says.

I can write this feature to any length you desire, and can deliver it, edited, with a week.

> With best regards,
> XXXXXXXX

Editing

What is editing?

Editing is the improvement—for reasons of space, accuracy and/or quality—of existing written, audio or video content. Editing is an open-ended process: it can be continued forever. So, there is also a time factor in the editing process.

Editing work is both a feature of writing and a career (part-time and full-time) in itself. There is little career training available; rather, editing as a profession typically draws people with a love of language and an aptitude for grammatical precision. As a writing feature, it is treated as a skill that is part of the professional writer's toolkit and is learned on the job.

Generally speaking, editing takes two forms:

- *Rough (or content) editing*—This work focuses upon the overall narrative in terms of logic, clarity and continuity. A content editor will regularly change the structure—and even the location—of chapters, remove large chunks of superfluous text, and call upon the author to create new material to be added to the copy. Rough editing almost always takes precedence over fine editing. Rough editing is sometimes done, at least in part, by the publisher in order to shape the text into the most saleable form.
- *Fine (or line) editing*—Once the manuscript has been pounded into shape by the rough editor, the work of polishing the text is given to the line editor. That person's task is, as the term suggests, to look at the individual sentences—lines—in the manuscript and make sure they meet the highest standards for grammar and rhetoric. The line editor will also check for factual accuracy and consistency in the spelling and use of a given term. The typical line editor is a contractor with a strong background in English or other language—a graduate student or PhD candidate, for example.

Why edit?

Because even the best writing can still be improved. Perfection is endlessly elusive. And even a small mistake that survives the production process and reaches the end reader can raise doubts about the accuracy of the entire work or the author's writing skills. Particularly egregious errors can lead to everything from bad reviews to lawsuits. In heavily empirical works—textbooks, operating and repair manuals, reference books—errors can cause catastrophic results.

It is also important for new writing to pass by more than one set of eyes. Authors typically have trouble seeing their own mistakes, while a dedicated line editor can ignore content and just focus on the words. By the same token, writers can also fall in love with their creations, and it sometimes takes a content editor (especially a publisher who can enforce their choices) to take an axe to large sections of unnecessary text.

Finally, no writing is above editing. T. S. Eliot's *The Wasteland* is generally considered one of the greatest poems of the twentieth century. But sometime take a look at Eliot's draft of the poem and then at the final version of the same poem after it was edited by another famous poet, Ezra Pound. There is no comparison: in cutting Eliot's poem nearly in half, Pound took an impressive, but indulgent work and turned it into a masterpiece. If one of the greatest of all poems needed a serious, even harsh, editing; then no other writer can ever claim his or her work is beyond editing. And, in fact, writers who have tried to build careers off first drafts—such as Sherwood Anderson—managed to produce some good work, but it always fell below their potential.

In the author's career as both a magazine (content) editor and a book (content and line) editor, he has worked with many of the world's finest authors and essayists. In his experience, the most successful of these writers not only let their work be edited, but actually embrace the process—to the point of trusting their editor's judgment on key matters of style and content as highly as their own. They know that a good editor is to be treasured—and used again and again.

What kind of writing should be edited?

Every kind of writing—from novels and poems to e-mails, tweets, business correspondence, legal documents even signage—needs to be edited. Speaking from experience, not editing can have some nasty consequences: just misspell a common word while typing an important note or memo and turn it into an obscene, racist or sexist word—and you will carefully edit your copy ever after. So why not do it *before* you ruin your reputation or wreck your career?

For most things, including tattoos, editing should take place before the final act of creation: having ink injected into your skin, sending off a manuscript to your publisher, writing a love note, firing off a memo to your boss, and so forth. You can't take those back. Happily, in the digital age a few things, such as blogs, can be retroactively edited.

If you want a reputation as a professional writer, you should get into the habit of editing *everything* you write, *every time*. In due course, it will become second nature and can be accomplished in just a matter of seconds. Along the way, you will be amazed (and a little appalled) by just how often you write incoherent, ungrammatical or incomplete sentences. And you'll wonder how many times you sent off similarly damaged copy in the past without knowing it.

How to edit

1. *Edit as you create*—Reread each sentence or paragraph quickly after you write it. Does it make sense? Do you not know a fact? Leave a "TK." Read word for word in your head for continuity, transitions and to check for run-on sentences. Do this quickly: don't let it impede the flow of creativity.
2. *When the text is completed*—I've already said this several times in this book, but I'll say it again: Put it aside (if you can) for long enough that you can read the work with fresh eyes. That may not be possible if you are under a tight deadline. If that's the case, then focus upon the lede, key points, quotes and the spelling of names—the first two for logic and content, the latter two for accuracy. If, instead, you are under a long deadline, put the work aside for a week or two, then return to it with new eyes. Don't skip over copy just because it is familiar, and you assume you know it—that's where you'll make your worst mistakes. The author of this book long ago discovered, from painful experience, that whenever he assumed he was knowledgeable about a topic, the spelling of a name, a job title, that was when he was at the greatest risk of being wrong—and he would have to make a public or private correction and apology. Learn from such failures. In the era of Google and Wikipedia, there is no excuse for not looking something up.
3. *If editing someone else*—Read the work all the way through first. This is less important with line editing, but if you are content editing it is a near necessity. Otherwise, you will add content that the author has already added a few pages later, draw incorrect conclusions and ask questions that soon will be answered. Furthermore, you need to read

the work first to understand its style, tone and pace so you can match or maintain those features in your edits.

4. *Set out a block of time to edit*—By the same token, try to get a block of work done in a single session. The obvious block of work is to edit an entire chapter or multiple complete chapters at a time. Short of that, edit distinct sections within a chapter, or a single topic in, say, an instruction manual. On the other hand, don't burn yourself out by trying to take on too much editing work at one time: just as with writing, the quality of your editing will deteriorate.

5. *Priorities*—Good editing is best pursued by following a hierarchy of attention. In fact, there are two such sets of priorities: macro, which looks at the big picture (typically used with content editing); and micro, the process of editing (typically used with line editing).

Macro: Attack the narrative by asking the following questions:

    a. *What is the overall theme*? Does the work stick with that theme or does it drift off into tangents?

    b. *What is the overall structure of the work?* Does the narrative stay within that structure? Are the chapters (or sections) of similar length? Is the formatting of the chapters/section maintained?

    c. *Does the text have a continuous, logical arc?* Is the logic maintained through the work? Are there any contradictions? Do each of the chapters contribute to that arc?

    d. *Does the text support its underlying claims?* Is that support reliable and fully documented?

    e. *Are the goals of the book stated at the beginning*?

    f. *Is the text complete in achieving its goals?* Does it achieve *all* its goals or just *most* of them? What is needed to achieve the missing goals—or should these goals be removed from the text? Are the chapters themselves internally logical?

    g. *Are the key points fully supported by facts?*

    h. *Are all the individuals described or quoted in the text done so accurately?*

    i. *Are the footnotes (if used) both complete and sufficient?*

Micro

    a. Use a red pen or red pencil for visibility and distinguish the edits from the surrounding text.

    b. Place check marks in the margin alongside sentences that contain your edits (so they won't be overlooked).

    c. Circle your edits whenever possible. This, too, keeps small edits (such as commas) from being missed. Also, if you add words nearby or in the margin, both circle that addition and draw an arrow precisely to the spot where it belongs.

d. Place a "TK" as a place-holder for information that is currently not available, but needs to be found and inserted.

e. Look for noun–verb disagreements, typically singular versus plural. This is a common error, especially in long sentences with lots of clauses. It is also often found when describing a grouping of human beings. Thus, "the team *is* having a good year", but "the members of the team *are* having a good year."

f. Check initial-capitalized nouns. The first letter of many words— brand names ("Ford") and technical terms ("The Scientific Method") in particular—are capitalized. On the other hand, you'll find—especially if you are in public relations—that people regularly, and improperly, capitalize job titles ("Assistant Deputy Marketing Manager for Consumer Goods") in order to inflate their image. Fight that trend: otherwise your press release will be almost unreadable to modern eyes.

g. Break up long paragraphs and long sentences. There is a tendency when writing sentences and paragraphs to keep writing them, piling on more and more content. There is nothing wrong with that if it makes composition easier. But don't let it survive the editing process. For long sentences use the *breath test*: read the sentence aloud, and if you run out of breath it is too long. Break it up, the easiest way being to just repeat the subject reference: "The car has inferior brakes. It also has lousy steering." For long paragraphs use the *commitment test:* Look at the paragraph on the page: if you hesitate to tackle such a huge block of text, chop it up and in that way put some white space on the page. Make the breaks where there is even the slightest shift in the narrative flow.

h. Write down the spellings of key terms and names. Just hand write them on a pad of paper or a digital tablet for easy reference. That way you can make sure the author (including you) remains consistent throughout the text—you'll be amazed how the spelling of a name will slowly change over the course of the narrative. Using spellchecker software may seem easier and more efficient—but the reality is that if a misspelling becomes another real world you may never find it.

i. Kill exclamation points and clichés. The only time you should *ever* use an exclamation point is when you are quoting someone who is shouting or exclaiming (hence, the term). Using an exclamation point in anything other than dialog is essentially demanding the reader exhibit an emotion he or she may not feel is deserved. For that reason, it is insulting—something you never want to do to a reader. As for clichés, we tend to use them in our speech because they are a simple shorthand for complex concepts. But, in writing, clichés are the mark of author laziness and suggest to the reader that the author has an unoriginal mind. Worse yet is to treat a cliché as if it is an original creation: "As I always say, 'a stitch in time saves nine.'" That makes you look like an idiot—not the best impression to make on someone you want to take you seriously. Clichés are pretty easy to spot in the writing of others, but much harder to find when editing your own work. The only answer is to develop a powerful cliché detector—it takes time—and then ruthlessly edit them out of your writing.

j. Run your editing results past the author. Make sure he or she understands your editing marks and can decipher your comments or written additions. If you are also expected to insert your edits, use editing software in the "track changes" mode. If you are the author and have performed a handwritten edit, insert your changes—or if you are using editing software, accept the changes and then read the entire text to make sure the edits are clean—inevitably you'll find that some spacing is missing—and that you haven't missed anything.

Editing jobs

The term *editor* covers a lot of different careers, many of them requiring only a tiny amount of time with a red pencil in your hand. Elsewhere in this book we deal in depth with those "other" editing jobs—most of them management positions with publications or publishing houses. Here, we will address those positions only as they relate to copyediting.

As with many other writing professions, editing work takes two forms—full-time work and freelancing, though in the case of editing, the preponderance of work is probably freelance and contract work.

Freelance editor—There are thousands of these jobs, ranging from occasional work to nearly full time, and for every type of publication from small-town newspapers to presidential memoirs to Nobel Prize–winning scientific papers to novels and screenplays. They can pay from nothing (if a side responsibility to another job) to the equivalent of a professional salary (assuming several book-length jobs per year). As with all freelancing, this type of work is also a business, requiring bookkeeping, marketing and all the other duties of being a sole proprietor. Though there are a few agencies and brokers out there that will manage this work for a fee, they are comparatively rare—and you need to determine if the added work is worth the cost.

Copy editor—Copy-editing work, especially part-time or contract work, can be found at almost every level of publishing, from local newspapers to national magazines to book-publishing houses. Only blogs and newsletters, because of their small operating budgets, and e-books, because they are self-published, typically go without the services of independent editors and require the authors to do their own editing work. Otherwise, all other publishing operations either contract editors by the job (if small) or employ full-time copy editors (if large). Large book-publishing houses typically employ editors in management positions who serve as the content editors of the books they purchase, and who hire freelance line editors for each book.

Line editor—Book editors typically employ a line editor to clean up a book's text in detail after they have finished with the rough editing work. Because most editors have several books in queue at one time, they often maintain a stable of line editors they can contract to work in parallel. These contract editors are typically recent graduates of top universities—with skills either in language and grammar or in a particular field of expertise, or better yet, both. Others are older versions of the same individuals currently at home raising families or between jobs or otherwise looking for an added source of income.

Section editor—Magazines, newspapers, and web 'zines are usually of sufficient size that they are divided into sections, each dedicated to a different topic (sports, business, news, arts and entertainment, and so forth.) Each section is usually managed by an editor, often with a copy editor in a secondary role. Section editor is normally the first step into a publication's senior management and combines the managing of reporters, the assignment of stories and rough editing of the finished result. This editing work is done quickly and focuses only on the lede and story organization. The rest of the work is done by the section copy editor.

News and assignment editor—The next step up from the section editor, the news and assignment editor is in charge of the "front" of the publication—that is, the "News" sections (local, regional, national, world). This job also entails managing a crew of senior copy editors who handle the editing of the stories in the "front of the book (publication)." Any actual editing by the news and assignment editor is minimal and focuses primarily on the lede stories of the day and headlines.

Managing editor—The various section editors (including the news editor) report to the managing editor, who directs the day-to-day operations of the publication. As the equivalent of a corporate chief operating officer, managing editors do little actual "editing"—not surprising, given their considerable management duties. But they will sometimes play the role of editor on major stories, investigative series, special sections, and so forth—considering the importance (and potential for lawsuits) of those stories.

Executive editor/editor in chief—As the CEO of publication or publishing house (the publisher is the chairman of the board), the executive editor/editor-in-chief does almost no line editing. But he or she may perform some content editing at the highest level—especially if the author is either a celebrity or has been paid an enormous advance (and thus the reputation of the entire publishing enterprise is at stake). Even then, the majority of the editing will still be assigned to others down the chain of command.

Career: The good

It is professional. Except at the top, editors don't get a lot of attention, much less glory, but smart writers know enough to value them. Leaving aside management-type editors, who enjoy all of the perquisites of power and position—even freelance editors are treated as professionals and as experts in their fields. Great line editors are never short of work; great content editors have almost unlimited opportunities in management.

It is for perfectionists. Perfectionism is a prerequisite for line editors. Your job is to fix the content and/or grammatical errors of authors—not to overlook or add to them. In this work there is no margin for error. That said, if you are a natural perfectionist and worry over every detail, this is one profession where your personality will put you at a distinct advantage.

You deal with important people. The better your reputation as an editor becomes the more influential the authors you will deal with. At the highest levels, you will work with—and contribute to—the work of the world's finest authors, writers and journalists, as well as heads of state, entertainment stars and captains of industry. And, more than likely, you will help turn a problematic work into an award-winner or bestseller.

You are considered irreplaceable. Smart writers, when they find a good content editor—even a great line editor—will stick with them indefinitely. Full-time copy editors at publications are especially esteemed, and often experience an esteem equal to executives.

It is a steady, very-long career. Great editors, at every level, enjoy almost unmatched job security. At some publications that especially value quality editing—such as the *New Yorker*—they can stay on the job for decades, more esteemed by the year and enjoying enormous power.

There are management opportunities. Though it is not true in Hollywood, in print, Web and television, being an editor is the standard pathway to junior, middle and senior management. That said, to climb that career ladder you must be willing increasingly to delegate actual editing and focus your time and energy on management, strategic planning and leadership—and supporting more junior editors.

Career: The bad

A career in the details. If you work in line editing, you may find over time that you get tired of seeing the trees and never the woods—that is, the job requires laser-like focus on individual words and sentences and you almost never get the chance to actually read (and enjoy) the entire work. One potential solution is to take on content editing work, even if you need to work at a discount to get the job.

It can be drudge work. Most people, in fact, find editing—particularly line editing—to be the ultimate boring, detailed work. That includes most writers; which is why they hire you. And even if you enjoy editing, there may come the day (as it does with most jobs) when you grow tired of it; when the fine detail and slow pace becomes excruciating. Once again, the solution may be to make a lateral move into content editing.

You'll encounter unappreciative writers. The writing profession contains its share of jerks. And for a profession that requires a certain level of intelligence, they can be pretty stupid, too, and never more so than when they don't appreciate the value of their editors. Some writers treat everyone like servants, not least editors. When this happens, no matter how famous the client, quit—no job is worth being treated like a slave. Find a client who appreciates your skill.

There's no recognition. Inside your publication, or with your book editor at the publishing house, your work may earn you respect and, over time, even veneration. But to the outside world, even if you are listed in a book's acknowledgements, you are invisible. That will not change, ever, unless you become a content editor and work your way up through management. If you can live with anonymity and don't crave personal fame, then you will be fine; but if you begin to envy the success of people you edit, then you may struggle with your career.

Turning points

Compared to most careers related to writing, a life in editing usually doesn't have a lot of turning points. That's because the career is largely self-selecting: since there are no college degrees in editing, this is work that you enter into consciously and stay in by choice. Still, there are moments when you will find yourself re-evaluating your career choice.

The move to management—If you are a successful editor, even as a freelancer, you will likely be given an opportunity to take on an entry-level management position. This is the moment when you have to decide whether to stay a line editor or move up the organization chart.

The editing pigeon hole—The first opportunity to enter management usually comes early in your career. If you are not interested, that is one thing, simply turn it down. But if you are interested, and the offer doesn't come, you may well find yourself trapped as a line editor for the rest of your career. If that happens, you need to signal your boss of your interest. It may be as simple as asking. Or you may want to take courses or get a training certificate in management. If you want to go all the way to the top, look into night MBA programs at nearby universities.

Forever the bridesmaid—Some people go into editing as a way to enter the world of journalism or authorship; as a placeholder until they find that writing job or sell that novel. Then, when those events don't occur quickly enough, those folks find themselves locked into a prosperous, but ultimately frustrating, editing career. There is no obvious solution to this other than not to give up: do your creative work on the side and try to build a new career. You may even be able to use your unique contacts as an editor to make submissions. The author has never known anyone who stuck with writing, even in the face of rejections, who didn't eventually become an author.

In the meantime, don't give up your day job.

Rejection

Every human being knows the definition of rejection in his or her life. "Rejection" in the context of professional writing is the experience of having a proposal or a completed piece of writing turned down by a targeted publication or other media venue.

Like other forms of rejection, literary rejection can be a deeply painful experience, particularly when you take that rejection as a judgment on your writing skills or, worse, your value as a human being. The key is to put that rejection in proper perspective and develop strategies for turning it into acceptance. In this chapter we'll look at those strategies in detail. (For simplicity, we use "publication" to represent all media.)

Basic rules

We start with some simple (but not necessarily easy) rules for responding to a rejection letter or e-mail from a publication.

1. *Learn to deal with rejection*. It's part of being a writer, as much as it is of acting, dancing and other arts. Want to know real rejection? Have a career as an actor: endless casting calls and tryouts, almost always ending in rejection, sometimes on the most personal terms. Compared to that, having your writing rejected is easy. Just tell yourself up-front that rejection goes with being a writer—even famous writers sometimes fail to sell a piece—and that you need to incorporate that experience into your working life.
2. *Get over it*. Having an article or story or book rejected is usually not an evaluation of you as a person, or even of your talent, but simply a bad fit between what you wrote and what the publication needs. Given that, why take it personally? Instead, find the publication or publisher where it is a good fit.
3. *Get back to work*. Get angry. Get over it. And get on to the next project or pitch. Don't dwell on rejection—it'll break your spirit and make you hesitate to pitch the next time. Great writing is built on confidence.

4. *Learn from it*. The tendency when you get rejected is to hide. Don't do that. Instead, ask the editor what was wrong with the piece. Be professional with your inquiry, not churlish, and try to glean as much useful information as possible to make your piece more saleable—and make that editor more receptive to your next pitch.

5. *Resell*. There is more than one venue for every writing job. Take what you've learned, quickly modify the piece, and get it out there again. If you can get a kill fee for the rejection, that too is revenue from your writing. And remember: four or five kill fees are worth more than one sold piece.

6. *Develop relationships*. You are more likely to have your work bought, even if it needs a lot of modification, if you have developed a personal relationship with the editor or have a history with the publication. Don't just communicate with that editor or publication when you are pitching the story. If you sell the piece, write and thank them when the article appears. Over time, as you become more a part of the "family," you will find that pitching, acceptance, editing and payment become much easier.

7. *Give it away*. In the age of the blogosphere, any piece you can't sell still can be placed on the Web for free and used as personal promotion. Nothing you write should ever be wasted. All can be added to your reputation.

Not all rejections are the same

Neophyte and amateur writers have a tendency to assume that rejection is just that: a complete turndown. Professionals understand that there are many different forms of rejection. And, further, that they can learn from a rejection—often even more than from an acceptance.

Rejection takes several forms. Use this taxonomy to determine how to respond:

1. *Pitch rejection*—This occurs when a pitch letter or an e-mail to a publication is responded to with the statement that the publication is not interested in the story idea being proposed. This type of rejection can take three forms:

    a. *Unconditional*—The publication simply rejects the idea with no further comment. Your response: quickly pitch it elsewhere. Don't try to pitch this story to this publication again, in any form or modification.

    b. *Conditional*—The publication rejects the idea but leaves the door open for further modifications to make that idea acceptable, but without guarantees (that is, they will only look at the replacement pitch on spec). Your response: Determine what your odds are of getting it right the second try versus pitching elsewhere. Make your decision and respond rapidly.

c. *Alternative*—The publication rejects the idea, but suggests another story idea, again on spec. Your response: pitch the current story idea elsewhere, quickly. Determine your odds of selling the new idea to the original publication. If you like the odds, take the job. If you don't like the odds, thank the publication for its consideration and leave the door open for future pitches.

2. *Pitch partially rejected*—This occurs when the pitch letter is answered with the suggestion to modify the original idea in some major way. This type of rejection takes two forms.

a. *On spec*—The publication wants you to revise your pitch, with no promise of giving you the assignment. Your response: decide if it is worth your trouble. Determine if you have the skills and contacts to do the alternative version.

b. *On acceptance*—The publication wants you to revise your pitch, with the promise to give you the assignment. Your response: Determine if you have the skills, interest and contacts to do that alternative version. If so, take the gig.

3. *Story rejection*—You have already gotten the assignment and have written and submitted the finished story. Now you have been informed by the publisher that the story has been rejected outright. Your response: Go somewhere else, immediately. Don't try to convince an editor; it is a done deal. Ask for a kill fee—after all, your idea was accepted, and you did the work. Better yet, have already asked for a kill fee in your original negotiations.

4. *Story rewrite*—The publication likes your story but now wants you to take it in a new direction; or it wants you to do additional reporting, add a thousand-word sidebar, and so forth. Your response: if a new direction, take the gig; a sale is a sale. If a major addition, ask for more money.

5. *Assigned story rejection*—A publication asks you to write a story. You complete the job only to have your assigned story killed because of content, space limitations or another reason. Your response: Demand a kill fee and the right to sell the story elsewhere, including to the publication's competition. If the latter is refused, demand the full fee and negotiate down. If the story is rejected for reasons other than content or quality, immediately ask for another assignment. They owe you one.

6. *Assigned story partial rejection*—Your story is accepted, but the publication tells you it needs a major rewrite. Your response: Agree. It's

a sale. But, you've wasted a lot of time, so ask for partial payment to get you through.

Ultimately, the most important thing about getting a story rejected is to learn why it happened in order to become a better writer. Again, don't take the rejection personally. It is very possible that your piece was rejected for reasons far beyond your control. For example, you send a poem to a literary magazine and it is rejected. It may be because the editor didn't like its subject matter. Or she was putting the latest issue to bed and had already laid out the content for printing. Or he has already accepted a poem with exactly the same subject.

In other words, there can be a hundred different reasons why your poem was rejected *that have exactly nothing to do with the quality of the poem or your talent as a poet.* If you let this rejection stop you from submitting your poem elsewhere, you will be doing yourself and your potential readers a disservice.

By the same token, don't let an acceptance convince you that you are a genius: your poem may have been accepted solely because another poet pulled her piece from that issue and your piece arrived at just the right moment and is of the right length to fill the newly created editorial hole. So, don't let that acceptance letter give you a big head (well, maybe a little bigger) and lead you to assume that your next pitch to the publication will have the same happy result.

Just stay focused. Do your best work always. And treat rejection (and acceptance) with the same skepticism—and as a stimulus to try even harder. Professionals don't let one setback, or one win, change their career plans.

A Writer's Life

Until now, this textbook has been about professional writing careers. We close with a look at the life of a professional writer.

The fundamental question

How should a writer live his or her life and conduct a career in order to achieve the greatest contribution, compensation, satisfaction and happiness? At the beginning of your working life this may not seem like a big deal: you're too busy with just trying to start your career, not worrying about how to finish it. But trust the author: there will come a time when you ask yourself whether it was all worth it, and what will be your legacy. The sooner you start asking yourself those questions, the better the odds that you will find (or more accurately, create) satisfying answers.

The following is the career wisdom of the author, acquired over the course of forty years as a professional writer. It is incomplete and, in some cases, perhaps even wrong—or at least a poor fit for your life. So, take it as you will, and keep searching for answers from every other professional writer you meet.

Recognize that you will change

Appreciate from the start that the person you are at 20 is not the person you will be at 40 or 60 or 80. Not only will your skills change, but also your interests and your dreams. Don't get stuck trying to live out fantasies that are no longer valid to your life—that is, just because at 20 you wanted to be a novelist, and told everybody so, doesn't mean at 50 you are still obliged to write that novel. No one cares. If something else inspires you instead, go after it—don't linger on the past.

Recognize that the world's perception of you changes as well

As you conduct your career, you will gain a reputation. Find out what that reputation is and don't delude yourself that you are seen as someone you are not. If your reputation is the one you want, then figure out how to cultivate and grow it. If it is not the one you want, then develop a strategy to change that reputation. And don't just sit where you are, trying to maintain the status quo, because your reputation will deteriorate if you don't tend to it.

Don't look back

Your past mistakes will only haunt you, while your past successes may depress you about the present. Save your nostalgia for retirement.

Learn from your biggest mistakes

The author once had a television series in which he interviewed the biggest names in high tech. What he learned was that while most people try to forget or bury their biggest screw-ups, really successful people regularly revisit them. They constantly pull them out, like talismans, and study them for what they can learn. They dedicate themselves to never making the same mistake again.

Don't fear past failures; use them to educate yourself. Erase their sting, keep them always at hand, and promise yourself to never do them again.

Take risks when you're young

The early years of your career are the time to roll the dice. Devote time to a long-shot idea; move to another city or country; quit a job on principle; go broke; write that novel. You can still do those things later in life—but it will be a whole lot harder when you have a mortgage and a family as hostages.

Always have multiple irons in the fire

Never trust an impending project not to fail—even sure things. And *never* bet your future on a single gig. Always have several other ideas in the works. It is virtually guaranteed that all but one or two will fall away. And on the rare occasion when more than two projects suddenly pan out, suck it up, put in the added time, and do them all. Use the extra income to reward yourself or to buy something you've been putting off.

Hit your deadlines, and deliver what you have been asked for

Don't get a reputation for being chronically late or needing a lot of rework. Leave yourself enough time to polish your writing to professional standards. Put in all headings, subheads, footnotes and so forth before you deliver the copy. If you are going to be late, have a very good reason, and notify your editor ahead of time. Never surprise an editor.

Cultivate your superiors and take care of your subordinates

This goes for almost any career, not least professional writing. It doesn't mean being a suck-up to your boss. But it does mean getting to know your boss, being a reliable subordinate, working to your mutual advantage, taking on the most challenging jobs—and in every way positioning yourself for promotion. By the same token, when you are placed in a management role, your job is to help your employees have the best possible career. This includes protecting them from unfair treatment, challenging them to do their best work and, perhaps the most difficult of all, helping them advance in the organization. Too many bosses see their subordinates as a potential threat and actively sabotage their careers. Don't be that boss.

Respect your elders and listen to their advice

Old-timers may talk your ear off, and they can be wrong in some of their arguments, but their opinions are hard-earned from experience. Listen, then try to escape their mistakes and build upon their successes. Someday you'll be that old veteran writer—and if there is any justice, you will be treated the way you treated your predecessors.

Celebrate your successes and learn from your errors

Life is short, enjoy it. Sell an article—buy a nice lunch. Sell a book—have an expensive dinner. Early in his career, the author used to celebrate a book sale with a new fountain pen (these days, he just pays the mortgage). True successes don't come along very often, so set those moments aside and honor them. By the same token, don't sweat your mistakes. Well, a little— at least enough that you learn from those mistakes, remember them, and don't make them again.

Enjoy the work you're doing while you're doing it

We all have a tendency to look beyond what we're doing now to the Next Big Thing. And while it's good to have a long-term strategy, and to keep your eye on the distant prize, it can also keep you from appreciating the here and now. A life spent thinking only of the future is a life of eternal dissatisfaction with the present. And what if you never do reach your goal—was your life then a waste of time? Learn to enjoy what you are doing at any moment. Find satisfaction in the small, the quotidian, and the as-yet unfinished.

Family and friends come first

The good news for writers in our mobile digital age is that you can do your work on a beach while on vacation. The bad news is that you *will* do your work on a beach while on vacation. Being a writer can be 24/7/365 if you let it. Don't let it. The work will consume your life and will become a vicious spiral in which, as you become more alienated from the rest of your life, you justify that alienation by working even harder. You get to see yourself as a martyr, and not the selfish person you really are. It is a cliché, but nevertheless tragically true, that nobody ever lies on their deathbed regretting they spent more time at the office—even if that office is just down the hallway in your house.

Your close personal relationships—family and friends—are the most important things in your life. Never forget that; no matter what the demands of work. And don't fool yourself either. Take it from me: walking around behind the bleachers talking on a business call while your children play on their sports team is not being a good parent. You are only there in body, not in spirit. Turn off the phone and go cheer your kids.

Cover your core

Determine your basic cost of living per month and do whatever it takes to guarantee that income. After that, focus on the projects you want to do. Remember Wilkins Micawber's famous line from *Oliver Twist:* "Annual income twenty pounds, annual expenditure nineteen pounds nineteen and six, result happiness. Annual income twenty pounds, annual expenditure twenty pounds nought and six, result misery."

There is a lot of wisdom in Dickens's words, especially so if you intend to pursue a career as a freelance writer. You need to have a very precise idea of what is your monthly expense nut—rent, car payments, food, your childrens' orthodontist. You must cover that cost any way you can—even if it means writing press releases under contract or taking a part-time non-writing job. If you don't, you will suffer—worse, your family will suffer.

Then, once you cover your core expenses you are free to either take on safe writing work that will pad your income, or (especially if you aren't married) tackle some speculative ventures—such as writing a novel—in hopes that you can supercharge your career or get rich.

Always go bigger

Don't stand pat. Never stop fighting for a larger audience, a higher-profile creation, a national platform, a bigger publisher's advance. The truth of the writing business is that there is a ratchet effect: while it is very difficult to get to the next level in your work, once you are there it is almost as difficult, if you keep working hard, to fall back down. It may take you twenty years to become a writer at the national level—but once you've arrived, your resume, your reputation and your connections will likely keep you at the level for as long as you want to be there.

Be multimedia

In the twenty-first century, it is not enough to be a good writer. You also need to know how to write in different styles and for different venues. Even more, to survive you have to know audio and visual technologies. You can't learn how to do this by reading a book; rather you need to spend time behind a camera, in front of a microphone, and sitting in an editing suite. One of the best ways to do this is while you are still in college is to take courses in broadcasting. It gets harder later: some of these skills you can learn on the job (assuming you work in the right place) or by taking night classes at a local community college. But get those skills; don't assume that you will live by writing alone in the decades to come.

Learn to speak publicly

Surveys have found that the average person puts public speaking second, just behind dying, as their greatest fear. And the reality is that some people are quite comfortable speaking in front of any sized crowd and don't understand what the big deal is for others. The fact is, you do not have to be an accomplished public speaker to be a successful professional writer— but it sure helps.

In the corporate world, a talent for public speaking—at corporate events, trade shows, conferences, and so forth—is a prerequisite for advancement to the vice-presidential or director level. As a television or radio reporter, part of your job description will be to emcee community events. And as a book author or novelist, you will be expected to do television and radio interviews as well as speak at book signings and other promotional events. In almost every field of professional writing, public speaking will enhance your reputation, capture new readers and could contribute a major portion of your income.

But if you do want to pursue public speaking and are nervous about it, there are a number of ways to overcome your fears. First, start with small groups of people you know (though confident speakers will tell you that small audiences, whose faces you can see, can be tougher than giant audiences of anonymous faces); prepare a stump speech that you can all-but memorize; and practice, practice, practice.

As for television and radio interviews, you can prepare for those with a friend and a video recorder. Watch your physical and verbal mannerisms and get rid of any eccentricities. Dress simply and plainly. Don't look at the camera. And give succinct answers.

Pro bono work

Samuel Johnson: "No man but a blockhead ever wrote except for money." You are a professional, don't ever write again for free—with one exception: your skill can be very valuable to nonprofit institutions, your kids' school, your favorite political candidate, and so forth. So, be a good person and a good citizen and donate your skills to your community. But never donate those skills to a for-profit institution ever again.

Your writing is a business, not an art form

We have said this again and again: treat your writing career as a profession, not a calling. Manufacture your product—words—but also take care of the rest of the business, including marketing, promotion, finance and billing and taxes. The better you run your business the more money you will make and the more time you have to do the writing you want. Run your business poorly—or worse, ignore it—and you will eventually find yourself taking on work you don't want to do, and at the expense of the work you want to do. If you can't do the business side of your profession (and don't kid yourself, you can) hire a bookkeeper. But to save costs, just go out and buy some bookkeeping and tax-preparation software.

Meanwhile, learn to negotiate the highest fee or advance. Invoice immediately. Keep track of your income and expenses. As your business grows, hire a good tax accountant.

Manage your money

If you have a full-time writing job, carefully budgeting your paychecks can buy you some time to do the writing you want or to attend a writers' conference. If you are a freelancer, you'll discover that payments for your writing—especially books—usually come in large lump sums. You need to learn to string that money out over time until the next payment. Train your creditors, bank, landlord and so forth to expect tardy payments combined with multiple payments.

Marry well

No, this is not advice on who to marry—only that it helps to have a patient spouse who can manage money. Writers can be difficult people to live with, not least because they have to swing back and forth from creative to promotional modes every few months. And, of course, there are the reviews. That said, too many writers like to excuse their boorish or selfish behavior because they are creative people. That is garbage. There is no excuse for treating the people in your life badly—or taking advantage of them by living off their wages while not working hard yourself. And shame on you if you try to teach the people in your life otherwise.

You've only got to be great once

Back when the author had an interview series on American public television, he had the opportunity to interview the novelist William Styron. We were talking about another novelist, Ralph Ellison, when I noted that it was tragic that Ellison had written the great novel *Invisible Man*—and never published another book in his lifetime. No, Styron replied, not tragic at all—you only have to write one masterpiece to make your reputation forever. Everything else will be forgotten anyway.

As I grow older, the more I'm convinced Styron was correct. Your fans may be disappointed, but your professional peers know that if you can write that one great story or book your reputation is set. The problem is, how do you know which book you start will end up being that Big One? You don't. Which means that whenever you get the chance, you should take your very best shot—in baseball parlance, you should always swing for the fences. Every writing job should be your shot at immortality.

Grow old gracefully

There's nothing sadder, or more pathetic, than aged person trying to be young. First of all, it can't be done. Second, it ultimately is a denial of who you really are—that is, you are living a lie. Finally, as a writer, it leads you to write about things you don't know instead of things that you do. So, don't try to stay hip. That's not to say you shouldn't stay informed of what is going on in the world around you; just don't try to live in a reality that isn't yours.

Finally, don't try to compete with younger writers, but rather carve out a safe place where they can't compete with you. And that place is the world and the experiences of your own generation. That will not only protect your career, but free you to help those younger writers.

Apply for awards and honors

Why? Because everybody else is, though most won't admit it. Instead, they'll act as if they are above all of the "glittering prizes." They aren't— and they will win awards that rightly belong to you.

Still, aren't literary awards just about writers' egos? Yes and no. Keep in mind that, for people outside your profession, literary awards are a kind of shorthand for them to get a sense of how your peers judge the quality of your work. It is also how future generations will likely first approach your work—and, in the case of the really big awards (Nobel, Booker, Pulitzer, National Book Award)—is a near-guarantee that your best work will stay in print.

That said, it is crucial that, even as you submit your work for these awards, you understand that they aren't the absolute truth—not an absolute measure of quality, but in part the product of bias by judges, politicking and sheer dumb luck. Never forget that or let awards go to your head: they never help future works, but can only hurt them.

Don't take on any bad vices

Never buy into the myth that drunks are great writers or that heroin makes you a better artist. Your art is created *despite* your vices. Of course, being sober and judicious isn't very romantic—not like being a Malcolm Lowry or William Faulkner spinning out masterpieces supposedly while blind drunk. But the reality is that *nobody* writes well—at least not for long—when they are drunk or high. You just think you're writing well. And you can be certain those great drunken writers did their best work between benders.

There is also the matter of life expectancy. It is romantic to outsiders to read about writers who "lived fast, died young, and left a beautiful corpse." Not only is that last phrase almost always false, but the whole idea of an early death for artists is incredibly wasteful. Most writers (along with most painters) only get better with time. Imagine the great work Rimbaud or Mary Shelley or Rilke might have created if they had lived until their eighties. Their loss is tragic, not thrilling.

No, as professional writer your goal should be to create the best work you can. And that will only be accomplished if you stay healthy, live a long life, and do the best work every step of the way. Then go off into that long night proud of what you have accomplished.

Don't be a jerk

I use a much stronger word when I'm speaking to my classes. But the meaning is the same: don't be a jerk—a bad boss, a bad employee, a company hatchet man or someone who is known for stabbing others in the back.

You are better than that.

If that isn't enough to convince you, then let's try the pragmatic argument: you may think that being a jerk is good for your career—and sometimes it will be, for a while. But then you will hit the wall. No one likes the corporate assassin—especially not the executive who hired him—and you will be fired. Your bad reputation will follow you wherever you go, especially in the Facebook era. Your fellow employees will go out their way to keep your reputation destroyed.

And even if that isn't enough to convince you to be an ethical human being, consider your legacy: being a jerk will be the only thing most people will remember about you. And if you do manage to be successful, your jerkiness and rotten behavior will be recorded forever in your biography. All those people you screwed over will get the last word.

Instead, treat other people decently and with respect. Be ambitious and aggressive, but don't cheat and don't stab others in the back. Let your work speak for itself—and let your integrity, along with a powerful body of work, be your true legacy. Does that sound idealistic? You'll discover that idealism is just pragmatism, maintained over decades.

Pass it along

Professional writing often seems like a solitary activity, but it is an ancient and honorable craft guild. And, as with any guild, it is your duty to share your acquired wisdom with newcomers to the profession, just as your elders shared theirs with you (one of the reasons for this book). It is also your duty in the years ahead to leave the craft stronger than you found it. The technology revolution—with Moore's Law at its heart—is transforming, not just the platforms of communication in our culture, but also language itself, and at a mind-boggling pace. It will be your challenge, not just to keep up with these changes, but to establish new standards of professional writing for all those aspiring writers who will follow you.

Good luck and have a great career.

FURTHER READING

Ultimately, you learn to be a writer by writing (and by being edited); and you learn to be a professional writer by writing professionally, that is, by pitching and selling your work. When you start out as a writer, it is easy—and dangerous—to substitute the actual work of writing with endlessly reading advice books about how to become a writer. This is a common mistake. But, in the end, there is no substitute for doing the work.

That said, once you do become a writer, there is every reason to perfect your craft, to make yourself a better writer and a better manager of your career, not to mention getting your work sold in ever more-lucrative and respected markets. The following books, covering many different careers discussed in this text, are among the most popular and influential works in their fields. If you gain one useful skill or piece of practical information from each of these books, they will be more than worth their price.

Note that these books are designed for practical application to your work. It goes without saying that a number of other books, good and bad, deal with the philosophy of writing, the creative process and getting yourself in the mood for writing. The author offers no opinion on those books, except that, in the end, you still need to do the work.

Bell, James Scott. *How to Write Dazzling Dialogue: The Fastest Way to Improve Any Manuscript.* Woodland Hills: Compendium Press, 2014.
——— . *How to Write Short Stories and Use Them to Further Your Writing Career.* Woodland Hills: Compendium Press, 2016.
Clark, Roy Peter. *Writing Tools: 55 Essential Strategies for Every Writer,* 10th Anniversary Edition. Boston: Little Brown & Co., 2008.
Field, Syd. *Screenplay: The Foundations of Screenwriting.* Little Rock: Delta, 2005.
Fox, Chris. *Write to Market: Deliver a Book that Sells.* Seattle: CreateSpace Independent Publishing, 2016.
Hardy, Janice. *Understanding Show, Don't Tell: And Really Getting It.* Online: Fiction University's Skill Builders Series, 2016.
Hatcher, Jeffrey. *The Art and Craft of Playwriting.* Los Angeles: Story Press, 2000.
Kramer, Mark. *Telling True Stories: A Nonfiction Writers' Guide from the Nieman Foundation at Harvard University.* New York: Plume, 2007.
Noonan, Peggy. *On Speaking Well: How to Give a Speech with Style, Substance, and Clarity.* New York: William Morrow, 1999.
Penn, Joanna. *Business for Authors: How to be an Author Entrepreneur.* Online: CreateSpace Independent Publishing Platform, 2014.

——— . *How to Make a Living with Your Writing: Books, Blogging and More.* (Books for Writers, Book 2) 2nd edn. Bath: Curl Up Press, 2015.

Petit, Zachary. *The Essential Guide to Freelance Writing: How to Write, Work, and Thrive on Your Own Terms.* Writer's Digest Books, 2015.

Ruberg, Michelle, ed. *Writer's Digest Handbook of Magazine Article Writing*, 2nd edn. Cincinnati: Writer's Digest Books, 2004.

Saleh, Naveed. *The Complete Guide to Article Writing: How to Write Successful Articles for Online and Print Markets.* Cincinnati: Writer's Digest Books, 2014.

Sayre, Henry M. *Writing about Art*, 6th edn. Washington, DC: Pearson, 2008.

Scott, Steve. *How to Write Great Blog Posts that Engage Readers.* Online: Kindle, 2014.

Sedniev, Andrii. *Magic of Public Speaking: A Complete System to Become a World Class Speaker.* Online: Kindle Edition, Primed E-launch LLC, 2012.

Sloan, Justin M. *Creative Writing Career: Becoming a Writer of Film, Video Games, and Books,* Writing Mentor vol. 1. Seattle: CreateSpace Independent Publishing, 2015.

Snyder, Blake. *Save The Cat! The Last Book on Screenwriting You'll Ever Need.* Los Angeles: Michael Wiese Productions, 2005.

Strunk, William Jr, and E. B. White. *The Elements of Style*, 4th edn. Foreword by Roger Angell. London: Longman, 1999.

Toscan, Richard. *Playwriting Seminars 2.0: A Handbook on the Art and Craft of Dramatic Writing with an Introduction to Screenwriting.* Oakland: Franz Press, 2012.

Trottier, David. *The Screenwriter's Bible: A Complete Guide to Writing, Formatting, and Selling Your Script,* 6th edn. Los Angeles Silman-James Press, 2014.

Turabian, Kate L. "A Manual for Writers of Research Papers, Theses, and Dissertations: Chicago Style for Students and Researchers." In Kate L. Turabian, Wayne C. Booth, Gregory G. Colomb, Joseph M. Williams, eds., *Chicago Guides to Writing, Editing, and Publishing, 8th edn. Chicago*: Chicago: University of Chicago Press, 2013.

Weiland, K. M. *Structuring Your Novel: Essential Keys for Writing an Outstanding Story.* South Yorkshire: PenforASword, 2013.

Zinsser, William. *On Writing Well: The Classic Guide to Writing Nonfiction,* 30th Anniversary Edition. New York: HarperCollins, 2013.

SUGGESTED ASSIGNMENTS

Chapter 1

1. Interview a friend, family member or interesting individual to produce a five-page interview. Obtain from the subject two topics in detail:
   a. Basic information on themselves, including name, title, job, birthplace, age, education, family members. Focus on being accurate by rechecking everything.
   b. A complete description by the subject of an interesting event in his or her life.
2. Take a breaking news story from a wire service or the Web. Interview someone in your life for his or her opinion on how that story will likely impact them.

Chapter 2

1. Take five sentences from a newspaper, wire service, the Web or a magazine story that is too long, pretentious or complex. Edit those sentences to make them shorter, simpler, with punchier verbs and simpler nouns.
2. Find five great metaphors in literature. Write a paragraph on each explaining why they work.
3. Write five original metaphors of your own. Beware clichès: conduct a Web search to prove they are all but unique (that is, less than five citations)

Chapter 3

1. Take the interview from Chapter 1—from either the entire interview, or from the anecdote told by your subject—and create the first four paragraphs of a feature story. Incorporate at least one quote from your subject in those paragraphs.
2. Take a popular song and convert it into a poem, with a complex meter, caesura and other poetic techniques.
3. Take a complex poem and convert it into a popular song, with a beat and workable chorus.

Chapter 4

1. Using a common consumer product—shoes, toothbrush, briefcase, flashlight, and so forth—and write a two-page press release that includes a lede, opening quote, bulleted list of features, closing quote, price, delivery and boilerplate.
2. Write a pitch letter for that product, one page, with contact information.
3. Using the Web, research and develop a 20-outlet (TV, print, Web) routing for the release and pitch letter.

Chapter 5

1. Form into a team of four or five members. Take a common consumer product—you can use the same item as in Chapter 4—and develop an advertisement for it. You may design it for print, radio or television. Provide both the tagline copy and the body copy for the ad.
2. Take an existing advertisement and rewrite the tagline and copy for a different target audience. Before you do, research that audience on the Web and justify your choices.
3. Using the ad from #1 or #2, determine a target placement for the ad. Investigate the term sheet for that venue and establish a budget for the ad buy.

Chapter 6

1. Write a 30-second introduction to speech to be given by a friend or family member. Include a greeting to the audience, a witty anecdote about the speaker and a closing setup.
2. Write the first three minutes of a speech. Include an opening, a setup to the speech and an outline to the key points of the speech.
3. Write a two-minute toast for a dinner or wedding reception.

Chapter 7

1. Choose a technology-related activity—for example, operating an app on your smartphone—and write a two-page description of how to perform that activity successfully. Focus on covering the entire process, including side activities, and on providing a simple and clear description of the steps.
2. Write a one-page explanation of a complex technology—the microprocessor, GPS, packet switching and so forth—in a manner understandable by someone who is not technologically astute.

3. Take the description you created in #1 and convert it into a video script, including simple storyboards.

Chapter 8

1. Using freeware, establish a blog. Create a homepage using words and images.
2. Using this new blog site, write four multimedia entries on a common theme.
3. Develop a blogroll. Notify those blogs listed and request to be listed on their blogrolls.

Chapter 9

1. Attend a public event, on campus or elsewhere. Write a four-paragraph story, including lede, details on the event, and a quote.
2. Take a story from the newspaper, wire service or Web. Rewrite it to give a local slant.
3. Take the box score from a sporting event. Convert it to a 150-word narrative.

Chapter 10

1. Write a 300-word review of a new music download.
2. Write a 300-word review of a book written in the last six months. Include all publication information, price, and so forth.
3. Write a 300-word review of an episode of a television series or a live performance.

Chapter 11

1. Write the first 150 words of an essay on a literary or arts-related topic. Include a strong thesis statement.
2. Write the first 250 words of an essay on a political or newsworthy topic. Explain the structure of the rest of the essay.
3. Write the first 250 words of a personal essay, beginning with a real-life anecdote and using it as the basis of a larger, universal concept.

Chapter 12

1. Write a three-page proposal on a book idea. Include:
   a. Overview of the idea
   b. Description of the book

    c. Plan for the book (pages, delivery date)
    d. Audience and marketing
    e. Author bio
    f. Table of contents, with two sentences describing each chapter
2. Write a cover letter to this package, giving a brief explanation of the book.
3. Conduct a Web search of potential agents for your book. Look for those who specialize in your field or have represented authors who are like you.
4. If advised by your instructor, contact a selection of likely agents. Write each in turn and send a pitch letter explaining why he or she should represent you; describe the nature of your book idea. This letter should be no more than one page. If you get a response, send the cover letter and book proposal.

Chapter 13

1. Attend a public event, on campus or elsewhere (it can be the same even as #1). Prepare a 30-second radio spot covering the story.
2. Attend a public event, on campus or elsewhere (it can be the same as #1 or #2). Prepare a one-minute television news story. Include description of video clips to be used.
3. Write a 150-word introduction to a television documentary. Provide suggested imagery to accompany this introduction.

Chapter 14

1. Using commercial screenwriting software or freeware, write the first five minutes of a television program or movie.
2. Write a one-page, single-spaced treatment of a movie or television episode.
3. Using standard format, write the opening scene of a play of your devising.

Chapter 15

1. Outline, in two pages, the plot of a novel or novella.
2. Write the opening scene of a novel.
3. Write a 150-word description of the protagonist of your proposed novel.

Chapter 16

1. Take one of your school papers and reformat it to fit a format shown in the *Chicago Manual of Style*. Properly format all citations and footnotes. Add a proper abstract.
2. Take a poem or short story you have written (it does not have to be for this course) and submit it online or via hardcopy to a literary magazine. Show evidence of this submission.
3. Prepare your curriculum vitae in standard form.

Chapter 17

1. Using Photoshop, mock up a poster—including a headline and body copy—for your favorite nonprofit group.
2. Using Photoshop, mock up a printer advertisement—including a headline and body copy—for your favorite consumer product.
3. Using prepared copy and your own voice-over, create a 60-second public-service announcement radio spot.

Chapter 18

1. Write a one-page pitch letter for a proposed story, of your idea, to a newspaper or major magazine. Describe your unique knowledge or access as part of your explanation of why you alone should get the assignment.

Chapter 19

1. Take a homework assignment (including from this course) from this term. Give it a careful line editing. Use standard editing symbols and markings.

INDEX

1990s 46, 197
2010 48, 112
60 Minutes 202, 204
"Blog" 111
"Blogosphere," the. *See* Blog, bloggers
"direct marketing" 43
"inverted pyramid" 63
Joy Luck Club, The 107
"Little Gidding" 25
"newsbites" 68
"Parable of the Cave" 162
"TK" 233
"Pocket Fisherman" 46
"Rashoman-effect" 9
"Vegematic," the 46
"writer's block" 59

Academy Awards 79
ad agency 49, 50, 51, 53, 54, 56, 58, 270
ad copy 27, 57, 61, 62, 64, 270
advertising 24, 27, 29, 43, 44, 45, 46, 47, 48, 49, 50, 51, 52, 53, 54, 55, 56, 57, 58, 59, 60, 61, 63, 64, 96, 102, 103, 114, 213, 247
advocacy blog 114
Africa 13, 16, 163, 184
after dinner speech 86, 87
Agee. *See* Agee, James
Agee, James 145, 148
agent 138, 175, 177, 178, 179, 180, 181, 182, 211, 236, 240
amateurs 20, 23, 63, 64, 116, 145, 178, 216, 218, 235, 260, 270, 271, 278, 294
Amazon 120, 146
Anchor/host 206
anecdotes 1, 74, 76, 77, 83, 86, 165, 224, 311

Anglo-Saxon 16, 17, 100
Apollinaire 150
Apple 38, 223
apprentice 1
apprenticeship 148, 199, 203, 213, 219, 222, 256, 263
Aran sweater 117
Aristophanes 144
Aristotle 162, 237, 238
art monographs 143
articles 23, 89, 96, 115, 117, 143, 144, 183, 184, 190, 222, 271
Associated Press 123
astro-turf 113
Atlantic Monthly 143
audience 29, 30, 37, 43, 46, 47, 56, 61, 63, 68, 70, 71, 72, 73, 75, 76, 77, 79, 82, 83, 84, 85, 86, 87, 88, 91, 97, 109, 112, 113, 116, 117, 118, 143, 146, 148, 149, 151, 153, 154, 155, 166, 170, 179, 195, 196, 197, 199, 201, 202, 203, 204, 205, 206, 207, 210, 212, 215, 216, 218, 219, 224, 227, 272, 300, 310, 312
author 2, 3, 13, 14, 20, 31, 39, 70, 71, 87, 100, 101, 113, 122, 123, 128, 130, 133, 134, 143, 144, 151, 152, 165, 167, 173, 177, 178, 181, 182, 184, 185, 186, 191, 192, 193, 198, 209, 212, 217, 223, 226, 239, 240, 255, 256, 261, 262, 271, 272, 283, 284, 285, 287, 288, 290, 292, 297, 298, 299, 301, 303, 307

backgrounders 35
Bacon, Francis 162
Balzac 30, 163, 226

banner 29, 47, 118, 120
banner ads 47, 118
Barnum, P. T. 126
Barratt, Thomas J. 44
Barry, Dave 144
Barzun, Jacques 150
Baudelaire, Charles 147
Bazin, Andre 150
BBC radio 145
BBS sites 111
beat 18, 59, 84, 118, 121, 122, 124,
    129, 130, 131, 132, 188, 199,
    200, 201, 206, 207, 309
Berlin, Isaiah 142
Bernays, Edward 44
bias 158
billing 3, 104, 105, 270, 275, 277,
    302
biography 174, 179, 279
bloggers 2, 30, 40, 43, 109, 111,
    112, 113, 115, 116, 117, 118,
    119, 120
Bloom, Alan 144
Bolger, Brenna 4
book 1, 2, 3, 4, 15, 20, 28, 59, 63,
    69, 70, 90, 106, 109, 119, 120,
    130, 141, 142, 143, 144, 145,
    148, 150, 154, 156, 158, 161,
    166, 173, 174, 175, 176, 177,
    178, 179, 180, 181, 182, 183,
    184, 185, 186, 187, 188, 189,
    190, 191, 192, 193, 216, 223,
    224, 228, 231, 232, 235, 236,
    257, 259, 260, 261, 262, 264,
    271, 272, 277, 284, 285, 286,
    288, 289, 291, 293, 299, 301,
    303, 305, 311, 312
book proposal 177, 181
Bourke-White, Margaret 36
brand writing 49
Breaking News coverage 198
broadcast 46, 68, 123, 128, 145,
    196
broadcasts 46, 130, 200
Bushman 13, 14
Byte magazine 112

cadences 71, 72, 73
California 10, 217
Car & Driver 148
Carey, Pete 4
Caribbean 16
Castiglione 162
Catch-22 180
Celtic 16
CEO 7, 33, 53, 89, 157, 258, 290
Chamber of Commerce 68, 71
Chesterton, G. K. 142, 163
Chief Joseph 67
China 44
Christgau, Robert 146
Churchill, Winston 67
Cicero 67, 162
clickbait 47
client 2, 7, 48, 50, 51, 52, 53, 55,
    56, 57, 60, 61, 62, 63, 72, 73,
    74, 75, 76, 77, 78, 79, 80, 81,
    82, 85, 86, 87, 88, 91, 92, 99,
    103, 129, 180, 267, 268, 269,
    270, 280, 281, 291
climax 84, 87, 244, 248, 252
Closing of the American Mind 145
Cloud, the 98, 233
CNet 143
CNN 91, 197, 204
"Coke is It"
    slogan 61
college textbook 3
columnist 2, 7, 91, 131, 142, 144,
    148, 196, 260
Comedy 84, 216
commentary 113, 114, 116, 142,
    144, 162, 166, 200, 202
compensation 143, 153
compuserve 111
conclusion 23, 24, 25, 26, 84, 87,
    161, 164, 167, 170, 199, 252
conflict of interest 151
congressman 71
Consumer Reports 148
copy 9, 21, 34, 47, 50, 51, 52, 55, 56,
    57, 59, 61, 62, 63, 64, 74, 75, 78,
    96, 97, 100, 101, 122, 136, 142,

148, 150, 151, 152, 157, 171,
178, 187, 189, 190, 197, 198,
210, 213, 214, 219, 247, 267,
269, 270, 271, 273, 280, 283,
285, 289, 290, 299, 310, 313
copywriter
ad 58
copywriters 48, 50, 51, 52, 53, 54,
55, 56, 60, 64
copywriting 45, 48, 50, 51, 53, 55,
59, 61, 62, 210, 269, 270
corporate writing 95, 109
Correspondent 205
cover letter 30, 32, 33, 34, 178,
190, 312
craft 1, 4, 13, 54, 58, 73, 89, 100,
106, 149, 152, 166, 211, 213,
218, 222, 256, 277, 279, 305,
307
creative collapse. *See* creative stasis
creative writing 23, 106, 107, 109,
214, 256, 259, 261
crime 122, 199
critic
music 2, 131, 142, 143, 146, 147,
148, 149, 150, 153, 154, 155,
156, 157, 158, 159, 163
critical analysis 144
critical biographies 144
criticism 141, 148, 149, 150, 152,
154, 157, 159, 163
critics 141, 142, 143, 145, 146, 147, 148,
150, 154, 155, 156, 157, 158, 159
Cronkite, Walter 197
Crouch, Stanley 146
cultural criticism 147
CV 78, 179

deadline 7, 9, 59, 84, 116, 121, 128,
129, 143, 145, 151, 154, 170,
181, 187, 188, 190, 210, 211,
235, 269, 271, 280, 285
deadlines 2, 113, 119, 124, 127, 134,
141, 142, 150, 154, 156, 157,
198, 199, 205, 279, 298
Degnan. *See* Degnan, James

Degnan, James 4
Democrat Underground 115
Descartes 162
dialog 85, 209, 211, 213, 214, 217,
218, 219, 221, 224, 231, 235,
242, 247, 248, 249, 251, 252
Diderot, Denis 147
draft 62, 73, 74, 75, 106, 130, 179,
182, 183, 233, 269, 273, 284
Drudge, Matt 112
DVD 145

Earth 4, 13
editing 3, 21, 28, 31, 50, 52, 61, 62,
63, 68, 71, 100, 101, 114, 128,
179, 184, 186, 187, 188, 198, 201,
205, 218, 233, 234, 235, 249,
257, 258, 259, 267, 273, 275, 280,
283, 284, 285, 286, 287, 288,
289, 290, 291, 292, 294, 301, 313
editor 2, 7, 8, 19, 26, 29, 34, 37,
43, 71, 102, 113, 115, 121, 122,
125, 126, 128, 134, 135, 136,
151, 155, 157, 158, 167, 169,
170, 184, 188, 199, 205, 214,
236, 257, 258, 259, 278, 279,
280, 283, 284, 288, 289, 290,
291, 292, 294, 295, 296, 299
Egyptian hieroglyphics 15
Eiseley, Loren 21, 163
Eliot, T. S. 25, 163, 284
Emerson 163
England 44, 147
The Epic of Gilgamesh 15
Epictetus 162
essays 24, 111, 143, 144, 145, 146,
156, 161, 162, 163, 164, 165, 166,
167, 168, 169, 222, 259, 260
Eudemian Ethics 162
experimental
novel 1, 109, 224, 225, 236, 262
e-zines 33, 35

Facebook 51, 117, 305
failure 3, 55, 61, 62, 90, 97, 112,
222, 223, 246

Faulkner, William 18, 304
FBI, the 135
feature 33, 131, 200, 260
feature writers 7, 132, 144, 204, 260
fiction 4, 7, 21, 23, 25, 26, 60, 90, 109, 111, 118, 144, 161, 173, 175, 179, 192, 211, 214, 219, 221, 222, 223, 224, 225, 228, 229, 230, 231, 232, 235, 236, 237, 240, 244, 247, 251, 252, 259, 260, 261, 307
fliers 44
Forbes 4
Forbes ASAP
   Forbes 4
Foreign Policy 144, 166
formal address 80
formal addresses. *See* formal address
Fortune 50 company 71
France 44, 147, 165, 226
fraud 52
Free Republic 115
Freelance. *See* freelancer
freelance technical writers 103, 104
freelancer 1, 2, 27, 56, 90, 102, 103, 104, 105, 106, 123, 142, 147, 153, 260, 292, 302
From Dawn to Decadence 150
Fry, Roger 147

Gaelic Irish 14
Germany 44, 226
ghost-written 52
Gide, Andre 159
Golden Sayings 162
Google 118, 285
grammar
   rules 1
Grammys 79
The Grapes of Wrath 67
graphics. *See* Logos
Greenberg, Clement 147
Gross, Teri 196

guidebooks 96, 256
Gutenberg 45

Hall, Justin 111
Hammerstein, Oscar 25
Hammett, Dashiell 21
handbills 44
handbooks 96
Hayes. *See* Hayes, Tom
Hayes, Tom 49
Hazlitt, William 147
Hentoff, Nate 146
Hewlett-Packard 4, 36
Hired-gun speechwriter 90
Hollywood 30, 46, 53, 79, 124, 153, 214, 290
honorary address 83, 84
honorary addresses. *See* honorary address
Hope, Bob 79, 90
Huffington Post 115, 120
Hughes, Robert 147
Hugo, Victor 18
humor 87, 144
Huxtable, Ada Louise 147
hyperbole 151, 178

index 80, 99, 152
India 16, 44
Industry Speeches 85
infomercials 46, 47
informal toasts. *See* untargeted toast
insider/outsider 58
Instapundit 113
intellectual courage 149
Internet reviews 142
Internet, the 7, 10, 36, 45, 48, 87, 111, 114, 115, 116, 148, 157, 164, 171, 205, 225, 227
interviews 9, 11, 81, 124, 125, 127, 134, 154, 179, 184, 190, 197, 199, 201, 204, 205, 206, 210, 212, 301, 302
inverted pyramid 63
investigative reporter 205

invoice
standard form 3, 171, 278, 280, 281

Jobs, Steve 38, 223
journalism 4, 8, 30, 35, 39, 40, 53, 63, 95, 114, 121, 127, 195, 221, 292
journalist 9, 29, 32, 34, 35, 37, 41, 70, 120, 130, 132, 133, 137, 148, 152, 196, 201

Kael, Pauline 145
Karlgaard, Rich 4
Kazin, Alfred 148
kill fee 102, 267, 294, 295
Kubrik, Stanley 143

lawsuits 133
le mot juste 16
lecture 82, 83, 85, 210
lede 20, 32, 63, 97, 122, 125, 126, 127, 130, 154, 169, 170, 197, 199, 235, 285, 289, 310, 311
legal documents 9, 10, 136, 284
Leonidas at Thermopylae 67
Leviestro, Christian 4
libel 9, 133, 136, 138, 165, 205, 206
lifestyle 40, 117, 131, 150, 200
lifestyle news 199
Limbaugh, Rush 196
Lincoln 67, 68
Lincoln at Gettysburg 67
lingua franca 16
Lippmann, Walter 142
Lives of a Cell 21
Logos 48
London Blitz 196
Lone Ranger, The 196
Long Island 10
Los Angeles Times 87
Lost Illusions 30
luncheon speech 86, 87
luncheon speeches. *See* luncheon speech

Macbeth 15
MacDonald, Dwight 148, 163
Machiavelli 162
Madison Avenue 44
magazine
business 2, 4, 8, 39, 53, 91, 96, 117, 120, 135, 145, 147, 155, 157, 163, 173, 176, 183, 184, 187, 202, 206, 257, 258, 284, 296, 309, 313
magazine reviews 142
magazines 28, 30, 31, 35, 44, 45, 114, 132, 142, 143, 145, 146, 147, 157, 160, 161, 166, 168, 202, 204, 259, 260, 289
The Maltese Falcon 21
manual 97, 98, 99, 100, 286
manuscript 174, 178, 180, 182, 183, 184, 185, 187, 188, 189, 191, 223, 262, 283, 285
Marcos regime 10
Marcus Aurelias 162
Marcus, Greil 146
marketing 24, 33, 54, 89, 119, 179, 188, 206, 287, 312
Marsh, Dave 146
masters of ceremonies 78, 79
masters of fine arts 180
mea culpa speech. *See* mea culpa speeches
mea culpa speeches 75
media 3, 10, 29, 30, 31, 32, 33, 34, 35, 36, 37, 38, 40, 43, 47, 51, 52, 68, 69, 80, 81, 95, 98, 109, 112, 117, 122, 152, 153, 158, 168, 176, 186, 189, 190, 195, 196, 197, 205, 206, 210, 211, 212, 213, 226, 227, 228, 271, 275, 293, 301, 311
medium 112
Melodrama 216
memory 186
meta-blogs 114
metaphor 19, 20, 241, 309
methodology 96, 119, 143
Metro 122

Milton, John 162
Mitchell, Jim 4
mnemonics 83
Moby Dick 67, 240, 251
momentum 84, 232
monologue 209, 252
Motor Trend 148
Murrow, Edward R. 196, 201
Muse 1
Muse, The 2

Namibia 13
narrative 11, 16, 20, 22, 23, 24, 25,
    32, 61, 84, 96, 97, 100, 117, 119,
    124, 175, 177, 184, 211, 212, 213,
    215, 230, 234, 235, 236, 240,
    241, 242, 244, 247, 248, 249,
    252, 253, 283, 286, 287, 311
NASA 100, 196
neo-magazines 114
network news 204
New Criterian 144
New England 21
New York Times 147
news release 33, 35, 37, 125, 199
newsletters 28, 31, 289
newsnight 202
newspaper op-ed sections 166
newspaper reviews 141
newsrooms 39, 121, 122, 198
Nicomachean Ethics. See Plato
The Night Country 21
Nixon 75
non-fiction 21, 23, 60, 173, 221,
    222, 223, 231, 260
Noonan, Peggy 69, 308
notebook 127, 231
novelist 2, 7, 56, 59, 71, 97, 107,
    142, 148, 173, 211, 212, 222,
    223, 225, 227, 229, 252, 256,
    261, 272, 297, 301, 303
novel-writing 3
NPR 145

O'Rourke, P. J. 144
official reports 9

Oklahoma 25
Olivier, Laurence 92
Opie and Anthony 196
opinion 166, 202, 259
Opinion Journals 166
Orwell, George 145, 163
Ovambo tribe 13

pacing 18, 169, 174, 198, 218, 222,
    234
paleolithic 43
Palmer, Volney B. 44
Paris fashion week 124
Parsons, Louella 196
Pascal 162
pathos 238
patois 73
Pears Soap 44
Pennsylvania 67
pens 127
philosophy 44, 193, 278, 307
piece 23, 82, 101, 125, 126, 128,
    150, 166, 170, 171, 183, 190,
    232, 234, 239, 242, 259, 279,
    280, 293, 294, 296, 307
pitching 3, 199, 222, 275, 277, 294,
    295, 307
Plato 146, 162
playwright 2, 144, 215, 216, 218,
    219, 229
playwriting 215, 217
poems 24, 168, 225, 226, 259, 284
Poetry 25, 26, 224
poets 7, 147
policy address 81, 82
Popeil. *See* Popeil, Ron
Popeil, Ron 46
*Popular Science/Electronics/
    Mechanics* 148
Porsche 117
portal blog 113
Pournelle, Jerry 111
PR 29, 30, 31, 32, 33, 34, 36, 37,
    39, 40, 49, 53, 54, 57, 89, 102,
    119, 125, 129, 152, 190, 270
    corporate 4

president of the United States 69
President Reagan 69
press conference 38, 81, 87, 130
press kit 34, 35, 38
press release 1, 24, 27, 30, 32,
    33, 34, 35, 36, 37, 39, 122,
    189, 221, 231, 270, 287,
    300, 310
press secretary of the president of
    the United States 75
producer 205, 206, 214
product guides 96
product handbook 99
product warranties 96
professional writer 1, 3, 4, 8, 13, 14,
    15, 17, 24, 51, 54, 59, 64, 168,
    262, 267, 271, 283, 297, 301,
    304, 307
professional writing vii, 98
promotion 29, 70, 119, 201, 206,
    256, 258, 262, 277, 294,
    299, 302
propaganda 44
proposal 177, 178, 179, 180, 181,
    278, 293, 311, 312
Proust, Marcel 18
PRx Inc. *See* Bolger, Brenna
public address 69
public relations 1, 27, 29, 30, 31,
    32, 33, 34, 37, 39, 43, 44,
    51, 58, 75, 89, 103, 125, 132,
    152, 255, 287. *See* PR, Public
    Relations
publishers 153, 176, 182
Pulitzer Prize 10, 136, 261

Q&A 35, 81, 85, 87, 279

R&D 57, 58
redundancies 83, 100
regional stations 203
rejection 3, 293, 294, 295, 296
reporter 7, 8, 10, 29, 33, 34, 35, 37,
    43, 59, 87, 97, 109, 121, 122, 123,
    124, 125, 126, 128, 129, 130, 131,
    132, 133, 136, 137, 138, 158, 198,
    199, 200, 201, 205, 206, 263,
    278, 301
reporting 3
  news 2, 3, 4, 7, 10, 34, 52, 53,
    109, 111, 113, 115, 121, 122,
    123, 124, 125, 127, 128, 130,
    131, 132, 133, 134, 135, 136,
    137, 138, 147, 195, 198, 199,
    200, 201, 202, 204, 205, 206,
    210, 213, 214, 271, 295
reports 9, 24, 52, 54, 96, 99, 124,
    130, 135, 161, 206, 258
research 9, 44, 50, 51, 61, 63, 70,
    78, 102, 105, 116, 142, 155,
    175, 179, 180, 183, 191, 257,
    261, 262, 271, 278, 310
researcher 205
resume 78, 114, 137, 155, 179, 203,
    256, 301
Reuters 36, 123
reviewer
  book 2, 142, 149, 150, 153, 154,
    155, 156, 157, 158, 159, 259
  movie 2
reviewers 141, 142, 143, 145, 146,
    147, 148, 150, 152, 153, 154,
    155, 156, 158, 160, 189, 190
Reynolds, Glenn 113
rhythms 18, 25, 26, 72
Ricochet 115
rising action 84, 252
Robinson, Peter 69
Rolling Stone 146
Roman Senate 67
Rosenberg, Harold 147
rough draft 74, 270
rulebooks 96
Ruskin, John 147

Sagan, Carl 100
salaries 27, 50, 89, 90, 204, 257,
    264
Salon 115
Samuel Johnson 162, 302
San Jose Mercury-News 4
San people 13

Santa Clara University 3
satire 144, 162, 166
scapegoat 58
scapegoated. *See* scapegoat
scientific papers 96
screenplays 24, 209, 210, 211, 213, 214, 288
screenwriter 2, 68, 97, 209, 212, 215
screenwriting 98, 209, 211, 212, 213, 214, 215, 217, 312
script 37, 50, 64, 78, 79, 90, 98, 209, 210, 211, 213, 311
Secretary of the Interior 71
self-discipline 150
Shakespeare. *See* Shakespeare, William
Shakespeare, William 17, 249
Shonagon 162
Sibilants 15
sidebar 33, 35, 126, 280, 295
Silicon Valley 3, 8, 36, 49, 87, 107, 134, 135
similes 19
Sirard, Jack 4
Siskel and Ebert 145
Skype 39
Slate 115
slogan 53, 56, 59, 62, 63, 64
social networks 30, 51
speaker 32, 68, 69, 70, 71, 72, 73, 74, 75, 76, 78, 81, 82, 83, 84, 85, 87, 88, 90, 155, 191, 202, 210, 211, 301, 310
speaking professionals 70, 71
speech 2, 27, 38, 39, 64, 67, 68, 69, 70, 71, 72, 73, 74, 75, 76, 77, 79, 80, 81, 82, 83, 84, 85, 86, 87, 88, 89, 90, 91, 92, 154, 155, 162, 179, 191, 192, 206, 222, 288, 301, 310
speechwriters 27, 68, 69, 70, 71, 72, 74, 75, 81, 83, 84, 85, 86, 87, 89, 90, 91
speechwriting 27, 53, 67, 68, 69, 71, 73, 74, 89, 91, 92, 268

Spin 146, 237
spoken word 195, 213
sponsorship 29
sportswriter 132
St. Augustine 147
St. Crispin's Day 67
stand-up comedy 84, 90, 144
stand-up comic 90, 228
Stern, Howard 196
Steyn, Mark 148, 164
story 7, 8, 9, 15, 26, 29, 30, 33, 35, 36, 37, 40, 41, 59, 61, 62, 63, 80, 81, 84, 97, 114, 120, 121, 123, 125, 126, 127, 128, 129, 130, 131, 133, 134, 135, 136, 137, 138, 142, 150, 162, 165, 175, 183, 197, 198, 199, 200, 201, 205, 206, 207, 211, 215, 216, 217, 219, 221, 222, 224, 225, 226, 229, 230, 231, 232, 233, 236, 238, 239, 240, 241, 242, 243, 244, 245, 248, 251, 252, 256, 260, 261, 277, 278, 279, 280, 289, 293, 294, 295, 296, 303, 309, 311, 312, 313
storyline 62, 176, 222
stressed phrases 88
structure 1, 23, 86, 87, 161, 211, 230, 234, 260, 283, 286, 311
style 1, 50, 61, 63, 78, 89, 95, 99, 112, 118, 119, 126, 148, 149, 167, 175, 188, 216, 224, 225, 239, 246, 252, 272, 278, 279, 284, 286
subject 5, 8, 9, 10, 11, 18, 20, 36, 52, 53, 55, 62, 63, 64, 68, 73, 75, 85, 97, 98, 103, 113, 118, 119, 126, 127, 128, 134, 136, 137, 141, 143, 144, 146, 148, 149, 155, 164, 165, 169, 171, 173, 175, 176, 179, 182, 192, 197, 201, 202, 215, 239, 268, 269, 271, 272, 277, 279, 287, 296, 309
Sumeria 15
Super Bowl 46, 197

Swaggert, Jimmy 75
Swarthmore College 111
Swift, Jonathon 144
syllogisms 68
syndicated news shows 203

table of contents 99, 152, 177, 179, 183
tagline 51, 62, 63, 64, 310
Tan, Amy 107
targeted gossip 49
targeted toast 77
technical paper 99
technical writing 95, 96, 97, 98, 99, 100, 101, 102, 103, 104, 105, 106, 107
technology reporter 132
teleconferencing 39
teleprompter 80
television host 2
Terkel, Studs 196
terminology 96
Teutonic 16
textbook 1, 20, 73, 96, 176, 186, 212, 217, 231, 264, 297
The Drudge Report 112
The Music Man 217
The Pillow Book 162
the post-Socratic philosophers 162
The Prince 162
The Scheduled Speech 85
The Winter's Tal 216
theory 3, 118, 257
Thomas, Lewis 21
Thompson, Hunter 148
Thompson, Virgil 146
Thoreau 163
thumbsuck 112
thumbsuck blogs 112, 118
tickler file 128
Times Review of Books 143
TKs 63
trade magazine 8
trade manual 3
trademark law 48

tragedy 216
transcribing 10
transitions 84
trend stories 199
tropes
    writing 63, 196
Tsurezuregusa 162
TV 37, 46, 48, 50, 55, 64, 122, 123, 153, 174, 195, 197, 198, 202, 203, 213, 310
Twain, Mark 144
twentieth century, the 92
twenty-first century, the 45, 51, 69, 98, 114, 116, 157, 163, 164, 187, 223, 227, 228, 301
Twitter 51, 112
Tynan, Kenneth 150

United States 30, 44, 69, 75, 113, 145, 163, 180, 196, 226, 227, 264
University of Tennessee 113
untargeted toast 77, 78
Updike, John 145
upmarket stations 203

Vikings 16
Village Voice 146
visuals 62, 86, 197, 199
VNR. See news release
voice 37, 45, 68, 119, 125, 126, 169, 170, 195, 197, 198, 203, 205, 206, 210, 212, 213, 239, 246, 252, 268, 313
Voltaire 144, 162

Wall Street Journal 143, 147, 148, 166
Washington, George 165
Web, the 10, 29, 30, 31, 34, 36, 44, 47, 48, 49, 51, 64, 112, 115, 117, 118, 122, 124, 142, 145, 146, 147, 153, 195, 197, 202, 205, 207, 210, 212, 233, 294, 310.
    See Internet, the
West, Rebecca 163

whisper campaign. *See*
    targeted gossip
White House, the 75
Who? What? When? Where? and
    Why? 126
Wilde, Oscar 147, 150
Wilson, Meredith 217
Winchell, Walter 196
wire service 9, 34, 36, 123, 214,
    309, 311
Wolfe, Tom 148, 163

writing career 3, 4, 50, 57, 95, 106,
    107, 177, 195, 214, 255, 256,
    277, 302
written manual 98

Yoachum, Susan 4
Yoshida Kenko 162
YouTube 33, 35, 37, 48, 98

Zola. *See* Zola, Emile
Zola, Emile 142